North America

Los Angeles
San Diego

Kawabunga's
South Seas
Adventure

Galapagos
Islands

D1171218

120°

100°

80°

KAWABUNGA'S SOUTH SEAS
ADVENTURE

KAWABUNGA'S SOUTH SEAS ADVENTURE

Charles Dewell

South Seas Publishing

Copyright © 1999 South Seas Publishing

Chart sketches copyright © 1999 by South Seas Publishing Company.
Kawabunga Sail Plan and Cabin Layout sketches copyright © 1999 by South Seas
Publishing Company.
Photographs copyright © 1999 by South Seas Publishing Company.

*All rights reserved. No part of this book may be reproduced or transmitted in any form by any
means, electronic or mechanical, including photocopying, recording or by any information
storage and retrieval system without written permission from the author, except for the
inclusion of brief quotations in a review.*

Published by: South Seas Publishing Company
14025 Panay Way
Marina del Rey, Ca. 90292 U.S.A.

Publisher's Cataloging-in-Publication Data
(Provided by Quality Books, Inc.)

Dewell, Charles Scott, 1953–
    Kawabunga's South Seas adventure / Charles Dewell.
    p. cm.
    Includes index.
    Preassigned LCCN: 98-61208
    ISBN: 0-9666472-0-3

       1. Dewell, Charles Scott, 1953—Journeys—Polynesia.
    2. Polynesia—Description and travel. 3. Voyages and travels.
    4. Sailing—Pacific Ocean. I. Title.

DU510.D49 1998   919.604
                        QBI98-1340

Manufactured and printed in the United States of America

FIRST EDITION

Photography: Margaret Dewell and Charles Dewell
Editor: Barry Norcross
South Seas Logo: Gilbert E. Wright
*Book title lettering, Chart drawings, Kawabunga Sail Plan Drawings, Cabin Layout
drawings, compass rose, sailboat illustrations:* Itoko Maeno
Dust Jacket Cover Design: Compliments of James Ross and Richard Tanzmann, of McCarron,
Kane, Ross and Tanzmann, Inc.
Scans for color insert: Ken Herzog of Scarab Graphics
Book design: Christine Nolt, Cirrus Design
Printing: Publisher's Press

**The chart sketches in this book are not suitable for navigation.
DO NOT USE the chart sketches in this book for navigational purposes.**

DEDICATION

This book is dedicated to my lovely and courageous wife Margaret. Her relentless encouragement and unwavering love carried me through many difficult times. Margaret shared my dream and helped it come true. She's the best first mate a man could ask for—on land or at sea.

and

Salvador Mendez, my father-in-law and our shore manager, presided over "Command Central" while we were away— collecting and organizing our mail, fielding telephone calls from worried family members and friends and hunting down elusive engine parts. Without his constant motivation and support, this book would not have been possible.

and

To my mentor and friend Richard Taylor who picked me up when I was down and showed me the way.

∿

ACKNOWLEDGMENTS

Many talented people contributed their valuable time and skill to the production of this book. I am eternally grateful for their efforts. Barry Norcross for his trusted counsel and endless hours proofreading and editing the book; Jim Ross and Richard Tanzmann for designing the dust jacket; Gil Wright and Lynne Haggard for designing our logo and for procuring engine parts for us while we were in Tahiti; Christine Nolt for the book design and her sound advice; Itoko Maeno for her lovely illustrations and Earl Hinz for his kind words.

CONTENTS

"He mocks the men who say, "I've always wanted to sail to the South Seas, but I can't afford it." "What these men can't afford is not to go. They are enmeshed in the cancerous discipline of 'security', and in the worship of security we fling our lives beneath the wheels of routine and before we know it, our lives are gone."

— Sterling Hayden

PROLOGUE

SOUTH PACIFIC SQUALL

The Pacific Ocean has wicked ways of demanding tribute from a sailor before she grants passage into her South Seas island paradise. Reckoning with squalls is one of the nastier tariffs for the sailor. South Pacific squalls are like living, breathing, sinister creatures, rampaging across the sea, turning the warm, gentle, tradewind nights into chilling, exhausting brawls.

The night before had been the type I had dreamed about for so many years. The autopilot steered *Kawabunga* towards the Southern Cross as the beautiful cruising spinnaker drew us gurgling along at 4 knots, hour after hour, on a downhill slide to the heart of the South Pacific.

Tonight was different. I had been fighting a series of squalls all night. Sitting in the cockpit at 0310, I spotted what appeared to be a gigantic, black mountain off my port quarter. We were in store for another nasty visit. Even though it was a warm, tropical night, I jumped into my bibs and pulled on my foul weather jacket, slipped the three drop boards into the companionway slots and pulled the sliding hatch closed. The jib had been struck and secured and a reef tied into the main hours earlier when the series of squalls began. There had been no sleep.

At 0320 the sky exploded. Torrents of icy cold rain blasted me. I quickly disengaged the windvane, taking the tiller in my right hand, while seizing the main sheet with my left, ready for the next assault. A split second later the wind speed skyrocketed from 15 to 40 knots, plunging *Kawabunga's* starboard rail underwater. Climbing to the port rail and clearing the main sheet, I struggled to right the little boat. After gaining control I headed straight down wind and ran off through the darkness, humbled by the savage force of nature, one intrepid adventurer, alone on a perilous sea.

For the next hour I wrestled with the tiller to keep us on track, running before the tempest, the driving rain stabbing into my shoulders like ice picks. This was the worst squall I had encountered and I longed to be under the shelter of the dodger only a few feet away, but I could not steer from there and did not dare trust the vane to steer under these violent conditions.

I ran off for an hour until the squall passed and the bright stars returned. The first few minutes after the attack was over, I slumped on the port bench, allowing my burning muscles to cool and my teeth to stop chattering. Then, I steered the boat back to our proper course of 220° magnetic, engaged the windvane and trimmed the main before stripping off my foulies, diving into the cabin, punching the "position" button on the GPS computer and bundling myself up in a blanket on the starboard settee. Fortunately, we were not blown off course by more than a few miles, as the wind direction was generally favorable.

LAND HO!

The anticipation of my first landfall was overwhelming. At 0430 my position was 8° 35′ 14″ S, 139° 30′ 58″ W, 35 nautical miles from our target, Nuku Hiva and 17 miles from Ua Huka. If my navigation was correct, I should be able to see Ua Huka off my port beam at first light. Fatigue fed my doubts and fears. What would I do if there were no island on the horizon when the sun came up?

The green mountains of Ua Huka were sighted at 0655, right where I thought they should be. Fifteen minutes later I was able to make out Nuku Hiva, dead ahead. Relief, exhilaration and exhaustion enveloped me. I would be safely swinging at anchor in Taiohae Bay on the southern coast of Nuku Hiva that evening.

This was my first offshore passage, a solo shot of forty-two long and lonely days. The fact that I navigated a twenty foot boat deep into the heart of the world's largest ocean to the Marquesas Islands, the furthest islands from any continental coast, implies either: (A) I am a great navigator/adventurer/romantic in the mold of Captain James Cook and Captain James Kirk. . . or; (B) Any idiot can make a transpacific passage with a well-found boat and satellite navigation. The people who know and love me have voted. I'm afraid it wasn't even close. The consensus was B.

The author's first sailing lesson from his big brother Ernie

"There is a thrill to launching a boat, a thrill that never dims in all the years to come."
— Phil Schwind

CHAPTER 1

DREAMING OF THE SOUTH SEAS

CLOSET VAGABOND

I have fantasized about sailing away to the exotic South Seas for as long as I can remember. Of course, I grew out of most of my childhood fantasies. Playing baseball for the Detroit Tigers, football for the Lions or roping cattle with Little Joe on the Ponderosa were all aspirations at one time or another during my formative years. Sailing to the South Seas was different. There was something deep inside me driving, encouraging and assuring me it was my destiny. Much like a newly-hatched sea turtle is driven inexorably toward the sea, I sensed that sailing the South Pacific was something I had to do.

My love for the sea, in my case the inland sea, came naturally. My grandfather Dewell grew up working on commercial fishing boats. By the time he was eighteen he had his own boat, the *Wildcat,* and began earning a reputation as a man who knew where to locate whitefish on Lake Huron. My father joined him when he was old enough to work the nets and they fished together until World War II.

My parents and older siblings exposed me to the enjoyment

of boats and water sports as a kid growing up on Lake Huron. Responsibility and water safety were always emphasized. We spent countless hours in many different types of craft off Pt. Lookout and Gravely Shoals Lighthouse on Saginaw Bay. We had sailing canoes, prams, aluminum runabouts, an Owens cabin cruiser, Rebels, Snipes, a Sunfish, duck boats and an Aqua Cat catamaran. My friends all had boats and we spent our summers sailing, perch fishing or water skiing.

During my college years I spent summers in the upper peninsula of Michigan at my sister Bonnie's cottage on Manistique Lake. My pal Joey Ketvirtis and I spent our weekends sailing our catamarans on the lake and dreaming of swaying palm trees, warm tradewinds and enticing island maidens in nature's garb. Not necessarily in that order. We promised ourselves we would sail together to Hawaii before we were thirty-five years old. To a couple of impetuous teenagers, sixteen years would give us more than ample time to carry out our pledge. It sounded like an eternity. We figured anyone of advanced years (over thirty-five) would be senile and probably too frail to make such a trip.

My fascination with boats did not wane when I moved to Southern California soon after graduating from Ferris State College in Big Rapids, Michigan. I used to spend weekends at King Harbor in Redondo Beach watching the sailboats come and go, longing for my own boat. Within nine months, my brother Ernie and I purchased a 23 foot fiberglass sloop named *Cookie Monster*. We moored her in San Diego where Ernie lived and I commuted down on weekends to sail on San Diego Bay.

I spent a small fortune on books and sailing magazine subscriptions and have read every cruising book and attended every cruising seminar I could find. Many weekends were spent aboard *Cookie Monster*, reading about other people's adventures. John Guzzwell's book *Trekka Round the World*, more than any other, stoked my cruising fires.

When I lived in Manhattan Beach I would walk down to the beach and watch the sunset from a lifeguard tower and imagine what it would be like to sail past Catalina Island, over the horizon. I told all my friends and family that someday, somehow, I was going to sail away. I was a dreamer and would still be a dreamer today if it were not for my wife, Margaret.

After our first sailing date I asked Margaret if she liked our afternoon aboard *Cookie Monster*. She replied; "What's not to like?" I knew right then and there I had found my soul mate. We were married in February of 1990 and it did not take long for my incessant talk of cruising to get to her. One day Margaret's bucket was full. She told me people were rolling their eyes when I talked about going cruising *someday*. It was embarrassing. I was given an ultimatum — either we were going cruising or we were going to quit talking about it.

We soon began sketching out a plan to shove off in ten years aboard a 40 foot boat on a three year cruise through the South Pacific.

FLICKA

Paul Payne, my friend from the Bay Club, first told me about Flickas in 1977. He seriously considered buying a Flicka before choosing a Pacific Seacraft Orion. I began studying the plans for the little ship and reading articles on impressive passages made by Flickas all over the world. Bruce Bingham had designed a hearty little vessel based on the Newport, Rhode Island, fishing boats from the early 1900's and named her Flicka, meaning "vivacious little girl" in Swedish. Pacific Seacraft's advertisements in the sailing magazines seduced me with shots of Flickas in romantic settings around the world. I went to the Long Beach Boat Show several nights in a row to study the boat and talk with Steve Chapkis, who had sailed *Alsvid*, his Flicka, to Tahiti. For several years I admired a green Flicka docked in King Harbor. I wrote to Flicka owners around the country asking them what they thought of their pocket cruisers. Flicka owners seemed to be an odd bunch. I would be a perfect fit. After more than a decade of study I was convinced that Flicka was the best 20 foot boat in the world.

Margaret and I enjoyed sailing *Cookie Monster,* but she was a day sailor. We wanted an interim boat to cruise Southern California's Channel Islands before getting our 40 foot cruising boat. Trying to explain why we should pay a hefty price for a boat three feet smaller than the one we already had seemed beyond the realm of reason to Margaret, who had never been aboard a Flicka.

We attended an open house at Pacific Seacraft in early 1992. We wanted to see their grown-up cruising boats; the Crealock 34 and 37. I had long before given up on the idea of buying a Flicka. Margaret climbed down into a lovely boat's cabin, its interior appointed with teak, heavy bronze opening ports, teak and holly cabin sole and standing headroom throughout. "This is beautiful. What kind of boat is this?" she asked. I could not believe my good fortune. "It's a Flicka, the boat I've been telling you about." I said. A smile flashed across her face as she said, "Let's get one of these!"

We met with Greg Baroque, the sales manager for Pacific Seacraft. By the time we started adding up the costs, a new Flicka was going to set us back $60,000 and we just could not justify paying so much for a 20 foot boat. We wanted a new boat, but were willing to keep an open mind on the subject. We had noticed an old, shabby looking Flicka up on the hard in the factory parking lot and asked about it. The boat had been taken as a trade-in for a 24 foot Dana. They planned to ship it to Maine where shipwrights would refit her over the winter and sell her in the spring.

Our hearts sank when we took our first close look at the distressed *Lucky Lady,* whose pale blue hull was dull and scratched, whose outside teak was cracked and in ruins and whose cabin we could not enter until the crew eradicated a wasp's nest filled with enraged wasps. She did not make a favorable first impression. It required a giant leap of faith in Pacific Seacraft to imagine how the shabby craft could be restored, but my research told me their fine reputation was well earned. After the dust had settled we had negotiated a deal in which we would buy *Lucky Lady*, have her repainted, refitted and delivered for less than half the price of a new boat. Our timing could not have been better as the luxury tax was killing the boating industry and Pacific Seacraft could take on the project.

On several occasions, while on my way to my Brea office, I stopped by the Pacific Seacraft factory in Fullerton to check on the progress of our new baby. I was always welcome to come right in and watch the craftsmen at work. Margaret presided over the interior design with Rita Branstetter while I met with Greg and Stan Broadfoot, the Shop Foreman.

During the total factory refit the little sloop was torn apart, cleaned up, and new equipment installed. On one of my visits the 7.5 horsepower, single cylinder Yanmar diesel engine was out of the boat so even the engine compartment could be sanded down and repainted before reinstalling the engine. She received a new teak bow platform and fir bowsprit. The old stove was replaced by a new Origo 4000 alcohol stove. The head liner and cabin soles were replaced. The teak cockpit grate was rebuilt. A new seahood was installed. Three solid teak drop boards were built. Three bronze cabin lights were replaced. The interior wood was stripped and oiled. The settee, V-berth and quarter berth cushions were upholstered. The six heavy bronze opening portholes were polished until they sparkled. Her cream decks and topsides were scrubbed and buffed out. Teak rub rails were installed on the sides of the hull.

What really crowned the refitted yacht was a new paint job. Her hull was painted with Sterling lacquer. Her color was changed to cornflower blue with gold trim. Her home port of Marina del Rey was painted across her transom. Her new name, *Kawabunga!*, was painted in gold letters across both starboard and port quarters.

I suspect Pacific Seacraft either lost money or made very little on this extensive project. Most contractors in America today would get part way into a project like this and back off, saying they needed more money or more time, or they would simply back out and leave you to contemplate litigation, suicide or homicide. We had drawn up an informal contract listing what we wanted done and indicating what we were paying. It was hand-drawn on a piece of notebook paper, un-witnessed and not notarized.

We had not asked for the teak cap rails to be replaced. We were hoping they could be salvaged. When the boat was nearing completion, Pacific Seacraft did not like the look of the cap rails and replaced them at no charge. This involved a lot of material and labor. There was never any request, inference or suggestion that we pay any more money than we had agreed upon. Pacific Seacraft simply would not allow a boat out of their factory unless it was perfect. Their commitment to quality, detail and customer satisfaction is unsurpassed. What more can you say about a company like that?

KAWABUNGA'S CHRISTENING

The boat was commissioned at the Newport Harbor Shipyard on Lido Island in Newport Beach. Flicka hull number 171, built in 1981, was eleven years old, but looked factory-new. Greg took us on a sea trial out of Newport Beach. She certainly turned heads. We were thrilled with her charming good looks and nimble performance.

A week after the commissioning we hosted a christening party for *Kawabunga* at Reuben's Restaurant in Marina del Rey. *Kawabunga* was dressed up in her flags and moored at the guest dock at Reuben's during the party. Our family and friends helped us celebrate our new boat.

We named her *Kawabunga* because the name expresses excitement, adventure and fun to us. The word has different meanings to different generations. To us, it was from Southern California in the 1960's surf scene. "Kawabunga dude!" In the 1950's The Howdy Doody Show had Chief Rain in the Face greeting Buffalo Bob with; "Kawabunga". In the 1980's the Teenage Mutant Ninja Turtles ate pizza and said "Kawabunga". Bart Simpson in the 1990's uses the term "Kawabunga dude!" In each instance it is a word expressing joy and excitement.

When we were cruising in the South Pacific many people asked; "Is that abo?" They thought the name was aborigine from Australia.

NEW PLAN

Our lives were changing fast. Both Margaret and I had been in the insurance claims business for twenty years. That is a total of about 120 normal-person years in any other field. We were both fighting on the front lines of the rat race and the rats were winning. In fact, they were preparing a victory party.

We both had the best jobs of our careers, were making good money and had an apartment on the beach with a view of Santa Monica Bay, but we were unhappy. Margaret was the Insurance and Risk Manager for UCLA and I was a Hearing Representative at CNA Insurance Company. We were spending our lives in meetings, court rooms or on the freeway. Little time was left over for ourselves. Our *things* owned us rather than the other way around. Life was slipping through our hands. We wanted more out of life. We wanted to simplify our lives. We wanted to follow our dream.

We both read Earl R. Hinz' book *Sail Before Sunset* about Earl and Betty Hinz' cruise through the South Pacific. A major theme of that book was to go now, while we still could. Don't wait until it's too late. That was very good advice.

We suffered a number of difficulties, including illness, career problems and financial setbacks, but we never lost sight of our goal. We simply changed our ten year plan to cruise in a 40 foot boat to a five year plan to cruise in a 20 foot boat. Our lives have never been the same since. Thank God we were getting free from the rat race.

BON VOYAGE

In late May of 1994 I met with DeAnna Hegel, my boss for the previous three years. I gave her four week's notice, told her she had been a great supervisor and told her we planned to shove off in July for Hawaii. DeAnna thought I was just going through a mid-life crisis and suggested it might be cheaper, quicker and more effective to simply buy a red Corvette and get on with it. She favored a more conventional approach.

We were in a full court press to get the boat ready for the cruise. Our "To Do" list mysteriously grew longer and longer as we approached our departure date. Everything took three times longer to complete than expected. My brother John put in many hours, helping us get the boat ready. We hauled the boat, and put on a new coat of green Interlux Ultra Kote bottom paint. While we had the boat out of the water our topnotch shipwright Laurence Sunderland and his skillful right-hand man Dennis Castillo installed an Autohelm Tri-Data transponder just forward of the keel. From this one instrument we would get depth, speed, (current, average, maximum), a distance log, a trip log and water temperature. I could not bear to watch as Laurence drilled a huge hole in the hull. He sealed over the previous knotmeter through-hull under the stove. The Magellan satellite antenna egg was mounted on top of a Shakespeare fiberglass mast and installed on the stern pulpit. They had already installed the Monitor windvane and the Simpson-Lawrence manual windlass. Laurence worked very hard to get the boat ready and told me, "If you don't leave on time, it won't be because of me." He was true to his word.

We wanted to say good-bye to our friends, but we did not have much money. We decided we would have a low-key "open boat" party to say good-bye. Margaret called some friends and invited them to stop by on Saturday July 16, 1994. We were still working on the boat and planned on a departure date of Wednesday, July 20. Our dockmaster, Dave Irons, gave us some very good advice. He said, "No forced marches. Go when you're ready and not before." He could not have been kinder to us during our stay at Holiday Harbor Marina.

On Saturday morning Margaret went out and spent $10 on sodas and chips. Margaret's mother and father brought over a van full of food, including a farewell cake. Margaret's entire family came, including her 91 year old grandmother. We were shocked at the response. More than 250 people stopped by the D-3700 dock to look over *Kawabunga*, sign the ship's log and to say "bon voyage". Everyone brought food and drinks, gifts, money, batteries and encouragement. Their generosity was overwhelming. It was one of the best days of our lives. I was particularly touched by a letter given to me by my buddy, Buzz Wright. He knew Joey and I had pledged to do this trip before we were thirty-five and had not made it. We were six years behind schedule. He wrote; "Thank goodness dreams don't wear watches and first mates are not all named Joe." Thinking of the letter still brings tears to my eyes.

On Monday night our world was turned upside down. Margaret was below, packing away provisions. I was outside, installing a second lifeline. The telephone rang at 2030 and a few seconds later I heard Margaret scream. Her father was calling from the hospital. Margaret's mother had been run down in a parking lot and killed by a drunk driver who had stolen a car and who was being pursued by the police.

Under these horrendous circumstances, we made a half-hearted attempt to push through the pain and loss and to carry on. We set sail for the Isthmus of Catalina Island on August 3, ostensibly to re-group and conduct sea trials, but our cruising plans were mortally wounded. We collapsed when we got to Catalina and knew we were in no condition to sail to the Hawaiian Islands. It was already quite late in the season for such a passage and we were following reports of two hurricanes forming off the coast of Mexico. We spent two weeks anchored in several different coves along Catalina's leeward coast before sailing to Newport Beach, Dana Point, Mission Bay and San Diego.

Ann Miller, our dockmaster-friend at the Bay Club on Shelter Island found a spot for *Kawabunga* in early September. We had decided to keep the boat in San Diego over the winter and shove off for the South Pacific in May of 1995.

A TRIP HOME

"Your old Scotch mother", as my mum described herself, invited us to fly to Michigan to stay with her for a few months. She was suffering from acute heart failure and was scheduled for open heart surgery after the first of the year. The stall in our cruising plans afforded us a golden opportunity to spend a lot of quality time with my mum, time we would never have had if we were still working. My father had passed away six years earlier. My mum lived alone at Pt. Lookout in a cabin in the woods we had built when I was a kid. We spent an enjoyable and rewarding three months with my mum, including Thanksgiving and a snowy Christmas at my sister Bonnie's house in the upper peninsula of Michigan.

Mum passed away one week after her surgery. Margaret stood at the foot of mum's bed while Bonnie and I stood on either side, holding mum's hands, kissing her and telling her how much we loved her as she drew her last breath.

Margaret and I were grateful we were not far away, in some foreign port, when our mothers died.

"One does not discover new lands without consenting to lose sight of the shore for a very long time."
— Andre Gide

CHAPTER TWO

TWO MONTHS BEFORE THE MAST

SETTING SAIL

Our friends and family were milling around the dock at the Bay Club in San Diego, waiting for us to declare *Kawabunga* ready for sea. Margaret and I had worked nearly around the clock during the last month to get our little ship ready to shove off for the South Pacific. There were still some last-minute jobs to be done before she was ready. Packing a twenty foot boat for a long offshore passage is a challenge. Water, canned food, sails and equipment all had to be stowed away securely, while at the same time the boat had to be balanced. We had raised the waterline four inches in the summer of 1994 and she was sitting on those lines now.

Time slipped away as Margaret finished installing the lee cloth on the bunk on the starboard settee and I lashed a second cargo bag to *Kawabunga's* little foredeck. We needed every bit of storage possible to make this voyage. Our last job was running down the gremlins in the bow navigation light. By the time we were ready it was 1700 on Mother's Day Sunday afternoon, May 14, 1995.

Finally, all was ready. I said good-bye to Margaret's dad over the telephone. He had been treated for six weeks in the hospital for a heart infection and had just been released. The doctors told Sal that he needed open heart surgery. We had been faced with a dilemma. We knew if we missed this window of opportunity we would not be able to mount a new campaign — our cruising dream would die. Margaret decided to stay with Sal while I sailed the boat to Tahiti. She would fly down to meet me there.

Before stepping aboard *Kawabunga* I shook hands with my two brothers Ernie and John and waived good-bye to our dock neighbors Earl and Sonya Harris. Daisy, the mallard duck we had adopted hopped into the cockpit and had to be gently shooed away. Margaret and I climbed aboard and backed out of the slip and motored out from the Bay Club, past the San Diego Yacht Club. There was still a lot of activity off Shelter Island as Dennis Connor and his Stars and Stripes syndicate had lost the America's Cup 0-4 to the Kiwi's the previous afternoon. We wanted a few minutes to ourselves, so we steamed through La Playa anchorage, one of our favorite places in San Diego. This would be the last time we would see each other for a very long time. We were both dog-tired. The night before we stayed up well past midnight packing the boat. We continued up the island until reaching the Harbor Patrol dock at the tip of Shelter Island where we met my old pal from college, Mary Wendland. I handed Margaret over to Mary, waved good-bye to my brothers and set off into a light rain. It had been a beautiful day and I hoped the rain was not a bad omen.

I quickly changed into my foul weather gear as I navigated out of San Diego Harbor, past familiar Cabrillo Monument and Pt. Loma. I didn't know who had the more difficult job; me, sailing the boat to the South Pacific or Margaret, unloading the car.

Most of the equipment on board *Kawabunga* has a nickname attached to it. The Autohelm electronic autopilot's name is Abe, because he freed the slaves from steering. I named the Monitor windvane Joey, for my friend Joe Ketvirtis back home. Although Joey could not be with me physically, he would be with me figuratively. Joey was stuck steering 99% of the trip, never complained about seasickness, never needed a break and was never hungry. He was the perfect crew member. Kawabunny, our little stuffed bunny with her own sailor's suit, kept me company.

I wanted to clear the coast as quickly as possible, so I started the engine early in the evening. That first night at sea was a chilly one and it rained most of the night, but we had a beautiful full moon peeking through the clouds, illuminating the sea as I steamed inside the Coronado Islands, past a fishing boat working with her nets. Late that night a freighter crossed ahead of me, heading north. I steamed for seven hours that first night.

The morning of Monday, May 15 broke as a beautiful sunny day with a light breeze, blue water and puffy clouds. The boat was sailing perfectly at 4.1 knots with the mainsail and working jib rigged. Joey was assigned the steering duty. The wind held steady as we cleared the coast. By 1500 we were making 4.7 knots and the color of the water was becoming a deeper blue with big, rolling waves. By 1600 clouds filled the sky and the wind started to drop away until we were dead in the water at 1800. During the first twenty-four hour period we made 80.6 nautical miles and we found ourselves directly west of Ensenada, Mexico.

U.S. COAST GUARD

My plan, after clearing the coast, was to steer a SSW course of 210° in order to pass Isla de Guadalupe to port by a margin of 50 miles and then to follow 120° west longitude past Acapulco where I would finally be hurricane-safe.

At 2145 four dolphin paid a call on me. What excitement and joy they bring. Within fifteen minutes I sighted another visitor, a boat that was headed right for me. As it got to within one mile an officer of the US Coast Guard Cutter *Orcas* hailed me on the VHF radio. My heart sank as I was sure that the cutter would launch a boat and send over a boarding party of several armed commandos to perform a "safety inspection" on *Kawabunga*. It had taken so long to pack the boat in some semblance of order, leaving room only to stand at the galley stove and lay down on the starboard settee that the thought of the Coasties pulling everything out and searching through every compartment was depressing. The officer was very cordial and we had a lengthy and detailed radio conference in which I told him my last port and my next proposed port, length and type of boat, the nature of my voyage, the navigation and the safety equipment carried. When I told him that my next port would be Taiohae Bay on Nuku Hiva, he was astonished. He found it hard to believe that my boat was only twenty feet long, but I assured him of the seaworthiness of the vessel. Apparently, the officer felt that no self-respecting drug runner would be crazy enough to be out there in a twenty foot boat. A boarding and search was not deemed necessary. The officer wished me good luck on my passage.

There was an amazing Coast Guard presence in the area. The next morning a USCG jet flew over, followed by another one fifteen minutes later. I heard on the AM radio that the Coasties had launched a search and rescue operation, looking for a motor boat with four people aboard who had sent out a mayday the previous night. The reporter said the Coast Guard suspected this was a prank! It was good to know that the Coast Guard could blanket the area if you needed help, but I was very angry that someone would pull such a stunt. Three days later on a bright sunny morning, a USCG prop plane flew directly over *Kawabunga* very low. I tried to make radio contact on the VHF without success.

THE ZONE

It is simply impossible for a single-handed sailor to post a lookout twenty-four hours per day. During the early part of the passage, I set the alarm clock to ring every half-hour so I could get up and stand in the companionway to take a quick 360° scan for ships. One of my favorite places to sit was atop the bridgedeck, wedged into the companionway. I was comfortable, secure, protected from the sun and rain by the dodger, and could see through the dodger windows.

It was not long before the alarm was discontinued as I slipped into what I have termed "The Zone". This condition can best be described as an existence marked by a continual state of cat naps. An innate chronometer would rouse me to consciousness at twenty minute intervals. At such times I would throw the sliding hatch back and stick my head out the companionway like a prairie dog looking out his hole. I would give the horizon a quick 360° sweep, check our course and speed and retreat to my bunk. In the interim I would keep an eye on the bulkhead-mounted compass to make sure we were on course. A clinometer was installed just below the compass so I could quickly determine *Kawabunga's* degree of heel.

ON DECK

At noon on Wednesday May 17 we were at 30° 41′ N, 119° 33′ W. I was very happy with the twenty-four hour mileage of 102.6 nautical miles. The boat was raging along under the 100% jib and a single-reef in the main at over four knots. We had hit a maximum speed of 6.4 knots the evening before. The night had been rather frightening as the boat charged through the darkness at close to 6 knots. There had been no moon until 2200. Joey steered well as I snuggled in my bunk, secured by the lee cloth.

At noon on the fourth day we were 200 nautical miles due west of Isla de Guadalupe and we came to course 185°, almost due south. The wind was from the NNW and it was difficult to hold this course as it was directly down wind. I rigged a preventer to hold down the boom. We were now settling into a routine at sea. *Kawabunga* seemed to be finding her stride. I was reading *"I" Is For Innocent* by Sue Grafton, eating my See's caramel suckers and relaxing.

A weather pattern seemed to be setting in as well. The wind had a tendency of dying away to nothing in the early morning hours. Around 1000 a slight breeze would pick up and build through the afternoon. By 1600 the wind would die away again, leaving *Kawabunga* to wallow in the swells with a terrible motion. About 1800 the wind strengthened and blew hard all night. I got into the habit of reefing down for the night.

I wore my harness nearly 100% of the time, whether lounging inside the cabin or working in the cockpit. When I climbed the companionway steps to the cockpit I simply snapped on to the tether, so I was always attached to the boat whenever I was outside the cabin. While sitting in the cockpit I would usually clip the tether to the high side stern cleat. When going forward to work on the foredeck, I snapped to either the port or starboard jack line. I often thought my undoing would be tripping over my tether. I was always getting tangled up in the darn thing. I have seen tethers that are elastic and that might remedy the problem. Oftentimes I felt as though I was a mountain climber, climbing along the side deck towards the bow, trying not to trip over the tether and hanging on for dear life with my free hand.

We had our dodger built by Sam at Pelican's Loft in San Pedro. He did a wonderful job for us, not only in designing and building our dodger, but in building our tropics awning, kite shade/rain catcher and full mosquito netting for the cockpit. The dodger held up well, considering what it went through. The money spent on this canvas work was a good investment and made our trip much more comfortable. Invariably, we seemed to have the coolest boat in the anchorage. Our extensive canvas, combined with our six bronze opening ports and large hatch forward circulated a lot of air. Rarely did we have to rig up the Wind Scoop as we were well ventilated.

Sam built a handle on the back of the dodger that was very handy and made working in the cockpit much safer. If I knew then what I know now, I would have had him build handles on both sides of the dodger to make it safer to transit the "death defying corner" getting to the side deck from the cockpit. This was the most dangerous part of the boat. In an effort to provide more security, I rigged a ¾ inch line on each side, running from the back handle on the dodger to the hand rails on the coach roof. A stainless steel handle would have been preferable.

While at sea I kept the bottom drop board in the companionway 100% of the time. As the conditions worsened, I would put in the second, then the third and pull the sliding hatch closed and latch it. I could lock the sliding hatch from either the cockpit or inside the cabin.

KATHRYN ANNE

With my morning chores out of the way and the noon position plotted, I curled up with *Forrest Gump* by Winston Groom. There I was, 400 miles from land, all by myself and laughing out loud. At 1410 when I took my quick 360°, I was shocked to see a sail off my starboard quarter! This was my fifth day out and I certainly didn't expect to see any other boats in mid-ocean. Our course was 208° and our position at the time was 28° 40′ 36″ N, 122° 06′ 18″ W. She appeared to be larger than *Kawabunga* and on the same course and I knew that she would come up on me. She was flying a cruising spinnaker. I could see her clearly through my Fujinon Polaris binoculars. She would disappear into the trough of a wave and then reappear on the top of a wave. Initially, I was unable to raise her on the VHF.

After a short while I was hailed by Jeff Sweeney aboard the 42 foot Moody sloop *Kathryn Anne*. He and his wife Kathy had left their home port of Santa Barbara and were also headed for the Marquesas Islands. We had a long conversation and Jeff remarked how unusual it was to meet another yacht in mid-ocean. They had made three prior offshore passages and had never seen another sailboat. I took photographs of *Kathryn Anne*, noting her classic, traditional lines. Jeff gave me the most recent weather fax report which showed N to NW winds of 10 knots for the next few days with no tropical depressions. It didn't take too long for our two ships to pass in the afternoon, and again I was alone on the vast rolling ocean, laughing away at Forrest Gump's exploits.

BANSHEES

By the end of the first week at sea the fatigue and frustration levels began to escalate. This was most apparent at night when the wind would fall away to nothing. Strapped and wedged in my bunk I could hear the water rushing by, the sails slatting and banging and feel the boat jerking about. When a little wind would come up I would unsnap the lee cloth, unzip the sleeping bag, climb out of my bunk, pull on my warm Patagonia gear, (When was it going to warm up?), and climb out on deck to get the sails set. After fifteen minutes of tuning and getting Joey set up I would go through the drill of climbing back into my bunk to warm up and read. Invariably, no sooner would I get cozy then the wind would stop, leaving *Kawabunga* to wallow in the swells. I hate the racket the mainsail makes when it slats back and forth with no wind to keep it full. Then, I would have to roll out of my snug little bunk again and take down all canvas.

During these early, long and frustrating nights, I had an uneasy premonition of disaster and I kept expecting the mast to topple down on deck at any time. I thought the incessant clatter would drive me insane. As *Kawabunga* lurched about in the big Pacific swells, I hunkered down in my bunk trying to read, while at the same time trying to ignore the disturbing sounds up on deck. During those times I would listen to the little banshees up on deck sawing away at the standing rigging with hack saws, trying to knock down the mast. One hundred years ago, Slocum, who was the first to circumnavigate the globe single-handed, had the pilot of the *Pinta* to deal with. I had banshees. I didn't have to eat rotten plums to hail the banshees either, they just showed up.

On the eighth day the wind began to pick up and the waves became measurably larger. We had quite a ride surfing down the face of those waves. As we would start down a wave, the wave would try to push *Kawabunga's* stern to port, but she would just raise her skirt and continue on. The wind was strong and steady and I would go for hour-upon-hour without having to touch a sheet or adjust Joey. I had plenty of time to sit and think. What did I think about? I thought it was an awfully long way to the Marquesas Islands!

One of the decisions I had made prior to shoving off came back to haunt me. In San Diego I had toyed with the idea of removing a block that was located about three-quarters of the way up the mast, on the stays'l halyard entry. This block proved to be a continual bane to me, constantly tangling halyards, the topping lift and anything else it could possibly ensnare, just to make my life miserable. This was particularly frustrating as I did not employ a storm stays'l nor a cutter-rigged fore stays'l. I had a storm jib that hanked directly to the forestay. My thinking was that a block up on the mast would come in handy in working on the foredeck with the dinghy or other heavy equipment, but I never engaged it in this fashion. Obviously, I should have removed the fitting along with the block and I would have been home free. Going up the mast now, in the middle of the ocean, was out of the question.

SOLAR POWER

On Tuesday May 23 the sun was AWOL and I noticed the cabin lights were getting dim. So, I decided I'd better crank up the old Yanmar and charge up the batteries. At 0500 I went into the cockpit and learned that bank number 2 would not turn the engine over. Bank number 2 consisted of two six volt batteries. No problem, I had been running under bank number 2 all along and bank number 1, consisting of one 12 volt deep cycle battery, would be more than adequate to crank the engine. It was dead.

Quite obviously, with the sun being on holiday the last several days, the solar panels were not able to keep up with my liberal use of the cabin lights for reading. Why bank number 1 was dead was a mystery as I had not even used it, but had kept it "in reserve" for just such an occasion. As we were completely socked in again I decided to shut everything down and wait for the sun to make an appearance so my solar panels could do their thing. All cabin lights, the Autohelm Tri-Data, the compass light, the VHF radio and the mast-head tri-color light were all suspended. I had only used the GPS computer for a few minutes each day at noon and could always disconnect the GPS from the ship's power and use its own power source if need be. The most painful consequences of shutting everything down was not having a distance log and not being able to read at night. We had prepared the boat in "low-tech" fashion so as not to have such problems. We have a manual windlass, no roller furling, no water maker, no Ham or SSB radio and no radar. All this was done with the bright idea that I would have fewer breakdowns and less time squandered, lingering in some distant port for parts.

The thought of busting up my knuckles by using the crank on the engine was not an inviting one. Fortunately, the sun came out and after two hours I was able to start the engine and charge up each bank for an hour. I put myself on a regular schedule of starting the engine every third day to run up the batteries.

PASSAGE BLAHS

I was in a mental slump and had heard of the *passage blahs,* but this was ridiculous. Depression, guilt, seasickness and loneliness were overtaking me. I was completely listless, forcing myself to make sail changes and keep the boat moving. Margaret and I had been together constantly during the last year, rarely away from each other for more than a couple of hours. Now, I had left her to care for her father while I sailed away on my life's dream. I was constantly worried about Sal, my father-in-law, and kept him and Margaret in my prayers. I couldn't believe that I was in the middle of what I had hoped for and constantly planned and read about for as long as I could remember and I just wanted it to be over. . . . I just wanted to know that Margaret and Sal were okay. Mild seasickness persisted. Not the pukey-kind, but it's as though you wake up with the world's worst hangover every morning, only you don't feel better as the day progresses. I had to force myself to eat. I felt much better after shaving my beard.

WARP SPEED

On the night of May 24th the wind speed accelerated and we charged through the night like a run-away train. I double-reefed the main and we continued barreling along at over five knots. This was very eerie as it was a very dark night and I could see nothing. It was as though we were traveling through space. It even sounded like warp speed from the original 60's Star Trek, when Sulu would be thrown back into his seat as they picked up speed to outrun the Romulens. Anything over five knots in *Kawabunga* is like going to warp speed and you have to hang on for dear life. It's a very physical experience.

On this particular night, as I stepped into the cockpit, the boat lurched and I went flying into a stainless steel fitting securing the dodger to the cabin top. I suffered a gash on my head about hair-line level, or what had been hair-line level about twenty years ago, and it throbbed in pain. I was stunned and dizzy, but quite surprisingly I was no longer seasick! A wet towel placed over the wound did the trick. I took a forensic photograph of the wound in case I was found dead in my bunk. I did not want anyone thinking I had just died of a heart attack or something. I had been wounded! Four days later, and just as the gash was starting to heal, I dazzled myself again, in exactly the same spot. As I was bending down to rummage through the storage locker I was launched into the corner of the solid teak electrical box. Oh my — the language!

On the 24th we were at the latitude of Cabo and Mazatlan and it looked as though it would take another four or five days to reach the latitude of Acapulco.

The wind really picked up on May 26 and by the next day we were running with all three drop boards in the companionway and the sliding hatch snapped shut. The boat sailed 103 miles on May 27, our thirteenth day out.

MELEE IN THE COCKPIT

The next morning I was awakened by an incredible uproar in the cockpit. A foot-long flying fish was flapping around, flinging blood, wings and scales all over the cockpit. It took some time to corral the mighty fish and toss him back to the depths. When the sun came up I cleaned up the scene of the struggle. Out on the foredeck I found another, smaller flying fish. Unfortunately, this one was not as lucky as his cousin and was found all dried out on deck.

WORSHIP AT SEA

As was my custom, I held informal worship services on Sunday mornings throughout the passage. I had some taped sermons from our minister David Hong at Calvary Church of Pacific Palisades and had brought along some grape juice and communion cups. Mostly, I just prayed and read the Bible. Believe me, I prayed selfishly for good weather, good health and a fast passage. I also prayed for Margaret and especially for Sal, who would be going through a terribly difficult surgery. I sounded a lot like the Israelites who escaped slavery in Egypt en route to the Promised Land. All I could do was gripe about things and look back to the days when I had a job, a home and a car. Here I was, finally out of my own slavery, and all I could do was moan. I was hopeless.

WARMER WEATHER

By this time the weather had warmed considerably. As the cruising spinnaker drew us on a course of 208° under broken skies with the wind out of the NE at 5 knots I had one drop board in the companionway with the forward hatch wide open and the fan going full blast. Interestingly enough, the water temperature on day 17 was 82°, 21 degrees warmer than two weeks earlier. Thinking of a cooling influence, I planned to read *Alaska* by Michener when the weather got hot. I imagined that while sweating in the cabin I could read about the cooler climate of Alaska. I calculated that by the time I completed the book, over 1,000 pages, I should be through the inter-tropical convergence zone (ITCZ) and well on my way to the islands.

One of my bon voyage presents from Tim Boatman was a harmonica. For a change of routine I would break out the harmonica instruction book and work on my "Happy Birthday" rendition. Pitiful. Tim is a professional musician, but even he would have trouble teaching me to play any instrument whatsoever.

We had great mileage on the last three days of the third week at sea, scoring 82, 106 and 109 respectively for the days of June 1, 2 and 3. We had clear skies with bright sunshine and strong NE winds causing rough weather with monstrous, breaking seas. There were many flying fish taking off in squadrons and flying for an extended period before smashing headlong into walls of waves, pursued by low-flying gull-type birds. Due to the blustery conditions I put in a second drop board but was able to keep the forward hatch open. The days were great, but the sunsets were extraordinary. What a wonderful ride.

Jupiter, a very bright planet directly to the east and low to the horizon, was the first celestial body seen every night. It was a comforting sight to see Jupiter in the same spot each evening. I also took solace in listening to the radio. Even though I had been at sea for nearly three weeks I could still get AM radio out of Los Angeles shortly after dark and looked forward to hearing

Tom Snyder's show each night. I missed those nightly shows after I ran out of range.

GRACIOUS LIVING

I fear many people will be appalled when I describe my typical meal at sea. I doubt Emily Post would approve of my table manners during offshore passages. Whatever meals were made were made in one saucepan, with one large spoon. That's it. No plates. No other utensils. No table setting. Most of the time I would simply open a can, say of Dinty Moore Beef Stew, my favorite meal at sea. I would plop the stew into the 1½ quart saucepan, heat up the stew while the boat danced about, trying to sling the stew about the inside of the cabin. Once heated through, I would turn off the stove, snap my tether to my harness, climb out into the cockpit and try to balance the pan and not burn myself while I ate. Après dinner, I would tie a lanyard to the pan so I wouldn't lose it while washing it. I would lean over the low side, scooping sea water into the pan to rinse it and use a Rubbermaid dish scrubber to wash the pan and spoon. I never lost a pan, but I did lose a few spoons.

I was happy with our two burner Origo 4000 galley stove. We had been concerned about it because it is alcohol, rather than propane and not gimbaled. But, I had been able to cook without significant trouble, utilizing pot holders to keep the pots on top of the stove. My real problem was I had not been the least bit hungry and had to force myself to eat. I had lost quite a bit of weight and strength. Thank God for saltine crackers.

Our marine head is situated under the V-Berth. We had packed the space surrounding the toilet with cleaning supplies, stove fuel and lamp oil. The compartment was locked and equipment was piled on top. Rather than the marine head or a cedar bucket, I used a tall, blue bucket with a removable toilet seat snapped on.

My daily (and very necessary) rides atop the big plastic crapper at sea can only be described as challenging. Picture yourself sledding down the Matterhorn atop a five gallon bucket. Each morning I would try to balance myself on the throne, my hands grasping the teak handrails at the companionway for dear life as the bucket veered from port to starboard, forward and back, on top of the teak cockpit grate, as *Kawabunga* surfed down giant tradewind waves. It took a while to master the motion.

SURFING TO PARADISE

At 0245 on June 2, I was most rudely awakened by those pesky banshees again. The wind was up, blowing strongly from the east, generating large, ugly, breaking seas. I had been running through the night under the main alone, at five knots, with two drop boards in the companionway and the sliding hatch open. Earlier in the evening I sat in the cockpit admiring the stars and had taken a few over-hanger waves into the cockpit.

The banshees were playing a new game. They exchanged their hack saws for buckets. . . . While minding my own business, confined to my bunk, enjoying a short time of slumber, I was most rudely awakened by a bucket of water dumped directly on my face! I jumped out of my bunk, toweled off and set about learning how a wave could have possibly found its way underneath the dodger, (that covers not only the companionway, but two feet into the cockpit), over the two drop boards and then make another 90° turn to splash me in the face. I've heard of magic bullets, but magic waves? I concluded it must be banshees, as waves are not like cruise missiles that can make such turns and squirms to get to the target. At least the annoying little scamps kept things interesting.

It seemed every time I stood in the companionway to scan the horizon I noticed the waves were growing larger and more intimidating. We were being bounced around quite a bit and were having trouble staying on a port tack as the wind blew directly from astern. The stern was showing a proclivity to fish-tail while surfing down the front of the waves and often, while reading in my bunk below, our starboard side deck would be immersed in water as the boat rolled to starboard. The large porthole over my head looked like an aquarium, with water half-way up the glass.

WATER STEWARDSHIP

On June 3 we had our first rain since leaving San Diego. The rain did not last long in the morning, but in the afternoon it rained very hard and I was able to soap up in the cockpit and had the shower of my life. I was able to shampoo my hair too! As Jackie Gleason would say, "How sweet it is!" *Kawabunga* had her shower too and looked much better after having the salt washed off her deck. The dodger spray shield had been very crusty and difficult to see through prior to the shower. By the time I started to rig up the rain catcher the rain stopped. Our robust wind started falling away and it became hot and muggy. Hot weather, no wind and squally. This was doldrums country. Our position at noon on the third was 9° 13′ 30″ N, 128° 49′ 33″ W.

Water tankage was also a concern on such a small boat. The water tank is under the quarter berth on the port side and holds only 14 gallons. I carried two 6 gallon jerry jugs secured underneath the center insert in the V-berth by bungee cords, snapping to bronze hooks. I put another 6 gallon jerry in the ice box, along with two 3 gallon jerries and several frozen water bottles. I also kept two 3 gallon jerries in the cockpit. All together, I left with 45 gallons. I was very careful with water during the voyage, making sure to have plenty in case of emergency. I used sea water for dishes and bucket-baths in the cockpit. The water in the ship's tank was used for washing my face and hands and for cooking while the other water was saved for drinking. We were one of the few boats out cruising without a ship's watermaker. We did have a Survivor 06 watermaker packed in the abandon ship bag for emergencies.

HEY, THAT'S MY HAT!

A minor tragedy occurred just after plotting our noon position on June 3. As I sat in the cockpit, wishing the wind would pick up, a big hand slapped me across the face, sending my glasses and my favorite hat overboard. While I had been day dreaming we jibed around with great vigor, sending the boom to port, ripping the main sheet across my face. There was no hope for my hat as I saw it bobbing in our wake, but I still held out some small hope for my glasses. Perhaps they had landed somewhere in the cockpit. Nope, afraid not. A desperate search for my spectacles revealed nothing. Luckily, I kept a spare pair of glasses in the abandon ship bag. These glasses were an old pair that had a weaker prescription, but they were much preferable to stumbling around as Mr. Magoo. I had to keep this pair on my face or resort to wearing prescription sun glasses. With that in mind, I pulled out the Croakies Margaret packed for me and wore them the remainder of the time while sailing offshore.

After losing my glasses, we continued to steam all afternoon. I shut down the engine at 1925 and noticed a new sound. Something between a jangle and a rattle coming from the prop area. I had never heard that sound before. I leaned over the transom as far as possible, but could not detect anything unusual. I wished I could send Joey over to check it out.

All in all, June 3 was an eventful day. On the up side, it rained and I was able to scrub the gunk off. On the down side, I lost my glasses, my favorite hat and had a foreboding sense about the new sound coming from the engine.

The next day we continued to steam as the wind had abandoned us. After steaming all afternoon, I untied the jerry jug from the side deck, took it to the bow and poured the remaining 6 gallons of diesel fuel into the tank. Oh, how I wished we had carried more fuel. Diesel fuel is quite a bit lighter than water and we could have carried several more 6 gallon jerry jugs of fuel on deck. I hoped we would run into wind before we ran out of fuel. We were in real doldrums weather. We continued to steam for 24 hours with Abe steering the boat.

THE TWILIGHT ZONE

By noon on the fifth I noted a disturbing new turn of events while attending to my daily duties. It took several minutes to pump out the bilge. We were taking in an inordinate amount of water from somewhere, most likely through the stuffing box. Perhaps this was the source of the noise I had first noticed two days earlier.

"What was I thinking? Stop the ride, I want to get off." When *Kawabunga* crossed into the latitudes between 10° N and 5° N, it was like entering The Twilight Zone. I was nearly driven insane during this period as I began to doubt I would ever escape this tract of ocean. In this horrible patch of hydrospace, I not only learned the true meaning of *confused seas*, but several other of life's most unpleasant lessons. Rain struck the cabin top so hard I thought I was standing under Tacquamon Falls in the Upper Peninsula of Michigan. Imagine, no wind, or when the wind finally came up, it came from the SW, directly where we wanted to go. I had back-to-back days of three miles made good! Unbelievable heat and the incessant squalls. . . .

To give you an idea of my frustration during this baffling period I will run down my daily mileage, (nautical miles made good), for the period from noon on June 4, at latitude 8° 39′ 18″ N, to noon on June 13, at latitude 4° 37′ 18″ N. Much of the mileage was achieved by steaming rather than sailing during this period, especially on June 5 when I steamed 24 hours. The daily runs were: 36, 101, 3, 3, 27, 16, 36, 35, 35 and 60 nautical miles.

We traveled a grand total of 352 nautical miles made good for ten days or an average of 35 miles per day. It would be much worse if you threw out the steaming miles. We finally broke free on June 13, 1995, charging along at 3 knots with 10 knot winds out of the SE. Ten days to travel 4 degrees south. These were hard-fought miles.

ALBATROS

During this agonizing cycle I experienced a truly extraordinary day. On June 8, I had hopes that we were shaking free from our torment. At noon we were making 3 knots with a light SE wind and brilliant sunshine. I was praying for the wind to veer east. It appeared as though a good afternoon of sailing was in the mix.

By 1300 I had run through my customary drill of plotting our noon position and bringing the log up to date and was relaxing on the settee reading *Alaska*. I was nearly two-thirds of the way through the lengthy book and I reasoned I would have to finish the book as the price to be paid for my release from the ITCZ. As I turned a page I heard an ear-piercing horn blaring! Now, that's not something you expect or want to hear at sea. Oh no, I'm about to be run down by a freighter! I literally flew off the settee into the cockpit. I was greatly relieved to see a sail boat approximately 100 yards off my starboard quarter. Our position was 6° 31′ 26″ N, 129° 45′ 23″ W.

We got so close that we were able to shout to one another and take photographs. I learned during our long VHF conversation that Mike and Gisela Curray, aboard *Albatros*, a heavy duty cruising ketch approximately 38 feet long, had left San Diego bound for Nuku Hiva also. As a matter of fact, they had been at the Kona Kai Club and had seen *Kawabunga* leave from Shelter Island. Mike and Gisela had been cruising for the last fifteen years. Since they were expected to arrive in Nuku Hiva several days ahead of me, they readily agreed to call Margaret upon their arrival to let her know everything was okay. I took Mike's father's telephone number in La Jolla, in the unlikely event that I would arrive first.

They had been experiencing the same conditions for the last several days but carried plenty of fuel and had been running the engine. They looked very comfortable, lounging under the canvas shade they had rigged over their cockpit. We spent an enjoyable hour talking and taking photographs before they throttled up and gradually pulled away.

Being a rookie, I had been worried as to whether I had made the right decision to cross the equator at my target of 132° West longitude. The fact that Mike and Gisela had 15 years experience and were in the same patch of ocean made me feel good about my decision.

This was positively phenomenal. I have talked with several blue water cruisers, both before and after our voyage, and it is extremely rare to ever see another cruiser at sea. And I had encountered two.

DID YOU HEAR A FUNNY SOUND?

I could still see *Albatros* at 1515 and decided to run the engine and keep up for a while. After twenty minutes my heart sank when I heard the engine make a sickening sound. It stopped before I could even shut it down. It was dead. Even a mechanical moron such as myself knew the engine had breathed its last. I would no longer have an engine to steam through the ITCZ, to run up the batteries or to navigate coral reef passes. What an emotional day. I had gone from great joy to agonizing despair within a few hours. *Albatros* and I remained in VHF contact throughout the afternoon and evening and we discussed my engine problem. It did not sound good. By the next morning they were out of radio range.

Even without running the engine we were taking an inordinate amount of water into the bilge through the stuffing box. After the demise of the engine I found that the bilge pump was not pumping water as it should. It would take twenty minutes to pump the bilge dry. The engine had thrown its oil all over the engine compartment and down into the bilge. The oil did a number on the bilge pump and the hose. I just hoped and prayed that it would hold together until we reached the Marquesas Islands. The mast-head tri-color light took its cue from the day's events and burned out. I would add these to the list of repairs to be made in Nuku Hiva.

I pulled out Marcia Davock's *Cruising Guide To Tahiti and the French Society Islands*. This is a very detailed guide book. I looked up the section describing the industrial section of Papeete, Tahiti and found where I could have the diesel engine worked on. More importantly, however, were the descriptions of the restaurants, stores and snack bars where I could buy ice cream.

I found it hard to believe that I had spent four weeks alone at sea on a twenty foot boat. It was very depressing. I missed Margaret terribly and prayed for her and her father constantly. Reading Davock's guide was good for me as it turned my thoughts to activity in the islands with Margaret.

One of the ways I found to pass the time was to try to remember the number of places I have lived throughout my life. I came up with 26, including all the different places I lived in college. I fiddled with the SW radio from time to time, but came to the conclusion that it just wasn't worth the trouble to rig up the antenna and worry about the radio getting wet. I was a terrible harmonica player and my practice sessions ceased. When the wind picked up I enjoyed standing on the cockpit bench, hanging on to the dodger handle and singing. My repertoire was limited, however, to the songs I could remember. Since my brain was turning to mush, the song selection was deplorable. Then there's that whole lack of the ability to sing. However, the lack of talent has never stopped me from diving into anything. It was sort of like singing in the shower. Who could hear me? Elvis on the great blue sea. With a sore throat. And without Ann Margaret.

SOUTHEAST TRADEWINDS

The sight of tradewind clouds brightened my outlook considerably. We no longer had waves bashing us, just long Pacific rollers with ripples of wind on top like cat's paws. The boat seemed to glide along with a gentle breeze out of the SE. As a bonus, we were treated to a fine sunset and a few hours later, a beautiful full moon. By 2000 we were racing through the night with the starboard rail awash.

By the sixteenth the SE tradewinds were really filling in. In the afternoon I had reduced sail considerably, first trading the

130% headsail for the 100% working jib and then dropping the jib altogether. I almost waited too long to drop the yankee, hoping the conditions would moderate a bit. They did not. Finally, I bucked up my courage, tied up my deck shoes real tight and charged the foredeck, hauling down the jib and securing it on the bow. We continued to blast through the waves under single-reefed main alone. The water was a beautiful combination of deep blue with white streaked through it. Every fifteen minutes it seemed as though a huge hand slapped *Kawabunga* amidships, sending water against the dodger and into the back of the cockpit. The boat would shudder from stem to stern. Then, the little boat would seem to clear her head, and be off and running again. I had thoughts of buying a log cabin with a stone fireplace in the mountains. I could always have a little sailing dinghy on Lake Arrowhead if I ever got the sailing bug again.

The SE tradewinds consistently blew 15 to 30 knots for the next five days and we began posting respectable daily runs of 92, 113, 115,130 and 97 nautical miles. *Kawabunga* was in her element during these boisterous conditions. In a boat with 18 feet of waterline you pay the price physically for any mileage over 100 miles per day. Simple tasks are made difficult. Essentially, it was crash, bang, hang on for dear life, serious rock'n'roll and surfing down long ocean rollers.

SHELLBACK

In the early morning hours of Sunday, June 18, I became a Shellback, crossing the equator at 132° West longitude. After five weeks at sea I was finally in the South Pacific Ocean. I decided I would celebrate by having a bath. Margaret had packed a special Shellback present for me. My curiosity nearly got the best of me several times, but I didn't want to spoil my surprise and had impatiently waited until now to delve into the plastic bags that protected my gift.

The small gift bag had a drawing of a dolphin playing on the outside. The handles were tied together by a blue ribbon. Inside

I found the perfect gift for the humid conditions; a small, hand-held fan. Next, I carefully pulled out a small brass box with an anchor engraved on the top, wrapped in its own canvas bag. Inside the box was a wee certificate to fill out, showing where I had crossed the equator. But it was the card that I prized most of all because it had Margaret's handwriting on it and I missed her so. It was wonderful just to see Margaret's handwriting on the envelope.

The boisterous SE tradewinds were steadfast and we continued to take regular shots to our port bow and spray exploded over the dodger into the cockpit. Thankfully, the glass is thick on the portholes as we were being struck at point-blank range. Mother Nature continued to amaze me. The sky was bright blue with puffy white clouds, but there was so much motion it was hard to rest or read below. Every half-hour a robust breaker would strike our port quarter and send us surfing down a wave. *Kawabunga* would make a wide arc, slamming the starboard cabin side into the blue water. I tried as best as I could not to have the boat slip into rhythmic rolling, also known as death rolls, that can lead to a broach. After several days of taking direct shots to the port side portholes, water began finding its way through both rear portholes. On the port side the water spurted into the stove. On the starboard side the water poured on to my pillow and bunk. Before long, my bunk was completely soaked, even though I had the portholes dogged down as tightly as I dared. This proved to be a continual problem on offshore passages. I had replacement gaskets for the portholes, but it was one of the "ugly jobs" I had put off. I was glad I had decided not to install the bug screens over the ports as they surely would not have survived this beating.

ICEBERG?

On June 20, my thirty-seventh day at sea, I sighted the only ship on this passage. We were experiencing a wild morning of sailing. Serious rock'n'roll. It was all I could do to simply hang on in the cockpit. At 0830 I spotted what appeared to be an iceberg! The gears started churning in my brain and I realized that there could not possibly be an iceberg at 3° south latitude. It was a large white ship and she was having quite a ride on those big Pacific rollers too. I watched as she climbed up waves and then disappeared into a trough and then reappeared on the next climb. It was so rough I had trouble training my binoculars on her. Her bearing through the binoculars was 320° magnetic. She appeared to be on a course of 270°, possibly bound for Tahiti. I attempted unsuccessfully to make VHF contact. She was gone within fifteen minutes and I was glad that we hadn't crossed paths any closer. A few days later I saw a photograph in the *South Pacific Handbook* of *Nivaga II*, which looked like the ship I had sighted.

My misery was kept in check by the encouraging daily mileage being posted each noon. The shake, rattle and roll was worth it, although I could not get used to the violent, sustained, unremitting motion. The boat was being pushed hard, to the edge of the envelope. I was elated to post a 130 mile noon-to-noon run on June 21, the first day of winter in the southern hemisphere. There was great joy among the crew. After plotting my noon position, I determined I had another 300 nautical miles to go, but realized I was coming in too high, too far to the northwest. Taking into consideration the 1 knot south equatorial current setting us west, I decided to steer a course of 215° for a day, running southeast and then plot a course for a glide path to the target.

The conditions moderated the next morning so I decided to take advantage of the calmer weather and have a look in the engine compartment. What a mess! The engine had thrown its oil all over the compartment and the engine was bone dry. I poured a half-gallon of oil into the engine. I had been worrying about sailing into a crowded anchorage without an engine and causing wholesale damage to shipping, lives and property.

We had the compass swung in Marina del Rey before we left. *Kawabunga* had no deviation. However, for the last few days the compass and the GPS computer did not agree on our magnetic course. It did not seem reasonable that simply crossing the equator could have caused the problem. I had placed a fire extinguisher in the starboard cockpit drain, only 1½ feet from the compass. Obviously, that was the problem and moving it to its proper spot remedied the situation.

STEERING BY THE SOUTHERN CROSS

At 0700 on June 23 several dolphin swam by to raise my spirits. My mood sorely needed elevating too, as I was reeling during the night from the effects of two squalls. Then the wind just stopped. It was becoming unbearably hot. Frustration was taking hold. My log began to be littered with depressing comments, such as: "This #$^* island better be worth all this @^*!" "No sleep (maybe two hours last night)." Nothing seemed to be going right. I had made only 16 miles from noon to 1800. This island group was making me pay my dues to get to it.

Finally, I was able to find the perfect combination for the light conditions. I flew the spinnaker alone and used Abe to steer. Even with very little wind we were able to average 3 knots on this magical evening. Although there was just a sliver of a moon, it was clear and the stars were brilliant. I was mesmerized by the countless stars. It was such a lovely night that I sat out in the cockpit and, between cat naps, took it all in. I hand-steered for an hour but could not keep it up. Luckily, the battery power was sufficient to run Abe.

On June 24 I made one of my memorable mistakes. I had been lulled into a false sense of security by the gentle breezes and starlit swells. At 1130 I saw a squall coming and I did not strike the spinnaker before it hit. It was a weak squall, as squalls go, but it was much too powerful to be flying a spinnaker. As I felt the blast from the squall hit, I un-cleated the spinnaker sheet. The small sheet ran out like it was tied to a passing jet fighter, roasting both hands. It was clear to me now why Margaret wore sailing gloves. I was able to get the spinnaker down without any damage. A big, black, square cloud roamed off to port. I had been very careful up to this point and was disappointed in myself for being so careless. This could, and should, have been avoided.

By noon I had figured out the equation. At sea, you either get 150% or 50% of what you need. Now it all makes sense.

During the afternoon the normal, blustery winds filled in and we again set to work reeling in Nuku Hiva. At 1800 we were only 45 miles from Nuku Hiva. If I was where I thought I was, Nuku Hiva should appear on the horizon at first light the next morning.

At 0655 on Sunday June 25 I sighted Ua Huka off our port beam. By 0710 I was thrilled to make out the outline of Nuku Hiva. The conditions remained boisterous all day. I was very grateful that I was on the doorstep of my first landfall after slugging it out with the Pacific Ocean for forty-two days. I went below and tried to organize a bit and thank the Lord for watching over me, keeping me safe throughout the passage. Climbing back into the cockpit in the mid-morning I sighted Ua Pou off to the south. As I admired the green mountainous islands coming into focus, a rainbow appeared directly in front of me as I made my way between Ua Huka and Nuku Hiva.

I had been waiting a long time to raise our French courtesy flag. I climbed out to the mast, braced myself and hauled down the starboard flag halyard. I snapped on the French tri-color above the yellow quarantine flag, then hauled them up to the spreader. A rush of excitement came over me as I saw them snapping in the stiff breeze.

For an hour we fell behind the wind shadow of Ua Huka as we made our way towards Cape Martin on the SE corner of Nuku Hiva. All I had to do was to clear Cape Martin and hang a right, run westward down the coast, past Baie Du Controleur, another 7 miles to Baie De Taiohae. By noon I was able to change from the ocean chart to chart number 3931, Archipel Des Ile Nuku-Hiva (French) with a scale of 1:69,800.

Closing Cape Martin was exhilarating. I have never seen such a captivating sight. I could not have dreamed of such rugged beauty. Truly, this is one of the Lord's most beautiful creations. Cliffs rise abruptly from the churning blue ocean, ascending to nearly 4,000 feet. Thick green vegetation grows out of the black, volcanic, seemingly pre-historic rock formations. I expected to see a dinosaur at any moment. I sat in wonder as we closed and then passed this magnificent outcrop of volcanic land mass. I could hardly contain my emotions as *Kawabunga* roared along the south coast of Nuku Hiva and was greeted by a pod of Pilot Whales. I had never encountered Pilot Whales before, but their blunt head gave them away. They are black, somewhat larger than dolphin and swim very fast and play just like dolphin. It was a delightful welcoming committee. I exhausted my film taking photographs of the whales and the mountainous coast.

At 1500 I identified the two bare and rocky islets guarding the entrance to Taiohae Bay through my binoculars. These islets are called Sentinelle de l'Est and Sentinelle de l'Ouest. At 1515 I sailed through the entrance into the deep, protected bay. It is about 1¾ miles from the entrance to the black sand beach on the north end. I had been having a very wild ride until I got into the bay and then the wind dropped away as we were surrounded by steep, lush hills on three sides. The mountains cut sharply down into valleys. I ghosted into the bay, every once in a while getting blasted by strong winds funneling down the sides of the mountains. I could see several cruising sailboats anchored at the head of the bay. White mountain goats stood out against the green and black cliffs.

The VHF radio crackled to life. It was Mike and Gisela Curray aboard *Albatros* welcoming me to Nuku Hiva. They had arrived a few days ahead of me and had telephoned Margaret to report our meeting in the ITCZ.

I was finally able to anchor in 58 feet of water at the head of the bay at 1730. I was anxious to get ashore, but by the time I got things organized and started inflating the dinghy, an Avon Redcrest with a 2 horsepower Suzuki outboard, it was dark. Since I was unfamiliar with the landing I thought I'd better wait until morning to go ashore. As a few lights came to life ashore, I sat in the cockpit and marveled at the scene. The smell of the rich vegetation of the island smacked me across the face. The sounds of chickens and dogs traveled from shore across the bay. I was exhausted. I looked forward to my first good night's sleep in six weeks.

I felt a great sense of accomplishment, knowing I had navigated my way through one of the world's great oceans to a remote, wild and captivating island.

Cape Martin, Nuku Hiva

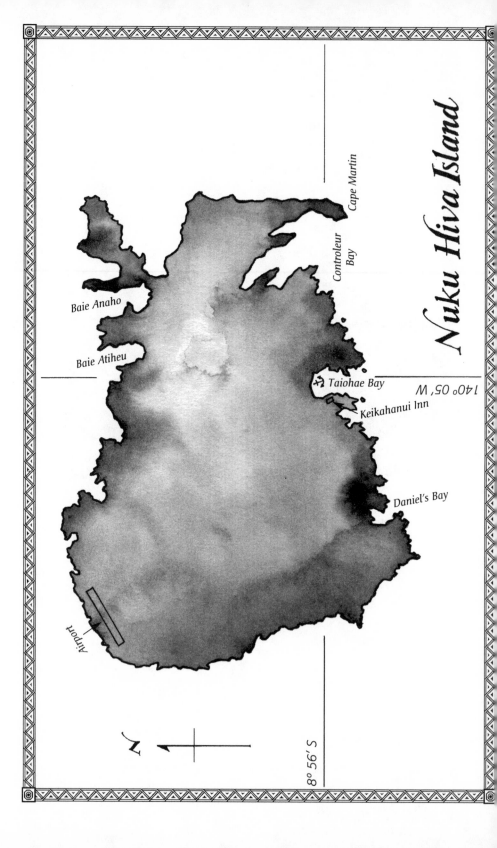

Nuku Hiva Island

Cape Martin

Controleur Bay

Baie Anaho

Baie Atiheu

Taiohae Bay

Keikahanui Inn

140° 05' W

Daniel's Bay

Airport

8° 56' S

N

"The ocean is a wilderness reaching around the globe, wilder than the Bengal jungle, and fuller of monsters."
— Henry David Thoreau

CHAPTER THREE

THE MARQUESAS ISLANDS

TAIOHAE BAY

Tropical sunlight radiating on my right cheek stirred me to consciousness. I had slept in the cockpit for eleven undisturbed hours and I awoke very disoriented. After *Kawabunga* was snug in the anchorage of Taiohae Bay I had collapsed. The stress of the protracted, solitary passage was finally lifted and my body and mind had collaborated to demand a leave of absence.

Between the swell rolling in, the wind funneling through the valleys kicking up a chop and the local fishermen roaring past in their bonito boats, it was rather uncomfortable. I could see very little activity by the cruisers at this early hour. I was amazed by how large Taiohae Bay was. The long, deep inlet was protected from the prevailing southeast tradewinds.

I surveyed the harbor with my binoculars. At the head of the bay I saw the little village and the concrete dinghy wharf and shower building. The gendarmerie would be northeast of the wharf.

My primary mission was to get ashore, clear in through customs and immigration and call Margaret. I set to work inflating the dinghy on the foredeck. Unfortunately, the foredeck area is so small, made even smaller with two cargo bags lashed forward, it makes it difficult to put the three plywood floor-boards in the dinghy while inflating it on the deck. I inflated the dinghy on deck, launched it, and rowed to the beach to install the floorboards.

As I began rowing towards the dinghy wharf, I had to stop and admire little *Kawabunga*, finally settled into a South Seas anchorage with a French courtesy ensign and bright yellow Q flag flying from her starboard spreader. I had dreamed of this day, of this scene; *Kawabunga* anchored in the foreground with lush, tropical flora as a backdrop.

It was a long pull into the little black sand beach adjacent to the dinghy wharf and I could tell by the pain in my shoulder muscles that I had lost much of my strength during the passage. Although there was very little surf, I was nearly capsized during my landing. I quickly pulled the tender out of the surf onto the dry sand and set about deflating, installing floorboards and re-inflating the dinghy.

After completing that task, I briefly scouted around the landing site. My legs were very wobbly and it was apparent that navigating on dry land would take some getting used to. Situated just off the beach was a colorful bonito boat on the hard for repairs. Hitched to the fishing boat was a small brown Marquesan pony, nonchalantly enjoying his breakfast.

I walked over to the shower and bathroom buildings. Big disappointment. These buildings were satisfactory a few years back but they had deteriorated to the extent that they were no longer tolerable. I had been looking forward to a nice long shower too! I had spent enough time ashore without formal clearance, so as swiftly as my quivering legs would take me, (I felt like a new born colt), I scrambled back to the tender and rowed back to *Kawabunga*.

As soon as I reached *Kawabunga*, I removed the canvas cover from the little 2 horsepower Suzuki outboard, freed it from its mount on the stern pulpit and affixed it on the Avon's motor mount. I was overjoyed when the outboard growled to life on the first pull.

THE SHOTGUN SAGA

I wanted to make a good impression on the local officials. In order to do that, a shower and a change of clothes was definitely in order. I filled the sun shower with three gallons of precious fresh water from a six gallon jerry jug, hung it from the boom over the cockpit and set about scrubbing behind the ears. I'm sure that any downwind crews were well-pleased with my decision to bathe. I had been saving my best khaki sailing shorts and aloha shirt for this occasion so I quickly dressed and set about retrieving my ships papers that had been packed in plastic bags and stowed in the forward locker. Jim and JoAnn Matthews had sewn a canvas shoulder bag for us as a bon voyage gift. I stuffed it with the ship's papers, camera and wallet, put on my good straw hat and headed for shore.

I took along my twelve gauge, double barrel shotgun that had been given to me by my dad as a Christmas present when I was thirteen years old. I had shipped the gun from Michigan to California just before shoving off and it was still in its cardboard shipping box. I was under the impression that all weapons had to be declared and handed over to the gendarmes at Taiohae Bay. The weapon would be transferred to Papeete and then on to Bora Bora and handed over when I cleared out of the territory.

The tide was out when I reached the dinghy wharf and the landing was two feet above my head as I stood in the dinghy. The dinghy wharf has room for roughly eighteen dinghies, but several of the spaces were occupied by local boats. I pulled the dinghy amongst the several dinghies already tied up. Taking the painter, I tied a bowline to a ring affixed to the concrete wall. It helps to be part mountain goat when scaling the concrete wall of the wharf. Bracing myself against the surge, I lifted the gun over my head and, while at the top of a wave, gently slid the weapon on to the top of the landing. Next, my canvas bag was tossed up and over. Using an outcropping of rough concrete as a foothold, I struggled up and over. I had taken classes in seamanship, celestial navigation and medical emergencies at sea, but had overlooked the all important rock climbing course.

Just as I finished my impression of a human fly, a friendly Swiss family walked up, peered over the wall and began discussing amongst themselves the best way of climbing down to their dinghy without shedding blood or splintering limbs. They took time out to give me directions to the gendarmerie, telling me to simply follow the road up to the right. I would pass the post office and eventually arrive at the gendarmerie. I could make a telephone call from the Post Office.

I wanted to call Margaret right away. Sure enough, there was a telephone booth out in front of the post office. However, I could not understand how to make a call as all of the instructions were in French. I had taken French at South Junior High School, but only because Mr. Jacobson, my French teacher, was also the baseball coach. As a seventh grader my ambition was to play for the Detroit Tigers, not join the French Foreign Legion. Therefore, very little French could be drawn from my frayed memory banks. My pocket French dictionary was of little help. After a few minutes I abandoned the idea and headed up the hill for the authorities.

By the time I reached the Gendarmerie Nationale it was 0930. I didn't know how trigger-happy the French cops would be, so as soon as I walked into the station I placed the box on top of the counter and announced that the box contained a shotgun. There were two cruisers in the station and two uniformed gendarmes. As soon as the gendarmes realized I did not have a handgun, they went back to their normal duties and generally ignored the shotgun. As I took a plastic seat to wait my turn to clear in one of the cruisers greeted me and explained that I was wasting my time trying to clear in without first securing my bond and a 3,000 franc stamp. I knew that a bond was required, but I thought that I should make my entry declaration first. Wrong again. I asked the gendarme if I could leave my shotgun with them as I did not think they wanted me traipsing all over Taiohae Bay with a gun. I knew the French exerted strict gun control over French Polynesia, so I was astonished when the gendarme told me in no uncertain terms that I was to take the gun — they did not want it left at the station!

The cruisers told me I could make collect telephone calls at the post office. I would have to go in and talk to the clerk and explain what I wanted to do. Mystery solved.

The post office was a very busy place. There was only one clerk to help several cruisers and locals. Fortunately, this young man was very friendly, patient and cooperative. I was unable to reach Margaret but I was able to contact my sister Bonnie and told her all about the passage. *Albatros* had called Margaret and Margaret had called Bonnie to let her know of our progress. Over and over again the operator would say that there was no answer when I called Margaret. The clerk kept my request on file so I did not have to fill out a new form each time I tried to call Margaret. I felt a little better, knowing that my family knew I was safe.

Again, I took up my canvas bag and my shotgun and headed out, this time for the bank. As I was walking down the hill I ran into Peter, a Swiss single-hander aboard *Paros*. Peter was in his late twenties or early thirties, very athletic, about five feet seven inches tall with blonde hair, blue eyes and a ready smile. He had just cleared in and we walked into the village together. As we walked along the road paralleling the bay, this happy-go-lucky sailor told me about being a champion skier in Switzerland. In the Polynesian islands the local girls are enamored with blond hair and blue eyes and Peter was inevitably in the company of beautiful young vahines.

We separated at the Banque Socredo. The bank was a modern building built across the street from the bay in the center of the little village of Taiohae. Again, I didn't want anyone to think I was a bank robber so I placed the shotgun in a corner and walked up to a teller window. I noticed that the bank was full of people, most of them sitting in chairs along the walls. Edythe and Dick Gantt who were cruising aboard *Celerity* approached me and pointed out that no one waited in line. It was obvious that I was a rookie and needed to convert to "island time". I was told to sit down, relax and go to the teller when it was my turn. Since I was the last one in, I took notice of the people ahead of me and sat down to await my fate.

While waiting, Gisela Curray from *Albatros* walked into the bank and introduced herself. We walked outside and hailed her husband Mike, who was talking with some locals on the beach. We discussed how incredible it was to meet another yacht in mid-ocean. In their fifteen years of cruising they had never encountered another sailboat at sea. Unfortunately, we would not have a lot of time to get to know each other as they were shoving off the next day for Hawaii. I thanked them for their kindness in calling Margaret and we parted.

THE BOND

When it was finally my turn I had a rude awakening. I was expecting to pay about $700 for a bond. They charged $990 plus $85 in exchange losses and $3.50 in fees. Ouch! The rationale behind the bond is to prove you have the funds to escape Polynesia. The French authorities do not want yachties thinking they can find a beach, move ashore and live off the land. The bond is supposed to be equal to a one-way ticket back to your country. In lieu of a bond, you can present an airline ticket to your country. As you can imagine, the bond was not a popular regulation within the cruising fraternity.

THE FORTY-TWO DAYS AT SEA DIET

By the time I concluded my banking I was starving. I wandered along the coast road, past the fish and fruit market, looking for a place to eat. As I strolled through the little village

I began to feel like Lee Harvey Oswald on his way to the Book Depository. The long box I was carrying did not look like curtain rods either!

I noticed a two-story hotel with tables and place settings on a deck overlooking the bay. It was 1100 and the waitress explained that the kitchen did not open until noon. There was little choice of sodas and no diet drinks at all. I rediscovered Coca Cola. The Coca Colas at 250 francs per can were very expensive, but tasted delicious. I never tasted anything so refreshing. My body craved the sugar.

I had lost forty pounds during the passage. I have been on many diets during my lifetime, but I can honestly say and attest to the fact, that the *Forty-Two Days At Sea Diet* is the very best for losing weight. I'm thinking of starting a bidding war between Jenny Craig and Nutri-System for my diet plan.

When noon finally rolled around I used my pocket French dictionary for assistance in ordering steak and French fries. The deck of the hotel sat elevated over the coastal road, looking south towards the center of beautiful Taiohae Bay. I could make out the island of Ua Pou in the distance. It was a spectacular day.

It was strange to hear all of the foreign, shore-side noises after being alone at sea for so long. Babies crying, dogs barking and roosters squawking, all added to the babel. In general, the populace are rugged, imposing, powerful, shy and congenial people. Many of them have decorated their bodies with tattoos.

After lunch I made my way back up to the post office to buy the 3,000 franc stamp for my passport. I learned the hard way that all business shuts down from 1200 until 1400 for lunch. I sat outside the post office for thirty minutes until it reopened. I was able to buy the stamp but unable to get through to Margaret in Los Angeles. I had no trouble at the gendarmerie in getting my three month visa after I produced my stamp and proof of my bond. I prepared a Crew List and a Customs Declaration listing my shotgun, ammunition, ship's equipment and stores. The customs officer told me I could keep my shotgun as long as I kept it stowed away.

At 1500 I lugged the gun and ship's papers back to the dinghy wharf. The tide was in, making it easy to climb into the dinghy. Once back at *Kawabunga*, I lowered my bright yellow Q-Flag. My formal responsibilities as captain of the *Kawabunga* were finally concluded.

EXPLORING

On the way back I took a swing through the massive anchorage, counting twenty-seven cruising boats of all designs, sizes and flags. There were wooden, fiberglass and steel hulls; sloops, ketches, cutters and yawls; traditional and high-tech; mono-hull and multi-hull; ship-shape and shabby. *Kawabunga* was by far the smallest, and by my eye, the most charming craft anchored in Taiohae Bay.

By the time I got back and got things organized it was getting dark. I wanted to save my ship's batteries so I filled a small hurricane lamp and a small anchor lamp with oil. I rigged the anchor lamp on the end of the boom and raised the boom several feet. It wasn't long before I was asleep.

The next morning I walked around the western side of the bay to the commercial dock where the island schooner *Aranui* was preparing for departure. Aboard the big white freighter, standing along the rail, were several passengers waving good-bye to family and well-wishers. They would take five days to reach Papeete, stopping in the Tuamotus along the way. This was a wild scene as the party had obviously started earlier and was now in full-swing.

It was quite a little walk back into the village and I thought if I walked along the road I might hitch a ride. Sure enough, a young man in a red four-wheel drive pickup stopped and gave me my first experience of motorized travel on Nuku Hiva. Unrestrained, wanton and death-defying pretty much sums it up.

The terror I experienced at the hands of the young Marquesan chauffeur apparently changed my luck because soon after he dropped me off at the post office I was talking with Margaret in Los Angeles. It was wonderful to finally hear her voice after such a long time. I was so happy to learn that her dad had not required the open-heart surgery after all. He was doing just fine. We discussed the pros and cons of her flying to Nuku Hiva and ultimately decided to meet in Tahiti on Monday, July 17.

After talking with Margaret I decided to do a bit of beachcombing. As I strolled along the coast road, westward past the village, I felt relieved and happy to have finally made contact with Margaret. On the other hand, I was disheartened that we were not together to enjoy the overwhelming beauty of Nuku Hiva. I continued along the water's edge as it curved southward, enjoying the brilliant sunlight shimmering off the palm fronds. I took several photographs of children playing in the surf and of a sailboat that had been lost and had fetched up on the sand.

KEIKAHANUI INN

Several yachties told me I should hike up to the Keikahanui Inn. I could see the inn nestled in the lush hillside, high above the black sand beach. It was a good little hike up to the inn, but well worth the effort. The inn had a typical yacht club setting with a South Seas decor mixed in. It had massive picture windows facing the expansive bay to the east. Several bungalows have been built nearby, hidden along the slope overlooking the bay. Mrs. Rose Corser introduced herself and gave me the history of the inn as I knocked back a few ice-cold Cokes.

Twenty years ago, Rose and her husband Frank left Newport Beach, California and set out cruising. They sailed into Taiohae Bay and fell in love with Nuku Hiva. They thought that Taiohae Bay was the most beautiful place they had ever seen and decided to put Frank's contracting experience to use and build an inn. At that time there was no electricity on the island and very few cars. There still are very few roads and the people get from valley to valley by horse over rough mule trails. Three years ago Frank passed on from cancer, leaving Rose to take the helm of the Inn in this challenging environment. She is a very genial host who acts as the guardian angel for the yachties in Taiohae Bay.

Rose invited me to examine and add *Kawabunga's* story to the renowned log books that she keeps at the Inn. These are the same log books that Maurice McKittrick had maintained at his store for years. Most of the yachties who arrive in Nuku Hiva have either drawn a picture of their boat or pasted a photograph of their boat in the log book, along with a brief synopsis of their crew and notes of their wayfaring. I decided to take a photograph of *Kawabunga* with my Captiva instant camera, write up a brief account of my passage from San Diego to Nuku Hiva and bring them back later in the week to add to Rose's log.

The next night I returned for dinner. Instead of walking from the village dinghy wharf, I drove the dinghy across the bay to the beach below and to the north of the Keikahanui Inn. The beach directly below the hotel is tempting but there is a coral reef extending out about one hundred feet from the shore at that part of the bay. I became intimately acquainted with this very reef later in the week.

I half carried, half dragged the dinghy up onto the beach and tied the painter off to a palm tree. It was late afternoon and the sun made a brief appearance as I climbed up to the restaurant. When I arrived outside the entrance I found a large assortment of boat shoes, reef runners and flip flops neatly arranged outside the entrance. I entered the establishment barefoot, after adding my footwear to the collection.

The inn was bustling with activity. There were several crew members from the boats anchored in the bay sitting at the bar and at dining tables having a good time. The crowd was affable and invited me to join in the festivities. Sea stories were traded and later we enjoyed Marquesan music from a local group. Several of the diners had spent the day on a Jeep excursion of the island arranged by Rose and they were raving about the waterfalls cascading down the sides of the mountains and the jagged coastline with its many bays.

After enjoying a hearty meal, entertainment and good company I said my good- byes, found my flip flops and pulled the hood of my foul weather jacket over my head. It had begun to rain. I found my way through the darkness to my dinghy and headed for *Kawabunga's* little cabin. I was very glad I had taken my jacket and flash light. The clouds opened up soon after I launched the dinghy and it was extremely dark. Before I left the boat for the evening I had switched on *Kawabunga's* anchor light. Even though I wanted to conserve power, I knew how dark it was in this bay when the sun goes down so I decided to use the power. I was very happy to see her brilliant anchor light guiding me home through the pitch-dark.

Kawabunga's anchor light is the brightest one I encountered during the entire voyage and I put it to good use on countless occasions. When finding your way home at night in the dinghy in a crowded anchorage, the prescribed method is to follow in the glow of a boat's anchor light until you are near that boat and then continue the process with another boat's anchor light. By that manner you lessen the chance of running into something in the darkness. It was always comforting to see her exceptionally bright light at the end of a long day.

SNACK BAR

I discovered a tiny outdoor snack bar run by a breezy young vahine who, between cooking food, waiting and bussing tables and taking care of the receipts, cared for her two year old toddler and mongrel dog in her spare time. The building was nothing more than a ten foot long by four foot wide kitchen constructed of wood, enclosing a stove, oven and sink. There were four covered picnic tables arranged on the craggy lawn aside the structure. The tables offered a priceless view of the enthralling island of Ua Pou off in the distance and of sparkling Taiohae Bay in the foreground. I ate lunch at this hot spot many times as the food was good, prices relatively modest and the entertainment unsurpassed.

The entertainment consisted of, but was not limited to, dodging coconuts plummeting from the towering palms. Fortunately none had my name on it, but some hit so close I suspect they had my initials! Rowdy roosters swaggered about, herding their hens back to their harems. Stray dogs took advantage of any distraction to promptly purloin lunch. The two year old boy staggered a few steps before falling on his face, sometimes perilously close to four-wheel drive vehicles speeding along the roadway.

The hostess had only two hands. She would pull the child away from danger, while taking orders and hustling back to the ramshackle kitchen. While the poor girl was under such assault, her mother-in-law sat comfortably at a shaded table savoring her cold drink, enjoying the seascape, but never lifting a finger to help nor offering a bit of encouragement.

POSTCARDS FROM PARADISE

After lunch I bought a fistful of postcards and spent the remainder of the afternoon writing to my friends. I filled out twenty-one before I realized that a stamp was nearly one dollar! With this in mind I pulled in the reins on my writing.

The only real "deal" for a yachtie is the French baguette, a long, thin loaf of bread. They are only fifty francs each, roughly 60¢. I loved the French bread in Polynesia. It was common to see the local people walking down the street with a brown paper grocery bag brimming with baguettes.

SHIPBOARD DUTIES

There was a lot to be done if I was going to leave on Saturday morning. A funeral had to be arranged for the engine, the bilge pump problem had to be solved, sails had to be inspected and stores had to be purchased and stowed away for the passage. The batteries had to be topped off with distilled water and charged up as much as possible. I had to plan the safest course to Tahiti. The hand-held VHF radio had to be charged up, and I had to assess the water supply.

The water at Taiohae Bay is not potable due to the contamination caused by the overpopulation of goats and pigs living in the catchment area. Taioa Bay, better known as Daniel's Bay, just five miles west of Taiohae, has good water. If I had to, I could put in there to top off my water tank and jerry jugs. Since I had two six gallon jerry jugs full and a few gallons left in the ship's tank, I decided I had sufficient water for the transit to Tahiti.

I let out fifty more feet of anchor rode on Wednesday morning as the weather changed from bright sunshine to overcast skies and powerful winds. It was not long before it began raining like crazy and the boat was bouncing around in the anchorage. The solar panels were useless in these conditions.

I spent the morning taking the bilge pump apart, cleaning it and re-installing it. It worked fine for a short period, but the oil from the engine had found its way into the bilge and was playing havoc with the pump.

In my telephone conversation with Margaret later that morning, I gave her a list of equipment that I wanted her to find and bring out with her. She had already ordered a new pair of eye glasses and a new pair of prescription sun glasses for me. The sunglasses I had were not dark enough for the intense sunshine in Polynesia. Margaret would order a new bilge pump for the cockpit and pick up a portable bilge pump to pack away for emergencies.

YACHTIE MISHAP

At the post office I met Mary Ann from *Briar Patch*. Mary Ann and her husband Max had been cruising for nineteen years, mostly in the Caribbean. They had been entertaining their daughter and son-in-law at Ua Pou. While climbing down their boarding ladder from *Briar Patch* into his dinghy, Max fell, suffering a serious fracture to his right leg. They sailed the boat to Nuku Hiva for help. Mary Ann had just loaded Max aboard a helicopter. He was flown to the little airport on the northwest side of the island and then on to the hospital at Papeete. The daughter and son-in-law had sailed on the island schooner on Monday and Mary Ann was left at Taiohae Bay to manage a fifty-one foot ketch. She had friends flying in to help her sail the boat to Tahiti.

HIKING TO TOOVII PLATEAU

The next morning broke bright and sunny. I had intended to buy fresh food to stock up the boat for the next leg, but was out of luck. There was a great deal of activity around the village and I was surprised to find that all the stores and businesses were closed down for the day. The people were getting ready for Tiurai, a festival where the inhabitants from all over Nuku Hiva and some of the other islands gather to hold dance contests and partake of the traditional Marquesan foods. This is all in preparation for Bastille Day.

I had on my hiking sandals so I decided an impromptu hike was in order. I had no real destination in mind, but I walked through the village and turned north up a steep road running up the mountain. I could eventually get to the Taipivai Valley on this road, but I knew it was too far for me to hike.

I had read Melville's novel *Typee*, based on his experience in the Taipivai Valley, known for it warriors, archeological findings, cannibals and human sacrifice. I doubted that I would run into any cannibals, but his descriptions of the steep mountain walls isolating the valleys and separating the tribes came to life as I hiked up the mountain.

The large valley of Taipivai is located to the southeast of Taiohae and opens up on Comptroller's Bay. This is the largest bay on Nuku Hiva's coast. There is still a small village there.

I came across a river so swollen from rain it was running over its banks and across the road. There were several children having the time of their lives playing in the middle of the road, which was now just another river tributary and swimming hole. It was not long before the road became nothing more than a two track trail, switching back and forth through the steep climb. I came across several horses from time to time tied up along the trail, apparently left there to graze and to be retrieved at a later time. After climbing for a few hours I came upon a majestic waterfall cascading down the side of a black volcanic peak mantled with lush green flora. I kept trudging up into the wild blue and green yonder and came across a man and woman cutting down banana stalks in the jungle with their machetes. I was a little hungry by that time but I decided not to bother them. They were busy. They had razor-edged machetes. Then there's that whole cannibal thing. . . .

At long last I reached the Toovii plateau, which I was told has an average height of 3,280 feet running along the top of the island. I could see most of the island from this lofty perch on top of Nuku Hiva. The panoramic scene of Taiohae Bay and the canopy of palm trees in the valleys was breathtaking. Aotupa Bay, just to the west of Taiohae Bay, was clearly visible. The contrast between the azure deep enveloping the emerald island was stunning. From that vantage point I could see the north shore, Atiheu and Anaho Bays.

Only an imbecile would not have a camera in this situation. Since my original intent was to buy stores, I had not brought along a camera. I will long regret this oversight, as I was treated to some of the most spectacular panoramas I had ever seen. I tried to make it a policy to always carry a camera with me from that time forward, but I stumbled on occasion.

I sat down for a spell to rest, drink in the beauty of the island and praise God for his glorious creation. Under the circumstances I found it hard to understand the attraction of solo cruising. This was definitely a moment to be shared.

EXCITEMENT IN THE AIR

The return trip was a cinch compared to the climb up and within two hours I was back in town. It sprinkled most of the way down, but the rain was most welcome as it had been steaming all afternoon. Passing through the village on the way to the dinghy wharf I could sense excitement in the air. The locals were running around, obviously keyed up, and all this activity piqued my curiosity about the next day's festival. The highlight of the celebration would be Marquesan dancing. I was told the food would be wonderful as well. There would be displays of their traditional wood and stone sculptures. There would be tikis and carvings of ancient Marquesan canoes, mainly carved from miro and tou woods. Human sacrifice was no longer on the program.

Traditionally, the Marquesans had adorned their bodies with tattoos. That tradition is alive and well in the islands today. Through my reading, I expected the islanders to be tattooed, but I was surprised to find a high percentage of yachties get tattoos either in the Marquesas or in Tahiti. Yikes! There was never a question as to whether I would lie down in the dirt and allow a Hinano-swilling virtuoso to give me a "souvenir tattoo". Not with the fanatical cowardice that overwhelms me whenever I come within close proximity to a needle of any kind.

I saw several men gathered around the dirt parking area of the market watching a game similar to shuffleboard. As I watched, the bystanders tried to explain the game to me. I could not understand the Marquesan language but came to understand that the object was to roll your steel ball, about half the size of a normal bowling ball, about twenty-five yards down the field. The next participant would roll his ball, trying to smash the first man's ball out of bounds, leaving his ball in the play area.

At dusk I left the village and motored back to *Kawabunga*. I had expected the nau-nau flies and mosquitoes to be much more of a nuisance and was happy to find that, in Taiohae Bay at least, the problem was under control. I heard far different tales from several cruisers that had been in the other bays and islands of the Marquesas group who had not only been pestered with the insects, but had come down with dengue fever.

I noticed *Viking Princess*, a Pacific Seacraft 31, had arrived in the bay so I drove over in the dinghy to welcome the new arrival to Taiohae Bay. I found Linda Broido, an attractive young woman with a white canvas hat crowning her long blonde hair, changing her engine oil. Linda was obviously a very capable sailor and was half-way around on her solo circumnavigation. I was very impressed with her ability to repair her on-board equipment. She is an electrical engineer from the East Coast of the United States.

On Friday morning I made a quick run into the village to pay my respects at the gendarmerie. I told them of my plan to leave the next morning. With official duties out of the way I walked down to the post office for my last call to Margaret. We had a little difficulty getting used to the fact that I was *two and one-half* hours behind Los Angeles time, (9 hours 30 minutes slow GMT), rather than two or three. Margaret had secured her airline ticket through Corsair and was anxious to join in the fun.

The rest of the morning was spent planning the passage to Tahiti. In the afternoon I jumped into the dinghy and headed for the west shore of the bay, greeting yachties as I steered through the anchorage towards the Keikahanui Inn. I was a bit slack in my piloting duty on my approach to the beach. My attention was drawn to the beauty of the hillside when I heard a sickening *thud* and the outboard kicked up, out of the water and the engine raced. The prop was no longer turning. The sheer pin was broken. Of course, I did not have a spare sheer pin with me. I rowed to shore and landed the dinghy so I could run up to the Inn with *Kawabunga's* photograph and my write-up for Rose's log. I had to row a half-mile back to the boat against a strong wind and chop.

I decided during the trek back to that I would forgo the row into the village and back in the dark for the Tiurai. Even though I wanted to witness the dancing, I deemed it more important to get a good night's sleep before weighing anchor in the morning.

It was a shame to spend only a week in such a lovely, enchanting setting. I should have spent at the very least a month in the islands, but the season was already slipping away. I can not say for sure that I ran into any cannibals while on Nuku Hiva. Rather than being man-eaters, the local Marquesans seemed to prefer a good beef steak, perhaps with breadfruit and a cold Hinano. The people complimented their environment. They were rugged, friendly and mystifying.

Marquesan pony, Taiohae Bay

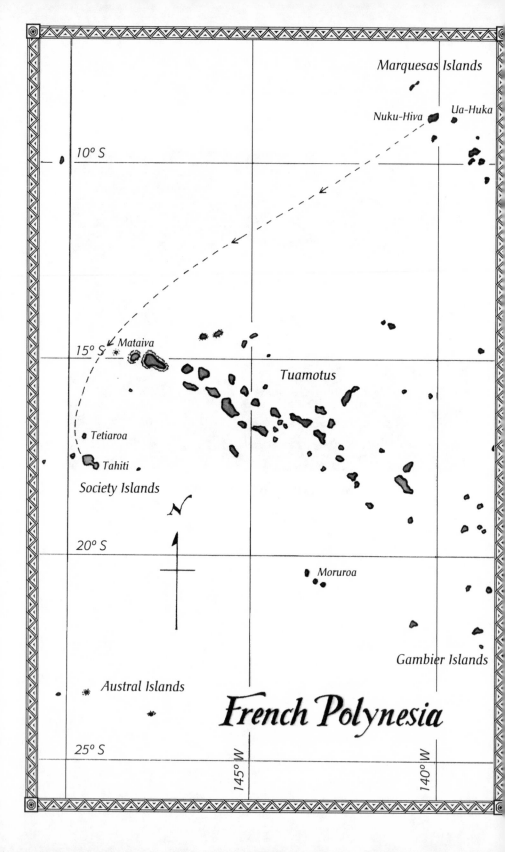

"I am the Captain of my craft,
My word is law, both fore and aft;
I am the cook and steward too,
I am the passenger and crew."
— Anonymous

CHAPTER FOUR

PASSAGE TO TAHITI

PASSAGE PLANNING

I planned my passage to Tahiti while at anchor in Taiohae Bay. I had charts, books and guides strewn about *Kawabunga's* little cabin. The Tuamotu Archipelago would be right on my way to Tahiti. I read about this interesting group of 78 islands, mostly coral atolls, stretching nearly 1,000 miles from the southeast to the northwest. I especially wanted to visit Rangiroa, a massive atoll with a crystal clear, navigable lagoon and knew it would likely be a once-in-a-lifetime opportunity to visit this atoll.

Being short-handed and without an engine, I decided not to sail the most direct route, which would take me through the Tuamotus, aptly dubbed the Dangerous Archipelago. Approaching these low-lying islands with their boat eating reefs was not a comforting notion. Also, without an engine, the strong tidal currents would make piloting in the passes prohibitively risky. Moreover, I did not have time to spend in the Tuamotu group if I were to meet Margaret in Papeete, Tahiti when she arrived on July 17. If possible, I wanted to be in Tahiti for Bastille Day, July 14.

With this in mind, I laid a more prudent course to the northeast of Mataiva, the most northwesterly atoll of the Tuamotu Archipelago. By this course I would evade all dangers by sailing "outside" Mataiva, then turn south toward Tahiti. The only danger would be Tetiaroa, which lies on a direct track, 30 miles north of Point Venus, on Tahiti. Nonchalant boat crews have been known to run up on Tetiaroa's reef on their way to Tahiti.

My course from Nuku Hiva to the Mataiva waypoint was 226° M for 634 nautical miles. I would then turn to course 173° M for 171 nautical miles to Tahiti. I thought it would take twelve days to make the passage.

THE HELL BITCH

I weighed anchor on the bright, sunny Saturday morning of July 1, bound for Tahiti. It was whilst weighing anchor, a 25 pound CQR with 60 feet of 5/16"chain and 300 feet of nylon line, that I came up with its nickname. From that point forward it was to be known as *The Hell Bitch*, in honor of *Lonesome Dove*. You'll remember that Captain Call rode the Hell Bitch, a magnificent horse, but a man-killer. Well, the CQR anchor is a magnificent piece of equipment, but it is a man-killer also. I needed to sail off the anchor and I was having trouble with the windlass. Once the anchor was broken out of the mud, *Kawabunga* began to drift swiftly downwind in the fresh breeze. I needed to get back to the helm as soon as possible in order to avoid playing bumper boats in the anchorage. Rather than fooling with the windlass any longer, I hauled the anchor rode, hand over hand, up to the deck. That was rough, slimy duty. As I lay in a crumpled heap atop the cargo bags, my hands cramped and muddy, my lungs ablaze and my heart executing a steeplechase inside my chest, I had an epiphany. Straining my ears I could hear a woman's voice. She was singing, low at first, but getting louder. Recognition flowed through me. I heard the lyrics of an old song taunting me; "You're not a kid anymore."

Within an hour *Kawabunga* glided through the Sentinels and put to sea. It did not take long to become re-accustomed to the rhythm of the Pacific swells, and to the routine of life at sea. The first four days out of Nuku Hiva I had splendid, off-the-wind sailing. I raised the cruising spinnaker and was able to keep the boat moving nicely in the light winds. I began reading the *Road to Omaha* by Robert Ludlum the day I left. What an enjoyable time; soaring along the blue rollers and laughing out loud reading about General MacKenzie Hawkins' and Sam Devereaux' antics. Rainbows, flying fish and a great book; the perfect combination.

INDEPENDENCE DAY PARADE

At daybreak on July 4, I sat in the cockpit licking my wounds. I had been slapped back to reality by four squalls during the night. The first squall hit at 1900 and lasted an hour. I was caught without my foulies on and was chilled to the bone. This was a bad one and I had not been physically or mentally prepared for a knock-down, drag-out fight. It took a lot out of me. Hand steering in an effort not to broach while exhausted and shivering from cold makes for an exciting evening. The cabin was soaked during the deluge as the storm had struck so suddenly I did not even have time to put the two top drop boards in the companionway. I was able to pull the sliding hatch back, but rain was blown inside the cabin. The other three squalls were all short-lived, lasting only five to fifteen minutes. I spent all night in the cockpit so I would be able to respond quickly to the weather changes.

Independence Day was a superb day I will never forget. *Kawabunga* was completely surrounded by hundreds of Pilot Whales from 0700 until 1300. I spent the morning in awe, watching my swim friends perform their antics for me. It was as though the call went out to all Pilot Whales to swim over to see

Kawabunga. As I stood on the bench in the cockpit, holding onto the handrail on the dodger, I could see whales on the horizon swimming towards me. Whales jumping and surfing as far as the eye could see. They took great joy in approaching *Kawabunga's* quarter in groups of four or five, surfing down those grand rollers and shooting under *Kawabunga's* keel. They looked like torpedoes zooming toward us. We had our own Independence Day Parade!

To celebrate the Fourth of July properly I had *two* cans of Beanie Weenie. Hot dogs and beans seemed to be an appropriate lunch for the occasion.

KEEP MY OPINION TO MYSELF

The passage was going very well. We averaged 87 nautical miles per day for the first five days out of Nuku Hiva, scoring 436 miles. I made a monumental error the very next day. I quote from the ship's log;

"Perfect sailing conditions. Exactly what you think of when you think of South Seas cruising!"

I remember thinking it might not be such a bright idea to actually write something like that down. . . . Well, the spell was definitely broken that very night. By 2200 I had reefed down the main and had a fight on my hands all night. The squalls were lined up, waiting their turn to ravage us. The wind was frightful, you could not see through the rain and the seas were immense and breaking. All in all, a miserable ride. I was beginning to show symptoms of SFS, (Squall Fatigue Syndrome). It got so that I hated the thought of night coming on — and it was dark for twelve hours. Again, quoting from my log;

"Worst seas yet this morning at 1000. I don't believe this. Man alive. Rock'n'roll — Full Auto! All kidding aside, I've had enough fun. It's really wild out here. I vote the wind and seas return to normal."

The howling winds, between 40 and 45 knots, lasted four days from the sixth through the ninth. Most of this time we ran before the gale under a double reefed main and no headsail. The scene was wild, with the sky angry and the sea completely white with foam blowing in streaks. Although the conditions made life aboard unpleasant, the crew's spirits were buoyed by the realization that we were making excellent mileage.

On the afternoon of the seventh I noticed the preventer I had rigged was causing a lot of stress on the lifelines. I decided to move it inboard of the lifelines. As I stood on the narrow starboard side deck grappling with this task I suddenly found myself with sea water surging up and over my right knee, the boat heeled perilously to starboard, charging along at 5 knots. I was tethered to the boat, but did not want to lose my footing in this predicament. It took every ounce of strength I could muster to hang on for dear life to the dodger's handrail until the boat finally came back up. The attack came suddenly and without warning, yet another lesson for the sailor to be prepared for the worst.

On the eighth we turned the corner and made our way safely around Mataiva. Unfortunately, the wind for our course was forward of the beam and we were hopelessly overpowered. For the first time, I hanked the storm jib to the forestay and this, along with the double-reefed main, balanced the boat beautifully. The motion improved considerably with the boat rigged in this fashion and we were able to make between 1.3 and 1.6 knots towards Tahiti. We were nearly hove-to, but able to make positive mileage. After twenty-four hours of this, the conditions moderated and I was able to strike the storm jib, put up the 100% jib, and go like a bandit for Tetiaroa.

BRANDO'S ISLAND

Tetiaroa Atoll is owned by motion picture star Marlon Brando. By noon on the tenth we were only 40 miles from Tetiaroa Atoll, with Tahiti another 30 miles down track. If we kept our current speed of 3.3 knots we would arrive off the dangerous atoll around midnight. We had been experiencing a very strong west-setting current the last several days. Taking these factors into consideration, I decided to change my course to the west, in order to run down its leeward side.

At 2100 I spotted a large cruise ship. I watched her for an hour and a half. It was very brilliantly lit up against the night sky. The full moon illuminated the sea for miles. At 2125 I sighted the north-end light of Tetiaroa, but even though we passed only seven miles off to the west with excellent visibility, I was never able to see the island. Unlike the rest of the windward Society Islands, Tetiaroa is an atoll and is very low. I was pleased with our satellite navigation. Brando may have waived at *Kawabunga* as we passed in the moonlight. It *could* have happened.

All was going well and my excitement was building. If the conditions held, we would be on station outside the Passe de Papeete at 0500, which would be perfect. We would be able to navigate the coral pass at first light, approximately 0620. I had visions of being anchored in Papeete Harbor at 0800.

Unfortunately, the wind began to gradually diminish. As the wind died away I was pushed towards the north shore of Moorea. The outline of Moorea looked wild and captivating under the full moon. I tacked away and got a good angle of attack for Papeete on Tahiti. At 0400 the wind vanished, to be heard from no more, leaving me midway between Moorea and Tahiti in the aptly named Sea Of The Moon. I figured the wind would reappear with the sunrise.

TIMING IS EVERYTHING

The sun came up. The wind did not. There was not a breath of wind as I sat in the cockpit dripping in sweat, three miles from the reef. Moorea and Tahiti were absolutely spectacular. I watched as the Moorea Ferry Boats raced the twelve miles or so between Passe Vaiare on Moorea and Passe de Papeete on Tahiti. I could also see large jet liners along with small, inter-island prop planes landing and taking off at the airfield located just south of Papeete. Reading through the guide books I learned that one can sit becalmed in this area for days, while just a few miles away at the northwest end of Tahiti there is plenty of wind. By 1300 the frustration level aboard became nearly unbearable. I questioned my sanity in such a venture. Would it not have been easier to have flown down and chartered a boat for a few weeks? I was in no mood to stay out another night and play around with coral reefs and passes with no engine. The ship's radio had drowned a week earlier. I pulled out my ICOM IC-M7 hand-held VHF radio and called the Papeete Harbor Master to arrange a tow. Well, it was a tow, that's for sure.

I expected a small power boat, twenty to twenty-five feet at most, to tow me in, something along the lines of Vessel Assist or Sea Tow in Southern California. I set about preparing the boat for the tow. An hour after our radio parley, I beheld a gigantic tug boat approaching little *Kawabunga*. I told the Harbor Master in my broken French that my boat was 20 feet long and four gross tons and he listened in his broken English and must have heard that I was the aircraft carrier *Nimitz*!

The captain and crew of the tug were very nice and towed me in professionally. I must say, I made a memorable entrance into the legendary harbor as little *Kawabunga* was towed into the anchorage by a monstrous tug boat. I had a huge audience as all the yachties in the anchorage were out on their boats watching the Tahitians in their pirogues (outrigger canoes) racing. Each pirogue had sixteen men paddling. The beach was packed with people watching the races and the lagoon was swarming with canoes. All of this activity was taking place on a Tuesday afternoon at 1430. I could not have imagined such a spectacle. I had arrived in the middle of the races held during the Heiva Festival.

As soon as I set *The Hell Bitch* I had no less than three dinghies surrounding me. They were all there to help. I was so touched I could have sat down and cried. Isabel from *Soul Massage*, George from *Kemo Sabay* and Val and Craig from *Cassiopea* all pitched in to get me squared away. I retrieved my two extra 250 foot anchor rodes, tied one to each stern cleat and tossed them to George and Val, who ran them to shore for me.

I tossed Isabel another line and she held me fast to her boat while the whole process was going on. The starboard line was tied off to a tree and the port line was tied off to a bollard along the beach. The kindness of the yachties was overwhelming. At long last, I was in Tahiti, but I was dog tired.

Public Market, Papeete, Tahiti

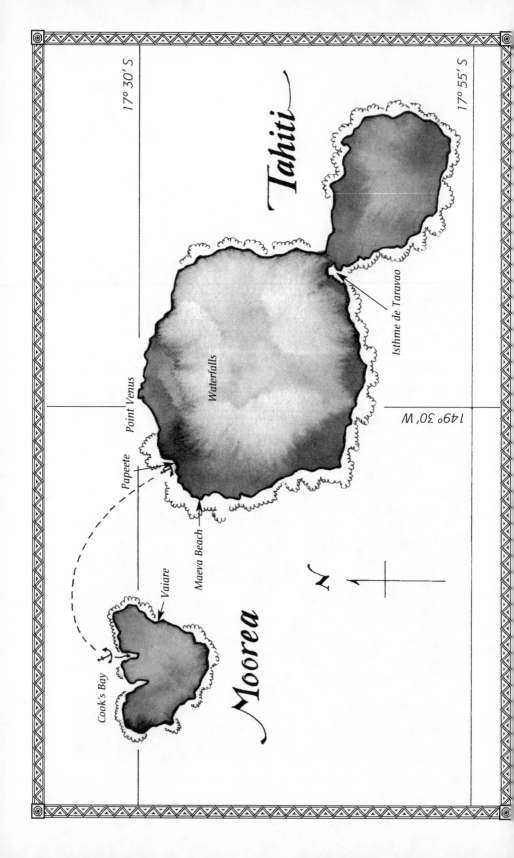

*"Live! Life is a banquet and most poor suckers
are starving to death!"*
— Auntie Mame

CHAPTER FIVE

TAHITI; THE ISLAND
OF LOVE

GETTING ACQUAINTED

Tahiti. The name evokes a mental picture of a sailor's earthly
Shangri-La; bronzed, seductive island maidens, balmy
tradewinds, swaying palm trees, erupting volcanoes, exotic
flowers, lush vegetation and an ideal clime. The coastal plains
and cloud-capped mountains were embraced by a colorful
barrier reef, broken at intervals by passes allowing access into
the protected crystal lagoons abounding in sea life. I was eager
to follow in the wake of explorers like Cook, Wallis and Bligh.

The first week was spent getting acquainted: acquainted
with Papeete, acquainted with my fellow yachties and
acquainted with the rejuvenating spigots strategically placed
along Hokule'a Beach. Unlimited fresh water for bathing and
drinking. True paradise.

Papeete is no longer the sleepy South Seas village it once
was. Young vahines no longer swim out to your boat, offering
themselves to the arriving seafarer. I speak solely for myself. All
those nails I stowed were of little use in bartering in 1995 as the
Tahitians use the French Pacific franc (CFP — Colonies

Francaises du Pacifique). I also arrived twenty years too late to belly up to the bar at Quinn's Bar, Tahiti's famous South Seas gin mill. Quinn's met the fate of the wrecking ball when the waterfront was redeveloped in the 1970's. There has been a substantial increase in tourism since Faa'a International Airport was opened in 1961. To put this into perspective; more tourists arrive in Honolulu in one day than in French Polynesia in an entire year.

Tahiti's staggering beauty, the mixture of Tahitian, French and multi-national cruisers, the undercurrent of protests over the bomb and the Tahitian's yearning for independence painted an intriguing scene. This was thrilling to a wide-eyed Michigan boy who had never traveled abroad.

Kawabunga was anchored in front of the Paofai Protestant Church off Hokule'a Beach. The beach was brimming with outrigger canoes that the local paddlers faithfully took out in the late afternoons. After clearing in with the port authorities, I had the option of moving to the quay but I decided to stay out of the "high-rent" district in deference to my modest cruising kitty.

The Port Captain, Customs and Immigration offices are all conveniently located in the same building on the Cruise Ship Dock. While clearing in I met Warwick Tompkins, a professional delivery skipper from Mill Valley, California. Tompkins had sailed to Tahiti several times and had been cruising the Societies for a month after participating in the San Francisco to Tahiti race.

Even though he was preparing to weigh anchor for Santa Cruz later in the day, he took the time to give me sound advice and introduce me to Papeete. We walked across the street and down a block to the Public Market where Warwick introduced me to Chris and Nedra Wagner who were cruising aboard *Magic Carpet*. They were moored at the Yacht Club de Tahiti. We picked out lunch from a Chinese vendor and took our plates up to the second floor where we were entertained with Tahitian music and dancing. After lunch we walked through the enormous market, admiring the fruits, vegetables, meat, fish, basket work, shell necklaces, flowers and pareus. Grass skirts and coconut bras were also for sale.

Papeete is the capital and administrative head of French Polynesia. There are approximately 150,000 people living on the island of Tahiti. The population of Papeete is 24,000, but the city swells to a whopping 94,000 daily when people drive in from the countryside to work. Of course, this creates snarled traffic on the only highway leading to and from the city.

Jeff and Kathy Sweeney from the lovely boat *Kathryn Anne* rowed over shortly after I arrived. We had happened upon each other two months earlier while at sea. It was fun to meet them face to face and compare our passage notes. Jeff took four years to restore *Kathryn Anne*, a wooden Moody 42´. She is precisely the breed of vessel you dream of backdropped against Shark's Tooth Mountain in Opunohu Bay, Moorea. We spent many enjoyable afternoons in Tahiti with this delightful couple and became good friends.

MOTORISTS — TAHITIAN STYLE

I was very surprised at the heavy traffic and dangerous drivers in Tahiti. As a general rule, the French were hopped up on a combination of nicotine and caffeine while the Tahitians were pie-eyed on either Hinano beer or marijuana, or both. This made for a perilous mix in the traffic flow. Crossing the street was an adventure in itself, always fraught with danger. I often thought how ironic it would be to plow the waves all the way to Tahiti only to be obliterated while attempting to cross Boulevard Pomare on my way to Acajou's for lunch by some wild-eyed lunatic at the command of a Renault. You took your life in your hands each and every time you crossed the street. Cross walks and traffic signals offered no sanctuary. You had to be quick on your feet. Picture Lou Whittaker stealing second base.

In the brief time we were in Tahiti, I personally witnessed two serious auto versus pedestrian accidents. One involved a young lady and one a little girl. Moreover, there were two multi-car crashes directly in front of the beach where we were anchored, one with multiple fatalities. We watched from the boat as they hauled away the bodies. We knew the poor victims were dead because the paramedics were in no hurry to get them out of the vehicle or away from the scene. It was commonplace to hear the screech of tires and then a horrible crash or even worse, a sickening *thump*. . . . All this within a two block area! Tahiti's mortality rate on the road is horrendous. There was a traffic school across the street from the anchorage which invariably had its classroom packed to the rafters, frequently with driving offenders overflowing out onto the parking lot.

HEIVA

The first week in Tahiti was very exciting as the Heiva Festival was in full swing. The Heiva has replaced the Tiurai Fête which paid homage the capture of the Bastille on July 14, 1789 during the French Revolution. The Heiva Festival began in 1985 to commemorate the territory's first anniversary of autonomy. Heiva is an extremely popular two week spectacle, featuring Tahitian dancers in their traditional dress at the ferry dock, outrigger canoe races in Papeete's inner harbor, and various ancestral athletic events. It is a huge party, rivaling spring break in Ft. Lauderdale. The difference here is that people of all ages go nuts, rather than just college students.

While living in Santa Monica, Margaret and I usually celebrated Bastille Day at a local French restaurant. We thought how cool it would be to spend a Bastille Day together either in France or French Polynesia. If only I could have made it to Tahiti a week earlier we could have made this dream come true. Unfortunately, the timing was not quite right. Bastille Day came to pass on my third morning in Tahiti.

President Chirac, France's newly elected leader, had declared his intention to resume France's nuclear testing program at Moruroa Atoll in the Tuamotus. Greenpeace had been protesting this decision and had organized a big demonstration in Papeete on Bastille Day. When I was in the Marquesas I heard over the radio that there had been protests at that time and the streets had been closed to traffic in Tahiti. I had noticed several French navy ships slipping through the pass into Papeete's deep water port during the few days I had been in Tahiti. While having drinks aboard George and Sarah's *Kemo Sabay* with Jeff and Kathy, we heard the French planned to bring in tanks to quell the demonstrations. I began to learn about the hotbed of turmoil surrounding Moruroa Atoll in the Tuamotus.

BASTILLE DAY

The anchorage was buzzing early on Bastille Day. At 0630 scores of Tahitians dressed up in island garb and waiving their home-made Polynesian flags mustered at the beach. The independence flags have a blue stripe on top, a white stripe in the middle and a blue stripe on the bottom with five yellow stars in the middle. The five stars represent the five archipelagos of Polynesia: The Marquesas, Tuamotus, Gambier, Australs and Societies. The nuclear protest flags were very similar to the independence flags but included a mushroom-shaped explosion graphic in the middle. Many people were wearing T-shirts protesting the bomb and French rule in Polynesia. The corps pounded their drums and blew their conch shells, inflaming the group's passions.

At precisely 0800 the French Navy shot off a twenty-one gun salute from a warship berthed at the Cruise Ship Wharf. The drums got louder and the shindig escalated on the beach. At 0900 the Greenpeace ship *Rainbow Warrior II* entered the lagoon through the pass. The Tahitians went bonkers! The harbor was teeming with outrigger canoes and dinghies scrambling out to salute and escort the *Rainbow Warrior II* to her berth at the Inter-Island Schooner Dock. What an entrance. The French were careful to berth the protest ship across the harbor, tucking it away from any access by the demonstrators.

In all the excitement, I half-expected the *Rainbow Warrior II* to fall to the same fate as her namesake. On July 10, 1985, Greenpeace's flagship, *Rainbow Warrior*, was preparing to set sail from Auckland Harbor, New Zealand to Moruroa to protest France's nuclear testing there. Before she could leave on her voyage, she was sunk by two bombs planted by French secret service agents. Nothing quite that spectacular occurred, but it was all very exciting just the same.

There were a few younger cruisers who donned island headdresses made of leaves, raised the protest flag and took their dinghies into the fray. I was invited to go, but felt I had no dog in this fight. Generally, the yachties stayed on their boats and took it all in from a distance. I was in the middle of cleaning the head compartment during much of the operation.

By 1130 the rally was over. The canoes triumphantly returned to the beach blowing their horns and conch shells and continued the beach party. At noon the French fired off several rounds from a warship at the Quai Bir Hakeim, where normally there are yachts tied stern-to the quay. This infuriated the Tahitians, whose ranks had dramatically fallen. The canoes had been stored away on the beach, but a few were lifted out of their cradles and carried to the lagoon. The protestors paddled towards the quay to meet the new challenge.

PREPARING FOR INSPECTION

My first priority was to get the little blue boat civilized before Margaret arrived. Cushions, laundry, duffel bags and blankets had to be aired out, laundered by hand and dried out. The boat had to be totally reorganized and transformed from a passage maker to a live-aboard. A great deal of equipment was hauled out and stowed up on deck and in the cockpit. We needed space to sit, cook and sleep. Believe me, this was no easy feat after two months at sea, but after a lot of spit and polish *Kawabunga* was ready for a visit from the gentler sex.

LES BROCHETTES

It had been two months since I had kissed Margaret good-bye. At long last, Sunday, July 16, arrived. Margaret was scheduled to arrive at 0700 the next day. I watched a glorious sunset over Moorea as I walked to the truck snack bars — also referred to as *les brochettes, les roulettes* or simply *les trucks*. Jeff and Kathy turned me on to *les trucks*, located along the waterfront behind the Port Captain's office. These thirty or so lunch wagons provide a variety of food, including Chinese, Tahitian, French, Italian and American, at a reasonable price. This was a very busy area, especially on the weekends when the cruise ships were in port. The aroma from the various stoves, barbecues and open fires which permeated the warm tropical breeze was worth the walk down to the wharf.

I pulled up a stool at Chez Jacqueline and savored Steak Frites. Jacqueline took orders and cut French bread while her husband barbecued the meat on a charcoal grill and her daughter bussed up dirty dishes. Each lunch wagon has from ten to twelve stools. Her's were almost always occupied. This became our favorite *les truck*. She and her family, all Tahitians who spoke no English, were always very pleasant.

As I waited for my steak to be barbecued, I had to hold back a chuckle as I thought of the days when Margaret and I worked together. When the pressure was on Margaret would say, "Someday I'm going to run away to Tahiti and live on bananas." More like steak and French fries.

RENDEZVOUS IN PARADISE

I was much too excited to row back to *Kawabunga* and wait for morning. Faa'a International Airport was only four miles from the cruise ship wharf, so I walked to the airport. As you can imagine, the airport is not a large one and it does not take long to see everything there is to see. I watched the Tahitian women make their beautiful flower leis and bought two for Margaret. One of the ladies, seeing how anxious I was for my vahine's arrival, gave me a third lei as a gift. It was a very sweet and touching gesture.

This was a very long night. The hours dragged on at an agonizingly slow pace. Eventually, 0700 rolled around, but still no arrival! The plane was two hours late. At long last the plane arrived and I was able to see her going through customs. She had a surprise for me. She had three huge bags with her. Margaret was also bringing down some replacement parts, including a new bilge pump and a big hand pump that she took aboard the plane as a carry-on. Where in the world would we find room for the new bags, new equipment and new crew member on little *Kawabunga?*

We had expected it to be hot and muggy in Tahiti and were pleasantly surprised to find the weather to be absolutely perfect. Margaret arrived on one of the most perfect days of the year. We hired a taxi and within a few minutes we were deposited at Hokule'a Beach. Let the loading begin.

Margaret noticed I had changed quite a bit since that rainy afternoon in San Diego two months earlier. I was forty pounds lighter and sported a white beard. Guess which of the two she didn't like? Apparently, the look I had been going for — that of a suave, seasoned passagemaker — fell short. She said I looked like a wolf man. I suspect she felt I looked like a burned-out old fool. It was strongly suggested the beard be removed posthaste. Very shortly after boarding *Kawabunga,* a photograph was taken of me and my beard before I was sheered like a New Zealand sheep.

Securing my first mate's extended visa was a monumental hassle owing to a combination of governmental bureaucratic catch-22, coupled with the airline's hiring of an imperialistic, lame-brained and lazy staff. The government would not give her a visa without an extended airline departure date and the airline would not extend the departure date without a visa. It took three days of reasoning, pleading, and veiled threats before Margaret got a little naked Tiki guy stamped on her passport.

LE TRUCK

We spent the next few weeks exploring Tahiti by *le truck,* by our dinghy and on foot. By far the most reasonably priced and entertaining mode of transportation was by *le truck.* This should not to be confused with *les trucks,* the lunch wagons. These open air wood-paneled busses were usually owned by the local driver and kept immaculately clean. Frequently, a huge Tahitian driver would be behind the wheel while his wife sat to starboard collecting money while simultaneously managing two baby Tahitians. Tahitian music would blare from the speakers. There were local trucks that ran throughout Papeete and long-range trucks that service the outlying districts.

We never had to wait long for *le truck* to come by. If you are walking, the driver will honk to see if you want him to stop. The drivers are very patient and will wait five minutes for you and your wife to climb a steep hill up to the road. Who ever heard of a bus driver waiting for anyone in Los Angeles? They may swerve onto the sidewalk to run you down, but they would never wait. We concluded the *le truck* drivers were by far the friendliest people on Tahiti. Each rider pays 120 francs and sits on a bench running along the open-air windows. From this seat you can drink in the flavor of the Tahitians with their baguettes, fruits and children — many children. We were told 75% of the population of Tahiti are under age eighteen. This has created dire social problems.

THE ENGINE CHRONICLES

Soon after Margaret's arrival we had to address the engine situation. Considering my vast mechanical experience — none whatsoever — and the in-depth diagnostic analysis I had already completed on our Yanmar, the engine looked gravely ill at best and had most probably fallen as a casualty of the first leg of the cruise. We had the option of rebuilding the engine or simply buying an outboard motor. Opting for an outboard would require figuring a way to mount a bracket of some sort around the windvane supporting frame, which takes up the entire transom area. The thought of reclaiming the engine compartment for storage was intriguing, but we wanted to get the engine repaired if it were at all economically feasible because we wanted the power generating capability of the little diesel and did not want the hassle of storing the outboard while at sea. I must say, however, that the thought of dumping that diesel engine into Papeete Harbor held a certain charm.

Armed with our trusty cruiser's map of Papeete, we set out for the industrial section of the harbor. The Tourism Office gave away maps listing boating services in Papeete to all yachties. We stopped at a popular boat and outboard dealer. We were greeted by a congenial Frenchman who was anxious to make a deal. I read somewhere that Johnson outboards, the outboards of my youth, were the overwhelming favorite in the South Pacific and that proved to be true. Nearly all the local fishermen employed Johnson outboards. The friendly Frenchman was selling Johnson outboards.

When our salesman asked me what type of outboard we currently had aboard I sheepishly told him we had a Suzuki. The man turned beat red as a grimace descended upon his face. He spit first to port and then to starboard. "I spit on Suzuki" he said. "But, if you want to buy a Suzuki, I have a cousin who works at the Suzuki dealership and will give you a good deal."

In the end, we decided against the outboard route. Chris and Nedra recommended Clouseau, a French diesel mechanic who did a lot of work at the Tahiti Yacht Club. Reportedly, Clouseau was not only an excellent diesel mechanic, he also spoke English. He was our man. The earliest he could meet with us was on the morning of July 31. Clouseau failed to appear at the appointed time and place and thus began the Papeete Engine Chronicles.

CLOUSEAU THE DIESEL MECHANIC

Clouseau blew off four meetings with us over the two month period that it took to have the Yanmar up and running. He had a yard on the motu across from the anchorage known as Quai des Caboteurs (Inter-Island Schooners) in the industrial section of the harbor. The only way you could get in touch with Clouseau was to telephone him at home at 2030. Sometimes he was there and sometimes he was not. I made countless missions into town to find a pay telephone to attempt contact with our mechanic.

Clouseau and his aide Kato arrived on August 2 and, after a brief examination, agreed with my diagnosis. The engine was in a bad way. They wanted me to take *Kawabunga* to their dock so they could remove the engine with their crane. I did not want to lose my prime anchorage so I set about taking down the canvas awning and dodger and rigged a block and tackle from the boom, using the gant line I have for my boson's chair. When Kato returned with his Tahitian vahine the next day it was an easy sell. Kato disconnected the engine in a few minutes and we were able to lift the little single-cylinder 7.5 Yanmar 1GM engine out of the engine compartment with the block and tackle, swing it out over Kato's work boat and gently lower it onto the bed of plywood positioned between the ribs of the boat. No muss, no fuss.

On August 8 we met with Clouseau and were informed the engine needed to be rebuilt. Water had killed the engine. We were given an extensive parts list. Although there was a large Chinese Yanmar dealership in the industrial section of Papeete, he did not have our parts in stock and Clouseau felt we could get the parts cheaper and faster by ordering them from the states. We faxed Margaret's father, a very experienced mechanic. He contacted several Yanmar dealers in the Los Angeles area for the best price and fastest service. R.S. Marine Engines in San Pedro fit the bill perfectly. They assembled the precious parts and shipped them off marked *Repair Parts For Yacht In Transit*, so we would not have to pay duty.

Three weeks later, on August 29, we finally picked up our parts at the airport. To say we were thrilled would be an understatement. In our excitement we forgot to take along our ship's papers and had to return for them before customs would release our parts to us. I won't even get into the run-around we experienced with our shipping agent as to whether the parts had actually arrived, or if they were at customs. It was the run-around ad nauseam.

That night I telephoned Clouseau and made a date to meet him the next morning on the beach in front of the boat. It looked as though we would be saying farewell to Tahiti in about a week.

THE TROUBLE WITH BLONDES

I must tell you, I feel a real kinship with Forrest Gump when I think of what came to pass next. As Winston Groom wrote, ". . . I'm beginnin to realize Mister Boone don't understand I'm a idiot, but he was bout to find out." Forrest and I can be a little too trusting. I got up bright and early, positioning myself on the beach where I had met good ol' Clouseau in the past. It was my mission to make it as easy as possible for him to pick up the parts and get to work rebuilding our engine. Sitting down on a bollard, I placed the prized box of parts next to me and entertained myself by another run through of Forrest Gump. As the morning wore on I talked with yachtie neighbors, busy with their own errands.

At 1030 I noticed our French neighbor Dreyfus was having a difficult time retrieving his anchor. He and a friend were planning to spend a few days at Moorea. They weren't going to make it without help. I jumped into the dinghy, delivered the engine parts to the safety of *Kawabunga's* cockpit, helped Dreyfus with his anchor, retrieved the package and returned to the beach and my lookout for Clouseau within a half-hour.

I strongly suspect Dreyfus was with the French secret police because his story of sailing to Tahiti did not square with his lack of seamanship. Also, he was emphatic about anchoring next to me when there was insufficient room to do so. It just so happened that Greenpeace had their office in the building directly in front of my anchorage and the reporters and activists congregated on the beach in front of *Kawabunga*. This was a perfect vantage point from which to maintain surveillance over the protesters, Greenpeace activists and reporters.

At 1130 Linda Broido from *Viking Princess*, whom I had first met in Nuku Hiva, came strolling up the street. Linda was yelling something to me from across the street but it was difficult to hear each other above the roar of the traffic. I was eager to tell her of our good fortune. Our yachtie neighbors knew we were anxiously awaiting delivery of our engine parts. Seeing an opening in traffic I made my break and scampered over to Linda on the other side.

The day before, some Tahitians rowed out and gave her an entire stalk of bananas. She was weighing anchor for Bora Bora soon and was worried they would all ripen at once and be wasted. We made arrangements to stop over later in the afternoon for cold drinks and our ration of bananas.

I proudly pointed to the box of engine parts, our ticket out of Tahiti, sitting a mere twenty-five yards away. Linda hurried on into town to send a fax. I dashed across the street to resume my book and my vigil. Something was different. What was it? Where was my book? Where was the shipping box? They had vanished into thin air. In a complete panic I looked around to see who had taken them and saw nothing out of the ordinary. I searched up and down the beach, to no avail. That box was out of my sight less than a minute or two. As Forrest would say, "Stupid is as stupid does."

After searching all day, my last hope was that Clouseau had pulled up in his van, snatched up the box and was busy putting the engine back together. At 2015 I finally contacted him by telephone and my heart sank when he said; "Oh Charlie, I am so sorry. I was too busy to stop by and pick up the parts today." Margaret had never been so angry at me. They even stole my book, adding insult to injury.

A quote from Captain James Cook seems to be in order. In speaking of the Tahitians in *Endeavor's* log of July 1769 he said; "They have all fine white teeth and for the most part short flat noses and thick lips, yet their features are agreeable and their gate graceful, and their behavior to strangers and to each other is open, affable and courteous and from all I could see free from treachery, only that they are thieves to a man and would steal but everything that came in their way and that with such dexterity as would shame the most noted pickpocket in Europe." Not much had changed in 226 years.

The next morning we picked ourselves up, dusted ourselves off and walked into town. We faxed R.S. Marine, explaining what had happened and asking them to assemble another shipment pronto. Our friends Buzz Wright and Lynne Haggard of Manhattan Beach came to our aid at this point as R.S. Marine did not accept American Express. Buzz and Lynne were kind enough to put the charges on their Visa card. We were spreading the misery around as Margaret's dad had gone through this entire drill the first time around. Luckily, thanks to Sal's earlier leg-work and Buzz and Lynne's plastic, Jack from R.S. Marine was able to rush our order through. The parts arrived in Tahiti twelve days later.

PROTESTS TURN UGLY

During the interim period, between the time we ordered the parts and their arrival, Tahiti had gone through great turmoil. Peaceful protests had turned to riots after the French began setting off nuclear tests on Moruroa. During the early part of the rioting, the airport had been attacked, the radar facility destroyed and much of the airport burned out.

On September 11 we disembarked from *le truck* at the airport, or what was left of it. We felt an eerie foreboding as we walked through the parking lot towards the terminal. More than one hundred rental cars had been turned over and set aflame in that parking lot during the first day of the riots. The charming area where the Tahitian women assembled the flower leis was completely destroyed. Workers were busy trying to clean out the blackened terminal. Our heart's sank as we approached the Customs building and the offices of our shipping agent.

The first floor was completely burned out. From what we could see, there was no way in the world the shipping office could have escaped the ravagement. We walked through the blackened stairwell, up the steps to the second floor and were astonished to find the office staff with buckets and sponges, busy washing the walls, ceiling and floors. They were up and running, or at least cantering, very shortly after the uprising. Their records showed that our shipment was in customs, but customs was downstairs, which had been completely burned out. The customs office simply did not exist anymore. The customs officers were sitting at a folding table in the middle of a warehouse. Miraculously, our parts had been saved and, after showing our ship's papers, we were off to *le truck* stand with our precious cargo.

As soon as we got back to *Kawabunga* I took the dinghy across the harbor to Clouseau's shop and hand-delivered the box of parts to Kato. I spoke with Clouseau himself later that evening and was told he could not possibly get to my engine until the end of the week. . . .

The next day we set about pumping two gallons of sea water out of the diesel tank! No wonder the engine coughed and died. The culprit was the air vent for the tank which is located just under the cap rail at the port bow. On the way down to the Marquesas Islands, this part of the boat was underwater a great deal. Obviously, a massive quantity of water found its way through the vent, down the hose and into the tank. I disconnected and tied off the hose from the vent and solved the problem.

KILL CLOUSEAU!

We were up at 0500 on September 18. Liberation day had finally arrived. Clouseau was scheduled to arrive at 0900 to reinstall the engine and we had broken down the awning and dodger, rigged the block and tackle and anxiously awaited his arrival. It pains me to tell you what happened next. Instead of Clouseau and Kato pulling up in their work boat, I saw Clouseau alone, walking along the beach. I hopped in the dinghy and pulled myself to shore to find him with a very sad look on his face. "What's wrong?" I asked.

"Something I overlooked when I tore the engine down. You need another part. You need a fuel-injection assembly. I am so sorry. . . ." He handed me a piece of paper with the part number written on it.

We would not be leaving for Moorea in the morning. I was torn between sitting down in the sand and crying like a baby or committing homicide on a French expatriate.

Margaret's father came to the rescue again, ordering the part from New York. After yet another no-show, Clouseau and Kato finally installed the rebuilt Yanmar on September 26 and 27.

We had planned to stay in Tahiti for three weeks, but due to the ongoing, ever frustrating and grossly expensive engine saga, we stayed eleven weeks. Not only was it expensive by way of monetary costs, (mechanics, parts, shipping, added expense of living in the most expensive place in the South Pacific), but cost us dearly in the irreplaceable entity — time. The cruising season in the Societies lasts until November 1, by which time you should be high-tailing it out of hurricane territory. As our cruising season slipped away, majestic Moorea, like the mythical Bali Hai, both beckoned and taunted us from only ten miles away.

Although the whole ordeal was very frustrating, we managed to have a lot of fun while in Tahiti and our extended stay allowed us to explore more of the captivating island and delight in her fascinating people during an exciting time in her history.

SEAMANSHIP

Before setting out on this cruise I was rather apprehensive about my seamanship skills. Although I had been sailing virtually my entire life, I had a secret fear that, compared to those other cruisers from around the world, I would come up a little short. I was dreading the day the fraud police would find me out, board *Kawabunga,* and drag me away to the phony-cruiser's brig.

After seeing some of the boneheads in Papeete, however, I no longer dread the comparison. What I observed was astounding. I had trouble believing some of the boats, many from as far away as Europe, had made it safely to Tahiti. The art of anchoring is apparently not stressed in some European circles. Perhaps blue is the color of the European bull's-eye as little *Kawabunga* was constantly the target of inept sailors rushing to launch the anchor, launch the dinghy, and launch themselves to the nearest bar before Tahiti ran out of Hinano beer and ukuleles. Just picture the Three Stooges abandoning ship. By the time we left I had the fending-off drill down pat. Strong winds, a muddy bottom and unattended boats made life interesting at the anchorage. I suspect a certain, G.P.S., push-button mentality was to blame.

While living in Tahiti's lagoon, I wore either a swim suit or shorts and Margaret wore either her swimsuit or a pareu. Margaret's search for the perfect pareu began shortly after her arrival. Margaret looked like a pretty native with her long brunette hair crowned in a colorful flower headdress and a pareu. She never went as far as the grass skirt and coconut bra though.

We decided to take the dinghy up to the Tahiti Yacht Club. Marcia Davock's guide was perfect for navigating within Tahiti's lagoon. We simply turned to the page detailing our route through the coral, placed our plastic Chart Book cover over it and zipped it up to protect it from the elements. It was important to remember that red right returning is backwards in French Polynesia. We grabbed our Pelican case with the ICOM hand-held VHF, spare sheer pins, a screw driver, water bottles and broad brimmed canvas hats. We took Margaret's umbrella to use as a sun shade and headed east-northeast towards Point Venus.

MORE BLONDE TROUBLE

A few days earlier I had learned a valuable lesson, one that I had learned as a kid and forgotten as a grown-up. *Always* take spare sheer pins with you. Margaret and I had taken the dinghy out for a little late-morning spin just to take in the sights. We had intended to spend fifteen minutes checking out the new boats in the anchorage but were drawn further down the interesting shoreline towards Faa'a and the airport. As we followed the channel west-southwest away from Papeete, we decided it would be nice to pull up to a restaurant along the lagoon's shoreline for lunch. Our opportunity to ask for local knowledge came when we spotted an attractive French maiden with strawberry-blonde hair, dressed in a chalk-white robe, strolling out on a wooden dock to a beach chair at the end of the pier overlooking the lagoon. As I left the channel and carefully threaded our way through the thousand and one coral heads, I tried to conjure up the French word for restaurant — duh!

As we approached within a few feet of the dock I stammered something in mangled French about a restaurant, pointing to the shoreline. An amused come-hither look spread across the damsel's face as she approached the chair, untied her robe and with one fluid motion tossed it onto the chair. My heart seized up a half-beat before the outboard did — my heart when I found myself gawking at a topless French girl — my outboard when it struck a coral head, shattering the sheer pin.

Of course the young lady found this all quite comical. Margaret did not. Lunch was definitely out. By this time, the afternoon breeze was building in earnest. The coconut palms were bent over 45° and, of course, the wind was blowing directly from the anchorage. It was a very long, quiet (except for the incessant mutterings from Margaret about the half-naked Euro-trash) and exhausting three mile row back to the anchorage against a nasty chop. This was the second time an attractive blonde dame had wrought disaster upon the captain of the *Kawabunga* during this cruise.

This made two broken sheer pins. I did not have spares in either instance. I carried spares from that time on and never broke another.

LIFE IN TAHITI

Our dinghy cruise to the Tahiti Yacht Club was a successful pilgrimage. We took photographs along the way and enjoyed seeing Tahiti's mountains from a different perspective. It is a rare occurrence to see the peak of Orohena mountain as it is usually hidden in the clouds. We were fortunate enough to see this sight for ten minutes in the early afternoon. We had a scrumptious lunch at the club before heading back. We needed to shove off in the early afternoon so we would have the sun overhead in order to navigate through the coral.

When we returned we noticed that Peter aboard *Paros* was anchored a few boats away from *Kawabunga* and we motored over to greet him. He always had a smile for everyone and developed good friendships with the Tahitians, spending his afternoons working out with a team of paddlers. They paddled over to Moorea and back before sunset. As in the Marquesas Islands, Peter was boffo with the vahines.

Reading is a luxury that the cruising lifestyle offers. To be able to kick back and enjoy reading a book through without interruption is rare in the spare minutes you can carve out for yourself in the work-a-day world. However, it was difficult to find English language books in Tahiti. The book store had a half-dozen English language books, mostly history books as I remember. They showed typical Americans at work and at play. Noticeable was the fact that these photographs were taken in the early 1960's. There were magazines for sale. The magazines,

International versions of *Time* and *Newsweek*, were at least a week behind in any news and the cost was prohibitive. The list price was 475 francs, but the local charge was 750 francs. During the riots the price went as high as 1150 francs. Trading paperbacks among the yachties was prevalent.

Before the book was stolen, Margaret and I took turns reading *Forrest Gump* to each other aloud. This was my third time through the book and Margaret began to worry because I was beginning to talk with a southern accent. Some of my favorite memories of Tahiti are of the two of us crammed in *Kawabunga's* little V-berth, acting out the chapters from Groom's book.

We quickly tired of the "Coconut Music" heard from the street corners and on the radio. This Tahitian music sounded like a weird twist on the music played by a 1930's singing cowboy, played on the ukulele rather than the guitar. Gene Autry and Roy Rogers would make good Tahitians.

IN SEARCH OF THE PERFECT PAREU

We will remember Margaret's birthday of 1995 as the one in which we circumnavigated Tahiti. We celebrated by renting a car and setting off to explore the island. We headed for Pt. Venus, winding along the road that circles the island. For the most part, the Tahitians live along the narrow coastal plains.

We had taken the wrong *le truck* on one occasion on our way to Pt. Venus and were treated to a winding road following the river valleys up the mountain. The area was filled with little huts, horse stables and many children. At one point the river had been dammed up, forming a perfect pool just outside a cottage. A deck had been built out to the pool and a dozen children were splashing and screaming to their heart's content. In our rental car we re-visited Pt. Venus. We had come out for the day by *le truck* a week earlier. It was exciting to see the Pt. Venus Lighthouse, designed by Robert Louis Stevenson's father. We walked along the beach looking out to historic Matavai Bay

where, in the eighteenth century, Wallis' *Dolphin*, Cook's
Discovery, Bligh's *Bounty* and Wilson's *Duff* had anchored. The
beach at Matavai Bay is exquisite and you could imagine how
hard it would have been for the crew of the Bounty to weigh
anchor after such a long and extraordinarily risqué stay.

Margaret was in search of the perfect pareu so when we
found Tahitian women stretching fabric out on the ground,
allowing it to dry in the tropical sun, we had to study their
methods. These pareus were much prettier and of superior
quality than the ones offered in Papeete. We bought a pareu for
each of our nieces and headed for the little food stand which, in
our judgment, had the best ice cream in Tahiti.

We left Pt. Venus, heading clockwise around the island, past
blow holes, waterfalls and dreamy beaches. There was a photo
opportunity around every curve and we stopped often to
marvel at the multitude of colors shading the lagoon to the port
while to starboard we gazed on the lush green hues rising
straight up from the coastal plain and the fluffy clouds capping
the peaks. We were surprised that there were no restaurants
once we left Pt. Venus, just "country" as they would say in
Hawaii. It was all very charming, but we were starved. There
were no Seven-Eleven's here. We found the people to be
friendlier as we traveled further away from Papeete, at least
until they got behind the wheel of a car. They had no patience
for looky-loos or for anyone driving anywhere close to the
speed limit. Double yellow line? Blind curve? "I spit on your
caution!" Defensive driving was a must. We certainly did not
want to get in an accident driving more than five miles per hour
in our Renault rental car as it would be crumpled faster than a
Budweiser can in the hands of Cap'n Ron.

We tooled our way along the windward side of the island to
the Isthmus de Taravao connecting Tahiti Nui (Big Tahiti) from
Tahiti Iti (Little Tahiti). This isthmus is only three-eight's of a
mile across, nearly cutting the island in two. Port Phaeton is
nearly land-locked and serves as a perfect hurricane hole. I was
told it fills up very fast whenever there is a hurricane alert. This

section reminded me of Catalina Harbor and the Isthmus at Santa Catalina Island in Southern California.

We were now approximately half-way around Tahiti Nui from Papeete, having driven 54 kilometers with 60 kilometers to go. We decided to drive along the north coast of Tahiti Iti for a few miles, enjoying the sleepy fishing villages and the spectacular windward coast before turning around and motoring back to the Isthmus de Taravao and then along the southeast coast of Tahiti.

It was a short drive from the isthmus to the Gauguin Museum and Botanical Gardens. We stayed only a short time as it was already late in the afternoon. This picturesque location is situated between the River Maara on the east and the River Tenaira on the west with Papeari Harbor and Pt. Motuovini looking to the south. The mountains and waterfalls are to the north. This is a very lush, tropical setting with plants from around the world. Gauguin lived and painted in villages close-by before sailing on to Hiva Oa, in the Marquesas Islands. I was surprised to learn that Gauguin was a circumnavigator as well as an artist. There are, however, no original Gauguin paintings at the Gauguin Museum.

There was a restaurant at the facility with a lovely setting. We chose a table on the sand overlooking the lagoon. Unfortunately, the French servers were acting like, well, French servers. Apparently, they intended to make us wait until we begged for service.   Not this sailor. Even though we were starving, we weren't about to take this treatment. The Frenchie's smirks we received as we left had the air of arrogance, practice and foreknowledge. It took us only a short time to realize our colossal error. We had to drive nearly back to Papeete before we found another restaurant.

We were ravenous by the time we drove into the parking lot of the Beachcomber Resort. Watching the sunset from this location was a special treat. While enjoying an ambrosial French banquet, we gazed out at the huts built out over the pale, azure waters of the lagoon. A mile offshore the deep blue ocean waves crashed against the shielding reef, exploding skyward in a spray of white spume as the sun sank slowly behind Moorea's craggy silhouette. Crème brûlée, Margaret's favorite desert, crowned the meal and her birthday.

COLONIALISM

For twenty-six years I daydreamed of sailing to the South Seas. Whether preparing a case for an appeals board appearance or fighting rush-hour traffic on the freeway, my mind would drift to my island paradise of Tahiti. My fantasies included bare breasted island maidens, crystal clear lagoons and volcanic peaks. Politics did not comprise even a small nap in my countless dreams of Tahiti.

It would be impossible to spend time in Tahiti without formulating an opinion on the French colonial system at work in Polynesia. Oh, perhaps you could if you flew in and out in seven days and stayed at one of the luxury resorts, protected from the daily life of the island inhabitants. In only a brief stay you would usually come away with the typical tourist view of things; how incredibly beautiful the scenery is and how interesting the people are. We were there for nearly three months, so we had an opportunity to interact with the people, learn a bit about their daily life and observe close-hand a truly colonial government and its effect on mankind.

Prior to coming to Tahiti I had not formulated any opinions on the French people. When I first arrived and saw the active protests against the French government by both Tahitians and yachties alike, I felt I should mind my own business. My opinion was that I was an American, a guest of this country and I should behave as a grateful guest. We never interfered in the local politics, but one can not help but become sympathetic to the Polynesian's plight after having experienced first-hand the colonial arrogance of the French.

The Tahitians can be hard to love too. They have been treated as second-class citizens in their own land for more than a century and many are in a passive-resistance mode. I have heard it termed *malicious compliance*. Many live a filthy, lazy existence with little ambition other than to get loaded and raise hell. It is telling, that on this island surrounded by an abundance of fish stocks, Tahiti has to import fish because they can not deploy enough fishermen to supply their needs. One of the most disagreeable traits the Tahitians have is that they routinely throw trash around when a trash container is only a few steps away. Many Tahitians have gladly handed over their freedom in trade for a welfare check, thus enslaving themselves — much like what we have done to some of our own people in America.

Of course there were exceptions. The Tahitians had their energetic and helpful *le truck* drivers and the lovely members of the Temple Paofai Evangelique congregation who always had a wide smile and kind word for us. Representing the good French was an old man riding *le truck* who helped us through our language difficulties to find Jeff and Kathy at Taina Marina between Maeva Beach and Taapuna Pass. The kindly Chinese were represented by Mr. Acajou, the owner of a fine restaurant along the waterfront where we enjoyed many delightful meals. Mr. Acajou was a very hard worker who built three successful restaurants and raised a large family on Tahiti.

Of course, there are ugly Americans and Europeans as well. Not many were yachties though. They were mostly tourists. On Sunday mornings these jet-setters visit the Temple Paofai Evangelique, not to worship but to chatter amongst themselves and walk around the second floor balcony overlooking the worshipers like they were some sort of zoo exhibit, straining to capture the specimens on video tape.

THE BOMB AND THE FOURTH ESTATE

By resuming nuclear testing at Moruroa Atoll, newly elected President Chirac was fulfilling a promise made to the French military during his election campaign. The third largest arms industry in the world and exporter of nuclear technology needed to test their devices. France refused an offer by the United States to give them simulation technology. Chirac wanted to do some Gaullist chest-pounding. More *gloire* for France. It seemed the more criticism his decision attracted, the more entrenched he became.

The largest demonstration was held on Saturday, September 2. There were thousands of people who marched peacefully through the streets of Papeete. As the parade advanced, one of the leaders utilized a bull horn to address the people in Tahitian, French and English. "Mr. Chirac — we don't want your stupid nuclear bombs in the Pacific. If you want to test your bomb, why don't you test it in Paris. I don't think the good people of France would want that. The arrogance. You pick on the people who are least able to protect themselves."

The parade ended at Bougainville Park, just outside the High Commissioner's House and Territorial Assembly. The demonstrators assembled at the Monument to Pouvanaa a Oopa where speeches were given. Pouvanaa a Oopa was a local "Free Tahiti" leader of the 1950's who was arrested and imprisoned in France.

There were many, sometimes overlapping, causes at work in this demonstration, including the anti-nuclear crowd, the environmentalists, the Polynesian independence movement, the anti-American bunch for dropping the first atomic bomb, the disarmament pack, people from Oceania who wanted the French expelled from the Pacific all together, drunken thugs and hooligans, French security forces and curious observers like ourselves.

We took time out for lunch at a French cafe a few blocks from the festivities. The French owner of the restaurant was very friendly and asked us how much longer we planned to stay in Tahiti. When we told him we were planning on staying another two to three weeks he said, "Oh, through the collapse!" A few days later this cafe was completely burned out.

We had seen many independence flags during the parade. They were beautiful and Margaret wanted one. On our way back to the rally we stopped a Tahitian man in his thirties and asked him where we could buy an independence flag. This was rather naive on our part since the flags were not manufactured but rather hand-made and the French surely would not allow them to be openly sold. The man looked at Margaret, glowing in her bright pareu and flower headdress, turned to one of the younger men carrying a flag, took it from him and said, "You don't need to buy our flag, you can have this one."

The young man looked a little down in the mouth, but acquiesced to the older man's authority and handed his flag to Margaret. We were astounded. Thus armed with our new Polynesian independence flag, we rejoined the rally in the park. We heard speeches from political representatives from New Zealand and Australia. I can't imagine a modern day American politician saying that he or she was "Royally pissed-off" but I rather think it would be a good thing if they did.

The beach in front of our boat was the scene of pep rallies and was used by the media for interviews. Many of the reporters were in some way connected to the Greenpeace organization which had an office in the building across the street. Prior to hopping a plane to this news hot-spot, I suspect most of them made a stop at Abercrombie and Fitch or Eddie Bauer for their "foreign correspondent uniform of the day". Any ensemble generally included a safari vest. These self-important journalists and photographer-types kept to themselves while searching out their stories. As a group they were not only aloof and ungracious but belligerent. As time dragged on without any violence or destruction to report, it seemed to me they tried their malicious best to incite an uprising.

Greenpeace had organized a "Peace Flotilla" to rendezvous with the activists on the *Rainbow Warrior II* outside the twelve mile exclusion zone at Moruroa. Boats were streaming in daily from New Zealand for the festivities. I dubbed these people *the drunken, self-important, publicity crazed environmentalists.* There were few camera-shy activists. I know this sounds harsh, but that was my observation.

In late August we spent a day snorkeling in Moorea with Jeff and Kathy Sweeney and Matthew Alcorn. When we returned to Tahiti we stopped for a moment on the beach to say our farewells. A big New Zealand sailboat had arrived in the anchorage dressed out in banners and painting on its sides proclaiming *New Zealand Lawyers Against The Bomb*. A pretty Japanese Lois Lane with her producer in tow approached us and began asking questions. She asked us if we were from the boat, pointing to the *New Zealand Lawyers Against The Bomb* boat. We looked at each other and Jeff spoke up; "No. We're Americans. We hate nukes *and* lawyers." The reporter re-loaded. She asked us if we knew how many lawyers were on the boat. We looked at each other and, in unison said, "Too many!" The joke was lost on this roving reporter. Apparently, this timid newswoman was taken over by panic as she quickly gathered her equipment and producer and high-tailed it out of there.

Some of the more adventuresome cruisers accepted charters on their boats, taking protesters and news people to meet the French navy off Moruroa. This was a very dangerous activity as the French Foreign Legion is not known for its sense of humor and it is against French law for a foreigner to charter his boat in French Polynesia.

The *Rainbow Warrior II* was seized while protesting off Moruroa and taken to the military base at Hao Atoll. They were not released for five months. We met with a French couple who returned to Tahiti homeless. They had sailed to Moruroa to protest and were arrested and their boat confiscated.

MARGARET MAKING NEW FRIENDS

My brother John had given us a wooden Chinese wash board to take on the cruise. It was a huge hit with the locals wherever we went. In late August, while finishing up laundry on the beach, I watched as a Polynesian voyaging canoe sailed into the harbor. Margaret and I drove the dinghy over to take some photographs. They were Cook Islanders and they had a big sign that said *Nuclear Free Cook Islands* on her sides. The captain and crew were very friendly. There was a German news team conducting interviews when we arrived. They needed a ride out to interview people on a German boat. I agreed to take the reporter, producer and camera-man in our dinghy. Margaret went aboard the Cook Island boat and was given a tour of the Polynesian voyaging canoe by the captain.

While waiting for the interview to end on the German boat I noticed Margaret waving frantically to me. She had caught the eye of a man who appeared to be half New Zealander and half Cook Islander. He had tattoos over the entire left side of his body and wanted kisses from Margaret. It was a friendly ship. The Cook Islanders laughed as he grabbed Margaret and kissed her twice as was their custom. I could see Margaret's face turn beet red in embarrassment all the way from where I was! In short order I rescued Margaret from the amorous Cook Island crew and returned her to her own boat. From that point on I kidded Margaret relentlessly about making new friends with the Cook Islanders!

RIOTS IN PARADISE

On September 5 the first nuclear bomb was detonated in Moruroa's lagoon. The members of the Fourth Estate finally had something to report. The French restaurants began to close down. A general strike was called. In a very short time there was no food in the restaurants or markets. The riots did not start in earnest until the sixth. From the anchorage we could see thick black smoke coming from the airport. Even we had known in advance that the Tahitians were planning on taking over the airport and we do not speak Tahitian. We are supposed to believe the French were caught flat-footed. I find this hard to believe.

As this madness began, the French had more than enough manpower to send three customs agents to *Kathryn Anne*. Jeff had posted a hand-written advertisement on his dock at Taina Marina, offering his inflatable dinghy for sale. This is taboo in Tahiti. So, while a plane was being taken over by armed thugs, the tires shot out and people held hostage, the Frenchies were searching every crack and crevice aboard *Kathryn Anne*, confiscating the dinghy and imposing a $360 fine on Jeff for his faux paus. Jeff appealed the decision. The fine was reduced to $180 and his dinghy was returned.

Later in the afternoon we began to see hundreds of young Tahitians, on foot and on motor scooters, rampaging through the streets. The term that comes to mind is *wilding*, like the senseless destruction by rampaging kids you hear about in New York City.

We became more concerned when these thugs began stopping cars right in front of our boat, turning them over and starting them on fire. Several accidents occurred when people tried to avoid the blockades. All I could think of was the Reginald Denny situation in Los Angeles. Now we could say we were in riots in two hemispheres!

We were in a rather precarious position. We were anchored only fifty feet from the beach with two stern lines running to shore and no engine. All hell broke loose as darkness enveloped the city. Soon, monstrous fires rose up from downtown Papeete. They were the biggest fires we had ever seen and we were amazed that the whole town did not go up in flames. Margaret and I walked out to the bow of *Kawabunga* and offered up a prayer for the safety of the people of Tahiti. Then I took out our double barrel shotgun, loaded up with 00 buckshot and positioned myself in the cockpit with our American flag waving overhead. There is strict gun control in Polynesia so the shop owners were at the mercy of the hoards. We were prepared to protect ourselves and our property. We were ready to rock and roll.

We shot video tape of the hooligans burning down parts of Papeete, Molatov cocktails exploding, concussion grenades going off, smashing storefront windows, trashing and looting.

The rioters, with T-shirts wrapped around their faces like Palestinian terrorists, used sling-shots and rocks. The authorities used stun grenades and tear gas canisters to disperse the crowd. Basically, it was Rioting 101. The battle cry of '95 was; "Shoot the French and hang the Chinese." The sights and sounds of the night were frightful. Windows shattering, bombs exploding, people screaming, dogs barking, alarms going off and the sight of downtown and the airport ablaze. . . . The tension was broken at regular intervals when gangs of motor scooter thugs drove down the streets. It's hard to take someone as a serious terrorist when they ride a motor scooter.

At 2300 army trucks began rolling in with riot personnel from New Caledonia and Paris. Most of the violence ended after 0200 on the seventh. I watched all night as the stores across the street from the anchorage were methodically looted. It made me sick to my stomach. The next day many young Tahitians streamed by with new sunglasses, bicycles and surf boards. The beach was covered with hangers, discarded after the garments had been ripped off. The liquor stores were looted. The book stores were not.

Explosions went off in the La Pizzeria Restaurant directly across from us. As the place burned I thought about how good their pizzas were. However, we always had trouble getting through to the servers. Even pointing to the menu would elicit a blank, glazed look. Here they had Tahitian servers, living in a French colony, working in an Italian restaurant taking an order from an American speaking English! How did we ever bridge this language barrier? There would be no pizza for a while.

While Papeete burned, Moorea's fine hotels were crammed with French soldiers enjoying the snorkeling in the lagoon ten miles from Tahiti.

During this madness, we were unable to get any local news reports. The French had closed off all media with an iron fist. All you heard on the radio was coconut music. We picked up our news on our Yachtboy 400 short-wave radio with reports out of New Zealand, Australia, the BBC and Voice of America.

Americans were not specifically targeted by the rioters. Burning out the French and the Chinese was the objective. Larry Shea from Vista, California and his crew Matt, aboard *L'Esprit De Mon Père*, who were anchored next to us, actually walked downtown with their video camera and shot tape of the Tahitians running amuck. They were not threatened.

Arlene McKinnan and Steve Hale, aboard the ketch *Summer Wind*, a Mariner 32 from Honolulu had been in the anchorage for a few weeks. They told a harrowing tale of losing both masts in a storm off the Tuamotus and drifting for ten days. At long last they were able to raise a fishing boat with their jury-rigged VHF antenna. They were given enough fuel to motor to Tahiti, where they were busy with repairs. On September 7, as the violence was waning, Arlene was in the galley making lunch. She looked out the port hole and noticed they had moved. She called to Steve, "Hey cousin, we're dragging!"

Steve ran to the companionway, looked to the beach crawling with little Tahitian hellions basking in their deviltry, and replied; "No — they cut our stern line."

One French expatriate, who had lived aboard his old steel boat along the quay for many years had his ensign burned twice. We happened along as he pulled down the tri-color from a nearby tree limb and put out the fire. He summed the Tahitians up this way; "They are like little children."

I wore my America's Cup T-shirt with the American flag on the left chest during this period. It was easy to mistake us for French and I wanted to distance myself from our NATO allies during this time.

Our last, and most serious threat in Tahiti, came on the afternoon of September 19. We made a late afternoon run to the Intermarket and were on our way home, carrying several bags of groceries. A Tahitian in a white pickup truck tried to run us over as we crossed Boulevard Pomare. We literally ran for our lives, diving into the center divider and rolling as the truck jumped the curb on the divider, barely missing us. We were very shaken and very angry. This was not our idea of paradise.

MARGARET'S FANTASY

On September 15, Margaret prepared banana crepes with maple syrup for my birthday. After breakfast we went ashore to search for a rental car. This was difficult because hundreds of rental cars had been torched during the uprising. As soon as we had a car we struck out for another visit to spectacular Point Venus to enjoy the circular bay, sandy beach, coconut palms and ironwood trees. After beachcombing for a time, we set our course for the north end of the island, up the river valleys into the mountains to our ultimate destination — the cascades.

We followed the winding road along the rocky coastline, pulling over a few times to allow the local drivers to fly by. Around the Arahoho Blowhole we turned off the coast road and headed toward the waterfalls of the Faarunai Valley. We parked and hiked into the falls. First we crossed over an interesting foot bridge that looked Japanese in design. There are three falls in this area, one very close to the parking area, about five minutes walk down a well maintained trail. The other two were thirty-five minutes hike away, following a river to the cascades.

The hike is a challenging one as you have to climb over large rocks and uneven terrain, hiking up and then down, following the general path of the river. It was raining on our way in and the clay-like mud was slippery. It was a beautiful hike through rain forest with exquisite views. The trees were incredible. They had weird jutting surfaces that looked like they came straight out of a fairy tale, covered with green lichens that looked like moss. There were all kinds of tropical vegetation, including Elephant Ear plants. After a half-hour hike we were able to see both Cascades Haamaremare Iti and Haamaremare Rahi. Iti was to the right of us and Rahi was to the left and set further back. There was a small pool at the base of Haamaremare Iti. We crossed the river by climbing from rock to rock and trudged up a hill and then down to Haamaremare Rahi. What an enthralling sight! Both falls were magnificent, but Rahi had a large, enticing pool of fresh water waiting to cool us off.

The sun came out just as we arrived. The rain earlier in the morning kept people away and we had the whole place to ourselves. We were dirty and tired from our hike. Taking off my shirt, I jumped into the pool, swimming toward the base of the waterfall. Margaret followed me and we had great fun, splashing, swimming and playing in our own secluded waterfall pool in the middle of the jungle. Margaret had always wanted to do this and we were finally able to pull it off. I had a wonderful birthday and Margaret had her fantasy fulfilled.

We hiked back, admiring the falls and smaller pool at Haamaremare Iti, and enjoying the lush scenery along the way. When we got to the fork in the trail we walked up what looked like a super highway compared to what we had been hiking on and walked up to Cascade Vaimahuta. This is where most of the tourists go. It is beautiful also, but there is a cement base laid out for the viewing area and the pool does not look as inviting. There were people there admiring the waterfall.

PROVISIONING

It was hard to leave the lovely mountains of Tahiti, but we took advantage of having the rental car to run some ship's errands. We visited two chandlers, buying two five-gallon jerry jugs for extra diesel fuel and two three-gallon jerry jugs for additional water to fit in the ice box.

We drove to three different supermarkets to provision. This would be the last place to provision until reaching Hawaii. As it turned out, the Cash & Carry was our best bet. Their products are somewhat dated, but the prices are cheaper than any other market in Tahiti. We were able to get boxes of canned beef stew, soup and Beanie Weenie.

We parked the rental car in the lot in front of a small cement wharf with a broken down crane. This is generally the domain of the little Tahitian devil children, our name for the fatherless children who run in hordes, vandalizing and stealing. They use the wharf as their base of operations, swimming from the wharf and diving from the top of the crane.

Margaret stayed with our supplies while I walked down the beach to get our dinghy, *Thumper*, which was anchored just off the shore. We loaded the little white Avon Redcrest to the very gills and shoved off for *Kawabunga*. I made two trips, leaving Margaret to guard our supplies on the wharf during my first transit. There was barely enough room for both of us to sit down on the second sortie.

PHONES AND FAXES IN PARADISE

By necessity, much of our budget in Papeete went to communications. We certainly could not depend upon the mail since a letter from Tahiti to California could, and often times did, take six weeks. In ordering parts and arranging shipping we made a lot of telephone calls and sent a lot of faxes.

They have quite a racket going in French Polynesia. You buy telephone cards in amounts of 1000, 2000 and 5000 francs. The charge is roughly 400 francs per minute so a 5000 franc phone card evaporates in twelve minutes. There is a little computer screen on the telephone and as you talk you watch the meter diving down, quite similar to a gas pump's meter going up — and at about the same rate.

GOOD-BYE TO MY ΣΦΕ LITTLE BROTHER

On September 1, I got up at 0300 to make one of the most difficult telephone calls of my life. Michael Green, my good friend and little brother in Sigma Phi Epsilon fraternity, had been operated on in New York the previous month and now lay suffering in a hospital bed at Hurley Hospital in Flint, Michigan. Michael was in his last days, fighting for his life against cancer.

Michael's family was a wrestling powerhouse. I attended Ferris State College in the early 1970's with the three Green brothers, Jim, Michael and Bill, all wrestling champions. Michael had been diagnosed with a rare form of melanoma in the spring of 1994 and given a very poor prognosis. During the holidays of 1994, while we were in Michigan visiting my mother, we drove to Flint to have dinner with the Green family. We were all aware at that time that Michael's condition was terminal. It was hard to hug him good-bye.

Michael was in terrible pain when I called. He had to struggle to talk but said, "I'm trying, I really am." I could not help but choke up. The loss of some engine parts or fighting a squall was so trivial compared to Michael's fight for life.

True to Michael's character, he was worried about our safety and our well-being rather than his own ordeal. He made me promise to be careful and to take good care of Margaret during the voyage. I told him I loved him and we said our farewells. We both knew it was good-bye forever. I was numb. I sat on the stone wall outside the post office looking over a dark, empty street and the quay beyond. Michael would not be taking me flying anymore in one of his airplanes, or water skiing in his jet boat and I wouldn't have Michael and his police badge to slither out of a scrape with the local authorities. My little brother in ΣΦΕ was a brave, dynamic and kind man.

NEW FRIENDS AND A NEW COURSE

Our original plan was to sail on to New Zealand but the dreadful expense of lingering in Papeete for so long wrecked that plan. Looking back, we can now see that there was a reason for this delay. We had to wait for Joe and Kaye aboard *Navi-Gator* and Rob and Sherry aboard *Time-Out* to sail into Papeete's anchorage before we would know where our next adventure would take us. We met these two cruising couples during our last two weeks in Tahiti.

While I was on the foredeck checking the anchor rode, making sure our fire hose anti-chafing gear was doing its job, Joe and Kaye drove up in their dinghy to ask for a recommendation for a diesel mechanic. They needed some work done on their generator. Clouseau's name came up. They chose another mechanic.

Joe recently retired as a captain for United Airlines. Kaye was an interior decorator in their home port of Miami, Florida. Prior to retirement, they cruised *Navi-Gator* "on a leash" for eight and a half years and had been out cruising full time for a year and a half when we met them.

The name *Navi-Gator* stems from the World War II days when Kaye was a little girl. Kaye was an army brat and her father was off to war, flying missions as a navigator. When people asked about her father, she told them he was an alligator!

Later the same day I helped move *Navi-Gator* from the anchorage to the quay. Rob Jordan was aboard helping Joe and Kaye with the lines. They had met each other in Panama several months earlier. After *Navi-Gator* was moved, Rob rowed over in his Fatty Knees hard dinghy with his girl friend Sherry Abdelnour. Rob was from Durban, South Africa and Sherry was from Dearborn, Michigan. We had already taken our dinghy over to *Time-Out* to admire her before ever meeting Rob and Sherry. *Time-Out* was a magnificent Hans Christian 38-T, very ship-shape and capable, like her owners. Rob was very interested in seeing *Kawabunga* because he had built seven Flickas in South Africa.

Rob and Sherry invited us over for dinner and we had one of our most enjoyable evenings in memory. Sherry had been in the hotel business in Avalon at Catalina Island for six years before joining Rob on this voyage. Rob had spent most of the last twenty years sailing the seven seas, circumnavigating two and a half times. *Time-Out* was the first boat he cruised in that he did not build with his own hands. I hung on to every word Rob had to say as he intermingled his sea tales with stories of camping in South Africa's bush. When Rob found out we were headed for Hawaii, he told us about Palmyra, a deserted, pristine atoll with plenty of fresh water and a lagoon teeming with fish, located roughly 1,000 miles south of Hawaii. It was a logical place to stop on the way home. Palmyra sounded like a true island paradise where we could live out our South Seas fantasy of living off the land on a deserted island.

Rob knew the caretaker of the island and was going to take over for him for a few months, allowing the caretaker to have some time away from paradise. Rob had convinced *Navi-Gator* to spend the hurricane season in Palmyra's lagoon and it did not take long to convince us. When he showed us video tape of the island the die was cast. We were going on a new adventure. We dubbed Rob the Pied Piper of Palmyra.

Bali Hai Club, Cooks Bay, Moorea

Tahitian Dancers, Bali Hai Hotel, Moorea

"For the truth is that I already know as much about my fate as I need to know. The day will come when I will die. So the only matter of consequence before me is what I will do with my allotted time. I can remain on shore, paralyzed with fear, or I can raise my sails and dip and soar in the breeze."
— Richard Bode

CHAPTER SIX

MOOREA

BALI HAI IS CALLING

It rained all morning on September 27, our *freedom from Papeete* day. Clouseau met me at 0900 on the beach and drove me into town to pick up a new battery. By noon we had a new battery installed in the hanging locker, the engine was actually hooked up to the electrical system and I had paid and thanked the mechanic. We were running behind schedule as the errands in town took longer than expected.

I had scrubbed the stern lines the day before. As quickly as I could, I retrieved them and began weighing anchor. Sweat streamed down my face as I cranked the winch handle atop the windlass in a clockwise direction, slowly raising the Hell Bitch from the depths and guiding the anchor rode down the hawsepipe and into the chain locker.

As I gazed across to the craggy peaks of Moorea, I thought back to the times when I felt we would never make that short passage across the Sea Of The Moon to our Bali Hai. Moorea teased me, much like the French women on that island, frolicking topless on the beach — "Look but don't touch." The lady island of Moorea had taunted us for three months. We had trifled long enough. It was time to tango.

The cranking got harder and harder and not just because I was old and weak. Finally, I could crank no more. My right arm and the winch handle had reached an impasse. It appeared as though *L'Esprit De Mon Père's* seventy-five pound CQR anchor was laying on top of our anchor. At least, I hoped that was the problem. There was always the possibility of our anchor being entangled in debris on the bottom of Papeete Harbor. At the very least, that would involve hiring a diver and there was no guarantee of recovering the anchor. My tryst with Moorea would have to wait a while longer.

Larry Shea was not aboard *L'Esprit De Mon Père* so I turned my attention to our outboard. We had an outboard motor lock on the little Suzuki, which was topnotch for theft protection. However, I had not lubricated the lock during the three months it was in constant use and the lock was jammed. I had struggled with the lock after returning from the run into town with Clouseau, but threats, cursing and slapping it with a hammer had no effect whatsoever. Since we were in a hurry, I simply removed the motor mount, with the outboard still attached and locked firmly in place, and deposited the outboard in the cockpit. I would deal with it when we got to Cook's Bay, just a few hour's sail away.

An hour later, I saw Larry Shea in his hot rod dinghy speeding for the anchorage. He was in the process of washing his clothes, and although I hated to interrupt a man hard at work on his laundry, I explained the situation and asked if we could re-anchor *L'Esprit De Mon Père'* after freeing *Kawabunga's* anchor.

This process took another hour and a half and was rather difficult as Matt, Larry's crew was in town running errands. *L'Esprit De Mon Père'* is a huge boat, probably 65 feet long and served as the center for party activity in Papeete during its stay.

I had been aboard on a few occasions and suffered from a mild case of "boat envy" as they had plenty of storage available, long, wide decks and a handsome cabin.

As soon as we raised *L'Esprit De Mon Père's* anchor we were free. Our little twenty-five pound CQR shot to the surface like a ballistic missile fired from the *Red October*. We bid farewell to Larry and headed for the pass.

THE CAPTAIN IS A BONEHEAD

I have always been a very conservative skipper, never venturing out in bad weather unnecessarily or taking chances with boat or crew. There had been times in Southern California when we left Catalina Island in less than favorable conditions due to work schedules. I had no such excuse this time. One important lesson cruising teaches us is not to make strict schedules. Go when the weather is right.

What I was doing now was completely against sound thought and my own rules of engagement. By the time we weighed anchor it was already 1445 and there was the probability rather than the possibility we would arrive off the pass after dark. Although the passage from Passe de Papeete to Avaroa Pass at Cook's Bay is only 17 miles, the channels between islands can be volatile, with confused seas and strong winds.

The intelligent call would be to re-anchor, regroup and reload for an early departure the next day, weather permitting. The old adage of carefully choosing your battles so you can live to fight another day would apply to the immediate case. Unfortunately, rather than being reasonable, rationalizing was in full gear. After all, *Navi-Gator* and *Time-Out* were expecting us and they would be worried. We had no way to contact them as our VHF signal would not reach them. But most of all, I wanted to leave Tahiti and start the next adventure.

Margaret thought it would be a good idea to simply take the boat northeast of the airport and drop anchor. This was only two miles away, would satisfy my irresistible desire for a change of scene and place us in perfect position to withdrawal from the lagoon early the next morning. Logic be damned — we were leaving!

The sun was shining as we slipped through the pass, coming to a course of 295° T, towards Pt. Aroa at the northeast end of Moorea. After setting the sails and tuning the windvane we sat back to marvel at the beauty of Tahiti from the sea. We held each other tight and savored the moment. The moment was soon broken by Margaret's projectile vomiting. It was sort of like "The Exorcist At Sea". Poor Margaret was not a happy camper.

The conditions deteriorated as the afternoon progressed. I put a reef in the main and tried to comfort Margaret. I had unwittingly contributed to Margaret's agony by not properly stowing the outboard. While on a port tack with the boat heeled 25°, the poor girl had to lie on the high side, fighting for fresh air, fighting her seasickness and fighting to hold on so she would not be impaled on the outboard prop jutting up from the cockpit sole.

By the time we reached the northeast end of Moorea, the sun was very low and it began to rain. We still had at least five miles to go to reach our waypoint to turn and begin our approach to Avaroa Pass. We had to sail past Cook's Bay to the waypoint and approach the bay on a course of 152° T. The approach is deceptive. If you identify the bay and head straight in you will surely run up on the reef.

I had been trying to raise *Time-Out* and *Navi-Gator* on the VHF all afternoon. If I could not reach them we would have to sail away from the island and heave-to for the night. Although the pass is marked with lights, there are range markers, and I had looked over the pass from the eastern shore of the bay a month earlier with the Sweeneys, we could not risk a night landing in heavy rain.

We were greatly relieved when we heard the crackle of Joe and Rob's voices over the radio. They volunteered to drive out to the pass in Joe's dinghy with flashlights and a hand-held VHF radio to act as our pilots. Maybe we would be saved from my boneheaded call after all. They cautioned us to stay well off the island as the outlying reef extends out a mile from the beach. We were giving the island a wide berth, especially with the hard rain which had reduced visibility significantly.

When we reached our waypoint to the northwest of Cook's Bay, we turned to course 152° T and started our approach. The magnetic course was 140° as the magnetic variation is 12° E in this area and *Kawabunga* had no deviation. I started the engine, struck the jib, disconnected the windvane and installed the autopilot.

A good pair of binoculars is a must when you are cruising. We bought the best pair we could afford, the Fujinon Polaris 7 x 50 binoculars with a compass and night light. Although they do not afford true night vision, you can see an awful lot with the Polaris binoculars at night as they pick up any ambient light. Standing on the steps in the companionway, with the dodger protecting me from the rain and spray, I availed myself of all the Polaris' features to search for the pass markers and our friends bobbing in a little dinghy off the pass. We were able to raise Rob and Joe on the VHF. I gave them our exact position from the GPS computer. In a few minutes we were able to pick out each other's lights from the darkness and rain. Joe maintained radio contact as Rob drew a bead on us with his flashlight. This reminded me of the movie *Top Gun*. This wasn't exactly a night landing on an aircraft carrier, but was as close as we would get. When we had Rob's blinking flashlight in our sights I radioed to Joe; "I have the ball." Joe, a former Air Force pilot, ignored my naval aviator lingo, but confirmed we were right on course.

When we arrived just off the pass, Joe ran his dinghy over to us and, in an operation reminiscent of the Navy Seals, Rob leaped aboard *Kawabunga* commando-style. I can't tell you how happy we were to see these two men. Joe, in his little white dinghy, fighting wind, rain and waves, led us through the pass and into the immense bay. Rob, wearing his foul weather jacket, but still soaked to the bone, acted as our on-board pilot. There was no way in the world we would have attempted to navigate through the pass without help from our new friends. This was only the first of many assists from *Time-Out* and *Navi-Gator.* When we were through the pass and well into the mouth of the bay we adjusted our course to steam directly up the middle of the deep bay. We anchored in sixty feet of water off Fisherman's Beach. As soon as we were sure the anchor was set, we scrambled into Rob's dinghy and set off for *Time-Out*, where we were treated to a warm shower and a spaghetti dinner.

COOK'S BAY

I climbed out of my bunk early the next morning and sat in the cockpit watching the sun slowly illuminate the vast bay. The spectacular beauty that my eyes beheld during the next hour made me forget about the long, lonely, miserable hours at sea it took to get to the South Pacific.

Mt. Rotui, rising 2,700 feet, separates Cook's Bay from Opunohu Bay to the west. Its rugged slopes were the first to be made alive by the sun's rays. Next to be illuminated was Mt. Tohivea, which faces the head of the bay. Mt. Tohivea, at 3,960 feet, is the highest mountain on Moorea and is located at the south end of the triangular island. Cook's Bay itself was next to come to life, as the morning sun's rays sparkled on the deep waters. As the sun rose higher, the eastern side slowly awakened. Mt. Mouaputa and Mt. Tearai flickered to life. Coconut palms, ferns and lush vegetation raise up from the bay, blanketing the stark lava and basaltic ridges and peaks, forming a staggering horseshoe bowl.

The eastern side of the bay is lined with hotels and shops while the western shore has been largely preserved in its natural state. The only man-made phenomenon identifiable on the west side is the Roman Catholic church, whose stark-white steeple juts out against the jungly bluffs.

Because we were surrounded on three sides by mountains, our days were cut short. The sun did not rise above the mountains to the east for quite a while after daybreak and withdrew beyond the peaks in the west long before sunset.

Mt. Mouaroa actually sits at the head of Opunohu Bay, but can clearly be seen while anchored in Cook's Bay. This mountain is also referred to as Shark's Tooth and was the mythical "Bali Hai" in the movie *South Pacific*. One of my goals was to get a photograph of Kawabunga in front of Shark's Tooth, so we grabbed the camera and Margaret and I hopped into the dinghy. Joe and Kaye had the same idea as it was an enchanting sunrise. We snapped several photographs of our boats with Shark's Tooth as a backdrop. We marveled at the stark beauty surrounding us. Kaye pointed out the three peaks with holes through them that could be seen from the bay. Mt. Mouaputa, pierced summit, is only a mile and a half southeast of the head of the bay. The peak is 2,592 feet high and you can clearly see blue sky through the hole near the peak.

The locals tell the Polynesian mythological legend about Hiro, who, along with several buddies, was in the process of stealing Mt. Rotui for Raiatea. Pai, apparently the Nolan Ryan of his time, seized his spear, wound up and hurled it from Tahiti, across the Sea Of The Moon to Moorea. The spear pierced the hole through Mt. Mouaputa. The incoming missile awoke the roosters and they in turn caused such an uproar it frightened the mountain-snatchers away. Imagine if you will, the mighty Hiro thrown into a panic by a flock of chickens. Not lions, nor tigers nor bears. Chickens! Hiro is no hero. He's not exactly in the same class as Superman or even Batman. Pai has potential.

PIG ROAST

Joe and Kaye invited us to go with them to a pig roast at the Bali Hai Hotel at noon. Rob and Sherry would not be going as they were preparing to leave the next morning for Huahine. At 1100 Joe pulled his inflatable dinghy alongside *Kawabunga* and we clambered in. We were soon to learn the advantage of employing a hard-bottom dinghy with a 40 horsepower outboard rather than a soft-bottom with a 2 horsepower outboard. You get to your destination much faster and have a lot of fun screaming across the waves. When we reached Pt. Paveau at the mouth of the bay we turned right, following the markers through the northeast channel inside the reef to the Bali Hai Hotel. This area would be a great place to anchor the boat for a few days in ten feet of crystal clear water. The channel runs about ten feet deep and is navigable by most sailboats about half-way to the Bali Hai Hotel. There is a dinghy passage from that point with many coral heads and depths of five feet or less. With the water so clear it was difficult to gauge depths, but Joe and Kaye were veterans of coral piloting and coached us as we carefully avoided coral patches.

The Bali Hai Hotel is located on the north shore of Moorea and can be approached from the sea through the Irihonu Pass. There is a beautiful anchorage just off the beach in front of the hotel. This hotel was built by three Newport Beach, California men thirty years ago. Jay Carlisle, Hugh Kelly and Don McCallum built the Moorea hotel first, followed by Bali Hai hotels on Huahine and Raiatea. They have also taken over a time-share condominium complex in Cook's Bay, naming it the Bali Hai Club. We found the Bali Hai establishments to be an oasis of hospitality.

We tied up to the hotel's concrete wharf and left the dinghy to the mercy of the local kids. We came to expect to find our dinghy crowded with youngsters whenever we returned from shore leave.

We spent a memorable afternoon at the Bali Hai Hotel. There were two anchors on display which had been lost by Cook and Bougainville during their Polynesian voyages. The tamaaraa, or Tahitian feast, was scrumptious. The spinach, of all things, was mouth watering. Joe and Kaye introduced us to Glenn and Shirley Burroughs who were cruising aboard *Odyssey*. Glenn and Shirley own a travel agency in Oklahoma City, Oklahoma. *Time-Out* and *Navi-Gator* had met this interesting couple in the Tuamotus and had become fast friends.

After the feast, the drums began to beat and the Polynesian dancing began on the patio overlooking the beach. Polynesian dancing falls somewhere between the Marquesan shuffle and Hawaiian hula. It's not stark and violent like the Marquesan dancing, and not as sensuous as the hula. The dancers, many of whom had been our servers during the feast, were adorned in traditional costumes made of leaves, shells, flowers, bamboo and natural fibers. We were thoroughly entertained in this beautiful setting.

A FOND FAREWELL

Time-Out and *Odyssey* weighed anchor the next day, sailing for Huahine. *Navi-Gator* followed the day after and we found ourselves in the gigantic bay with only one other cruising boat. It was near the end of the season and most of the cruisers were either in the leeward islands or further down stream, in the Cooks.

We enjoyed the laid-back Moorea lifestyle. Although only a few miles from Tahiti, the contrast was striking. The road was not a race track. There were very few cars. The people were few and friendly.

Do you know where you were when you heard about the O.J. Simpson murder trial verdict? I was talking with my sister Bonnie from a public telephone booth in the tiny village of Paopao. Ah, paradise.

One of the best views of Cook's Bay is from the patio of the Bali Hai Club. We used the club as our base of operations. They allowed us to land our dinghy at their dock, so we were able to leave the dinghy without fear of theft or vandalism. We enjoyed several lovely meals in the South Seas dining room and many hot dogs out at the snack bar on the patio and met some interesting people. The club is a time-share enterprise complete with a pool, tennis courts and thatched roof bungalows built out over the bay.

We had visited the Cook's Bay Hotel, located near the mouth of the bay, with the Sweeneys a month earlier. We returned in our dinghy to find the place overrun with French soldiers, apparently there to protect the hotels from an invasion of reef fish because, as far as we could see, they spent their time in the lagoon snorkeling and scuba diving. Walking along the pool after a very mediocre lunch, we saw three French soldiers in our dinghy. Margaret and I yelled at them and as fast as my little legs could carry me I ran to the dinghy before they could shove off. When they saw us coming they scrambled out of the dinghy and sat on their haunches under a nearby tree like three monkeys who had just had a stalk of bananas ripped from them. Frenchies!

EXPLORING MOOREA

One of the things we missed about Tahiti was their dependable and economical *le trucks*. The only way to get around Moorea was on foot, bike, scooter or rental car. A few days after arriving in Moorea we rented a little tin car from an agency across the street from the Bali Hai Club and headed inland, through the wee village of Paopao, past the pineapple plantations and wound our way up into the mountains, through the woods to the Belvédère Outlook. There is a little snack truck at the site where we bought an ice cream cone and marveled at the view. From the Belvédère you see both deep bays, Opunohu and Cook's, to the north. To the south, the view is of the island's interior volcanic crater and craggy peaks. After enjoying the astonishing view from our perch, we descended the mountain, past the sites of several decrepit maraes, through the valley to Opunohu Bay. We visited Robinson's Cove where so many famous sailors have anchored. We had originally intended to anchor in this bay for a few weeks but, due to our late arrival in Moorea, we had to pass this up. There was only one boat in this incredible inlet.

The blacktop road circling the island was in perfect condition. We continued counter-clockwise around the island. After passing the western shore of Opunohu Bay we came to

Papetoai Village and quickly found the Octagonal Church built on the beach. We had read about this historic place where missionaries from the London Missionary Society began their work in the early 1800's, publishing a Bible and a Tahitian/English dictionary. From this place Christianity was disseminated throughout the South Pacific.

We continued along the north coast of Moorea, stopping for lunch at the Moorea Beachcomber Parkroyal, a luxury hotel at the northwest corner of the island. After lunch we headed for Pt. Paroa at the southern tip of the island, passing the little village of Haapiti. There were no big resorts on the southeast coast. We found it to be pleasantly quiet, with the locals inhabiting humble villages, setting about the business of life with little thought to the occasional visitor that drove by in a rental car or scooter.

Making our way north, along the east side of the island, we stopped in Afareaitu, Moorea's major town. This was a bustling little town with carefree school children bounding out of class for the day, an ideal anchorage and a large market. We were able to pick up some tools and a variety of canned goods.

A short drive from Afareaitu brought us to Vaiare, where we had landed in the ferry six weeks earlier with Jeff and Kathy Sweeney and Matthew Alcorn. Little more than a mile past Vaiare stands the Sofitel la Ora. This posh French-owned hotel offers lovely thatched bungalows along a fabulous white sand beach with an awe-inspiring view of Tahiti. We visited this Xanadu on our earlier excursion. The hotel management had been very kind to us, allowing us to enjoy their beach and facilities. The luxuriously-long *hot* shower was the first for me in four months. The snorkeling was fantastic. It was at that point that I really thanked Margaret for insisting I spend the money for prescription lenses for my dive mask. This was a topless beach with topless snorkeling. There were many topless mademoiselles, the water was crystal clear, my vision 20-20. You do the math. Oh yeah — the reef and schools of multi-colored fish were cool too.

So, it was with an anxious heart that I turned into the Sofitel la Ora. Since we were late for lunch and early for dinner we took a brief look around and continued on our way, counterclockwise around the heart-shaped island. The road rises immediately after the Sofitel and climbs to a lookout high above the beach. We stopped and took photographs of the deep blue Sea Of The Moon channel between Tahiti and Moorea, and of Vaiare Bay and the east coast of Moorea. The island's green craggy peaks, magnificent reef structure and multi-colored lagoon were spread out before us, a feast for our eyes. We went exploring north of the airport, along Pt. Aroa. We found during this hour-long detour that the locals did not particularly appreciate outsiders driving off the beaten track. There were many *Tapu* (Taboo/forbidden) signs, dirty looks and shouts. Our interest in a jeweler was piqued when we began following his lovely wooden signs promoting his black pearl shop. We never did locate the shop. Apparently, you can't let your finger's do the walking in Moorea. You need a four-wheel drive vehicle. We were finally able to find our way back to the main road and returned to Cook's Bay. Although the circuit around Moorea is only 37 miles, we took the entire day to scout the most beautiful island we had ever seen.

THE HIDDEN SHOWER

We were surprised how hard the wind blew down through Cook's Bay. At night the gusts screamed down through the canyons, setting up a chop and buffeting us about. I veered out another 75 feet of rode soon after arrival and we never dragged. We did not have to worry about swinging room as there were very few boats in the enormous bay. It was like three or four Wolverine fans tossing the football in Michigan Stadium. We had the playground to ourselves.

Each morning we took the dinghy over to Fisherman's Beach on the western shore of the bay where a few pirogues were pulled up on the sand. We would anchor the dinghy close to the water's edge, step into the warm water and walk to the coconut-strewn beach to a concealed spigot. We enjoyed our daily clandestine showers on one of the loveliest beaches imaginable. This was quite a switch from Tahiti where we took our morning showers at the spigots on a busy beach. Margaret preferred a warm Sun Shower in the cockpit while in Tahiti for this reason.

BREAKING CAMP

After a short stay in Moorea we began to feel pressure to weigh anchor. It was getting late in the season and we had to get a move on. As it was, we would have to race through the leeward island group. We had dreamed of coming here for so long and now were leaving so soon. We would have enjoyed staying in Moorea for several months. We had barely scratched the surface of her lagoon, beaches and mountains we so longed to explore.

The Leewards are approximately 186 miles northwest of Tahiti. Four of the islands are atolls; Mopelia, Tupai, Scilly and Bellinghausen. Five are mountainous; Huahine, Raiatea, Tahaa, Bora Bora and Maupiti.

In preparation for departure I topped off our 14 gallon shipboard water tank and made runs to the village dock and fish co-op to fill all our jerry jugs. Margaret made a run into the Chinese magasin (store) in Paopao, then set to work packing everything away. It took nearly a day to make ready for sea.

After studying the charts, *Charlie's Charts of Polynesia* and Marcia Davock's *Cruising Guide to Tahiti and the French Society Islands*, we plotted three waypoints which would make a safe approach around the southwest end of Huahine-Iti and the barrier reef that stands 1½ miles from the south and west coasts. The passage would be 92 nautical miles on a magnetic course of 287°. In planning the hop from Moorea to Huahine, we felt our worst-case scenario would be a 26 hour run, if we were reduced to 3½ knots.

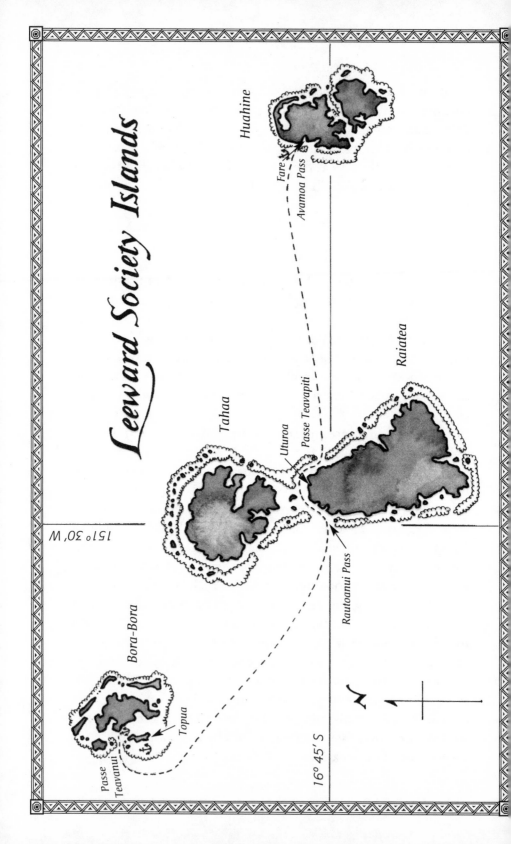

Leeward Society Islands

151° 30' W

16° 45' S

Huahine

Fare
Avamoa Pass

Tahaa

Uturoa
Passe Teavapiti

Raiatea

Rautoanui Pass

Bora-Bora

Passe
Teavanui

Topua

"For will anyone dare to tell me that business is more entertaining than fooling among boats? He must have never seen a boat, or never seen an office, who says so."
— **Robert Louis Stevenson**

CHAPTER SEVEN

HUAHINE AND RAIATEA

SETTING SAIL FOR THE ISLES SOUS LE VENT

The Hell Bitch was weighed at 1345 on Monday October 15. Our Simpson-Lawrence windlass had worked perfectly since leaving Nuku Hiva. Even so, I envied fellow cruisers who had electric windlasses. The French seemed to have the right idea on this issue. Inevitably, whenever a French couple weighed anchor, it was the petite, bikini-clad wench who was sent out to the foredeck to wage war with the manual windlass while the man stood at the helm smoking a cigarette, enjoying a cool drink and bellowing commands. I doubt this will catch on in the States.

We marveled at the beauty of the north coast of Moorea. I thought back to the night four months earlier as I was approaching Tahiti, ghosting past the incredible north shore of Moorea outlined by a full moon. It was such an enchanting spectacle.

We had a perfect afternoon's sail from Avaroa pass. The SE tradewinds were blowing 15 knots, the sky was painted blue and decorated with puffy white cumulus clouds. We charged WNW at 4½ knots. By 1800 the sky had become overcast, the SE wind had dropped to 10 to 15 knots and we were making 4 knots. We had looked forward to a dreamy, South Seas, star-filled, overnight hop to Huahine. This was not to be. The conditions deteriorated throughout the early evening and by midnight we were quarreling with heavy rain accentuated by intermittent squalls. We were blasted by gale-force winds, confused seas and unrelenting rain. It was a chore to remain alert, reduce sail and keep warm in the cockpit. This turned out to be a very long, cold, wet night. The storm subsided by 0430 leaving little wind and diminishing seas. The rain continued.

By dawn we were able to make out Huahine and update our plot. We had come in too high on our rhumb line, blown off course by the storm's onslaught. We found ourselves ESE of the island and began carefully making our way around the south end of the island under power. We were well aware of the dangers presented by the barrier reef extending deceptively far from shore. From time to time the island would simply disappear in the rain only to reappear twenty minutes later. When we made it past Huahine Iti the sea became very calm — we were protected from the NW swell by the volcanic island. The rain never stopped.

FEAR MAKER

Generally, there is a dramatic drop-off along the outside of a barrier reef. A depth sounder is of little value in approaching a coral island or atoll as you can go from several thousand feet to fetching up on a reef within a boat length. Sound is a welcome ally in approaching an island with a barrier reef as you will hear the booming roar of the ocean crashing against the reef, sending white spray high into the air.

We arrived off Avamoa Pass at 1115. The pass lived up to its Tahitian name meaning "Fear Maker". Every sailor knows the best time to pilot into an unfamiliar coral pass is with a bright sun over your shoulder and a lookout (armed with large brimmed hat, Polaroid sunglasses, clipboard, chart and binoculars) posted as high in the rigging as possible. A slight ripple is preferable to a flat calm. These are the best conditions for eye-balling shoals and coral heads. Why is it then — every time I enter a new coral reef pass it is raining pitchforks?

When the water is deep blue you know you are in deep water. The color of the water lightens as the depths get shallower. Brown or purple patches indicate coral heads while yellow or yellow-brown denotes a reef. Only a few feet in water depth over a coral sand bottom would show as pale white. When it is raining or overcast you can not make out the different water colors, much less coral.

We took our time studying Avamoa Pass before we committed to entering. We could see breakers on both sides of the pass and there was a 2 knot current running out of the lagoon. We set up in the middle of the two breaking sides and steamed into the pass on a course of 126° T, steering a magnetic course of 114°. Once through the pass, we followed the channel to the anchorage just inside the reef. We anchored in 4 fathoms of crystal clear, turquoise water, just north of the pass between the Bali Hai Hotel and the Temarara Cafe. An old, overgrown cemetery and a beach-front home occupied the beach just south of the Bali Hai. While we were in Moorea the owner of the Bali Hai told us to be sure to anchor in front of the hotel and feel free to use their showers and enjoy their beach. We did.

FARE VILLAGE

This is normally a very popular anchorage, but at the time there was only one other boat riding at anchor in this idyllic setting. A very short time after we set the Hell Bitch, Adam Reid motored over in his dinghy. Adam and his girlfriend Veronica were cruising aboard *Blue Moves*, a 27 foot English boat purchased in New Zealand. Adam, an American from Hawaii and Veronica, a French citizen, had been cruising the Societies for a few years. Adam cruised all over the world with his father when he was a teenager and had been cruising for twenty-two years. Adam was very familiar with the islands and gave us advice on interesting places to visit on Huahine and Raiatea and where we could get supplies. Adam's boat was ship shape. Veronica was gorgeous.

Several months later we met Ned Dring at a party at Honokohau Harbor near Kailua-Kona, Hawaii. Margaret and I were invited to a Valentine's Day party at the Hawaii Big Game Fishing Club. We were introduced to Ned who told us about his cruising, including his last crossing seven years earlier, taking him from Japan to the west coast of the United States with his son Adam. He told us his son had visited him a few months ago and had returned to Moorea where he was repairing his engine. We were astonished when he mentioned the name of his son's boat — *Blue Moves!* Either it's a small world or it's a small fraternity in a big world.

Huahine is actually two islands spliced by a bridge across a narrow strait. Mt. Turi, at 2,200 feet, towers over Huahine Nui (Big Huahine) to the north while 1,515 foot Mt. Puheri rises above Huahine Iti (Little Huahine) to the south. The garden isle of Huahine is only eight miles long, running north to south, and about five miles wide at it's broadest point. It has only 28 square miles of surface area. Huahine is known for growing watermelons, melons, bananas and pineapples. The island is also a treasure-trove of archeological sites, especially along the south coast of Lake Fauna Nui at the north end of the island. In 1972, while building the Bali Hai Hotel, more archeological strikes were made. Many of the artifacts are now on display at the Bali Hai Hotel. The people of Huahine resisted French rule and were not conquered until 1888, nearly four decades after Tahiti was taken. Pouvanaa a Oopa, a political hero to the Tahitian people, came from Huahine.

We found the people of Huahine to be warm and congenial — considerably friendlier than any other island in the Societies. Everyone had a smile for us and were as helpful as they could be. The beauty of their lagoon was unsurpassed.

By 1500 I was able to launch the dinghy and take it to the beach for a thorough scrubbing. While I was sponging up, Max sauntered out of his lagoon-front cottage to welcome me to his slice of heaven. Max stood a head taller than me and his thick Tahitian shoulders overtaxed the faded red T-shirt he wore. Max was genuinely interested in our voyage so I recounted a few of our adventures while he sprawled under a coconut palm at the water's edge. We ran into Max several times during our stay on Huahine. He appeared to be in his natural element burning up the road on his red motor scooter, blue smoke belching out of the exhaust.

Fare is a quaint, old-style, laid-back, South Seas town. Margaret and I walked along the shady main street, with the commercial wharf on one side and small shops on the other, watching people going about the business of life. Although Fare is the major town of Huahine, it is very small.

OFFICIALS IN THE BOONIES

I made a quick trip to the gendarmerie to check in. This is an informal procedure, just letting the officials know where you are, how long you intend to stay and what your next port will be. Normally, the gendarmes work in teams, with a French officer in charge and a Tahitian subordinate. I am the only one I know of who actually checked in while visiting Huahine.

The Tahitian officer examined my ship's papers, handled my business expeditiously, was pleasant and courteous. The big Tahitian and I had no problems making ourselves understood. While the Tahitian attended to his duty, the scowling French officer shuffled papers in an ineffectual attempt to appear engaged in work. It was obvious he was listening to the entire parlay. Thanking the Tahitian officer, I made my move to leave. The Frenchie sprang from his swivel chair battering me with questions in French. I told him I spoke very little French. He told me in English I was rude to travel to a French territory (the more accurate word is colony) and not speak the language. He told me whenever he traveled to England or Canada, he spoke

English. Seething, I stood up and said, "Good for you". Lame as it was, it was the cleverest retort I could think of at the time. I felt it best to shove off before reminding the conceited twit that the Frenchies had not cared whether we spoke French or not when we came to their rescue not once but twice this century. If not for English speaking people, the galling little turkey would be speaking German, not French.

We were boarded at 1000 the next morning by two French officers. We had seen a French patrol boat steam through the pass and take up position 200 yards away. A Zodiac was launched with six sailors aboard. They zoomed directly over to *Kawabunga*. They were obviously disappointed when they saw Margaret and me. They were expecting to find the elusive *Scout*, with a shapely, young, mademoiselle single-hander, known for dancing on the foredeck in her bikini. *Kawabunga* was confused for *Scout* more than once and we had been asked several times about *Scout* during our Polynesian interlude, but never ran into her. She must really be a knockout.

The officers had little interest in us after determining we were not *Scout*. Disappointment was etched on their faces. I handed over our ship's papers. They could not believe we had the shotgun and ammunition on board and began blustering about us being in some sort of trouble. I pointed out I had declared the weapon in each and every port we had been in and the gun was never confiscated. I had even tried to give it to the gendarmes and they would not take it. The officers seemed to think this was highly unusual. Since we were nearly out of the territory, rather than taking the gun, they put it and the ammunition into the blue bag we had and bound it with an official French custom's seal. The seal was not to be broken until we left the territory.

MY VAHINE

Margaret and I walked over to the Cafe Temarara for a late afternoon lunch. We had read about the Cafe Temarara in Marcia Davock's book and were anxious to give it a try. The cafe sits on the beach adjacent to the dinghy landing area. We had the cafe to ourselves. A fetching young Tahitian girl seated us and took our order. We asked her —fuzzy language again — if they took the American Express card. We took a smile, a nod and a "oui" as affirmative. We ordered two chicken dishes; Margaret the ginger chicken and fried chicken for me. What a treat. This was the best meal we had enjoyed in a long time.

The pretty server took our card for payment. She returned a few minutes later, explaining they did not accept the American Express card after all. We had no francs. We negotiated an agreement. I would stay as hostage while Margaret walked down the street to the bank.

After Margaret left, the young girl asked, "Is that your vahine?"

I looked at her curvy pareu, the Tiare arranged in her long, straight, brunette hair and her dark enticing eyes. "Yes, she is my vahine." A look I would like to describe as crestfallen came over her face. She turned and traipsed back to the kitchen where she joined the older women. I turned my attention to little *Kawabunga* anchored in the sparkling lagoon, thinking I should pinch myself to make sure I wasn't dreaming. Margaret returned to the seaside cafe within the half-hour carrying the artistic French Pacific francs (Colonies Francaises du Pacifique or CFP) that would liberate me from my cozy confinement.

THUMPER IS WOUNDED

The rain finally quit on October 12. The morning broke clear and bright. The lagoon was dazzling. We took the dinghy to shore for breakfast and to pick up some groceries. We planned to spend the afternoon snorkeling.

Arriving at the commercial wharf, I pulled alongside the rusty ladder running up the side of the cement landing. The surge pushed us into the ladder and we heard a rip and then a hissing sound.

I looked down at the ladder and saw a sharp piece of metal sticking out from the ladder. *Thumper* had been skewered like a shish kebab and air was escaping from an inch-long hole cut into the port side of the dinghy. Of course, my first reaction was, "#%&*@".

Margaret was appalled at my vulgar tongue. She said, "What are you so upset about? It's only — aaaiiirrr! The realization of what happened came midway through her sentence. She, however, did not swear.

We were only ten yards from shore, so there was little chance of us drowning. Nevertheless, we wasted little time paddling to shore and pulling the dinghy up on the dry sand. We plopped ourselves under the nearest palm tree and contemplated our next move.

I brought out the Avon patch kit and began reading the directions. I had never patched a dinghy before, but had patched countless bicycle tires in my day. How hard could it be?

The hole was situated above the waterline in an awkward spot due to the thick rubber trim girding the boat. I had to cut away some of the trim so I could have a flat surface to attach the patch. I cut out a circular patch, smeared rubber cement on both the patch and the dinghy and covered the wound. The directions said we had to wait 12 hours before we could inflate the boat. They weren't kidding. After waiting all day ashore, we decided eight hours was surely long enough. Faux pas.

CLUB BED

After patching *Thumper*, we walked across the street to Chez Guynette for breakfast. This hostel, lovingly known as "Club Bed", is owned by Alain and Helene Guynette, a very amiable, enterprising, and generous French couple. Alain is from France and Helene is French-Canadian. We were astonished to learn Alain had spent time in Marina del Rey, and even more surprised to learn we shared a love for the same local Mexican hole-in-the-wall restaurant there. They have a wonderful life in Huahine and are able to get away for vacations to Hawaii. Yes, people even need vacations from paradise.

Club Bed is strategically located across the street from the town wharf where the inter-island schooner *Ono Ono* ties up. Each day, a steady stream of backpack-laden passengers stagger off the *Ono Ono* in various stages of mal de mer, looking for the comfort of a motionless, cozy bed at the hostel.

Incidentally, I'm not sure how much confidence can be derived from a ship named *Ono Ono* (pronounced Oh No! Oh No!).

Every morning we had breakfast on the patio at Club Bed. Alain and Helene took us under their wing, having their staff do our laundry, allowing us to fill our jerry jugs at their water spigot and letting us use their showers. Club Bed is a very popular place, the only hotel we saw in French Polynesia with accommodations for the backpacker-tourist.

The wharf is the center of activity for Fare. People congregate to wait for loved ones to arrive aboard the inter-island schooner and to pick up supplies shipped in from Paris. The covered cargo shed on the wharf comes in handy when the sky opens up with bullet-sized rain drops.

One morning, while having an American breakfast at Club Bed, (the apricot jam on French bread was awesome), we were stupefied by the sight of an entire Tahitian family crammed inside an antique jeep, with all their baggage, trunks and recent acquisitions somehow loaded aboard. There were stray arms, legs and even a wheelbarrow hanging from the rattletrap as they sped away from the wharf for, what was for them, an ordinary Sunday drive.

We rented a car and spent a day exploring one of God's unspoiled creations. It's only 37 miles around the island. We chose the perfect day to wander the mountains and coastline of the island. The sun animated the lagoon in various nuances of blue. Of all the Polynesian islands, we found the colors of Huahine's lagoon to be the most vibrant. We were treated to a mythical South Seas sunset with Raiatea, Tahaa and Bora Bora in the foreground.

RAIATEA BOUND

At 0830 on October 15 we weighed anchor under overcast skies and a very light breeze and took a course of 265° T, bound for Raiatea. We had an enjoyable motor-sail to the north end of Raiatea, a short hop of only 24 miles. Several days earlier we had heard Rob over the VHF radio give the coordinates for Teavapiti Pass entrance buoy. Teavapiti Pass was incredibly beautiful. Outside the pass, we lined up with the range markers ashore, taking C-270° T, and entered the pass, keeping Taoru Island to the port and Ofetaro reef motu to starboard. We followed the prescribed course into the lagoon, past the marked reef Toamarama before coming to C-146° T for a short while until we were directly abeam to the center of Vaiurua Bay and then turned starboard to C-167° T for about a mile until we were past the Bali Hai Hotel and off Pt. Tonoi's marker where we turned to port on a heading of C-327° T and motored past Uturoa, Raiatea's principal city and administrative center for the Leeward Islands.

We continued to follow the channel past Uturoa until we located the new marina situated between the airport and Uturoa on the north coast of Raiatea. We headed bow into the dock, picking up a mooring for the stern line at 1430. This was *Kawabunga's* first marina in five months. The dock would afford a nice platform to effect the minor repairs that had been adding up.

Whales through the port hole

Boisterous Northeast Trades

Taiohae Bay Anchorage, Nuku Hiva, Marquesas Islands

Keikahanui Inn, Taiohae Bay — Shipwreck

Mountains behind Taiohae

Margaret aboard *Kawabunga*, Hokule'a Beach anchorage, Tahiti

Margaret's Fantasy:
Cascade Haamaremare
Rahi, Tahiti

Protesting "le bomb"

Monument to
Pouvanna a Opoa —
Papeete, Tahiti

Cook Island Polynesian Voyaging Canoe —
Hokule'a Beach anchorage, Tahiti

Approaching Bora Bora from Raiatea

Dinghies anchored off Topua for barbecue — Bora Bora lagoon

Topua Anchorage — Bora Bora Lagoon

Topua Iti, *Kawabunga* and Topua

Luti, his pirogue and the author — Christmas Atoll lagoon

Our friend Luti

Christmas Island feast — Luti's fare — Thanksgiving '95

Luti's grandchildren — Christmas Atoll

Seaplane ramp & Roger's camp — Palmyra Atoll

Swimming Hole —
Palmyra Atoll

Jungle Bathtub —
Palmyra Atoll

Beachcombing — Palmyra Atoll: Margaret, the author, Joe McCarthy,
Kaye McCarthy, Bill Pool & Roger Lextrait

"Lycra Boy" — the author relaxing on Palmyra Atoll

Mommy & baby Boobie Birds — Palmyra Atoll

Jungle Hike — Palmyra Atoll: Roger Lextrait at the point, Bill Pool,
Joe McCarthy, Diane Pool and Margaret in the foreground

Our flight will be delayed. . . Palmyra Atoll

Kawabunga anchored in
Center Lagoon —
Palmyra Atoll

Kawabunga at rest — sunset at the Hawaii Yacht Club — Oahu

Sunset over Moorea — Sea of the Moon in foreground

UTUROA

The setting was out of this world. Directly in front of us, across the channel to the north, was Raiatea's sister-island Tahaa. The hourglass-shaped coral reef encompasses both Tahaa and Raiatea. Both volcanic islands can be circumnavigated within the lagoon. To the south were the lush mountains of Raiatea, the second largest island in Polynesia.

We sailed in on a Sunday, so nothing was open, including the marina office. Uturoa was a ghost town. We walked into town looking forward to a nice late afternoon lunch, but the only business open was an old Chinese woman's food stand. We settled for bao and some candy bars. Bao, a Chinese white bun filled with pork, was so delicious we bought several to take back to the boat.

The next morning we were awakened by a pounding on our hull. I rolled out of my bunk and met our friendly Tahitian dockmaster who led me back to his office where I checked in and paid for three days wharfage.

The first project to attack was our dinghy repair. The patch I had put on in Huahine was leaking in the worst way. I pulled the dinghy up on the dock and was able to put on a good patch. This time I allowed it to dry for well over 12 hours, which did the trick. The next job was to put in new gaskets on all six portholes. We had ordered the gaskets from a firm in Florida but had not taken the time to put them in prior to leaving San Diego and I had been kicking myself ever since. The job took much less time than I thought and was a much simpler task than I had imagined. I thought that would remedy the problem of water coming into the cabin through the portholes, but I was wrong. What I needed to do, in addition to changing the gaskets, was to caulk around each of the portholes. If I had done so, my passages would have been much more comfortable.

Joe McCarthy drove up in his dinghy on Monday morning. *Navi-Gator* was anchored in Faafau Bay around the northwest end of Raiatea and Joe was out scouting about when he saw

Kawabunga. We made a date to go into Uturoa the next day to play.

Monday afternoon we hitchhiked over to Apooiti Marina in an effort to pick up some spare fuel and oil filters for our diesel engine. They were unavailable in Tahiti and we were told we could pick them up in Raiatea since it was a major charter boat center. Unfortunately, we were unable to get the filters we needed. This would come back to haunt us.

We had an enjoyable time hitchhiking. We were picked up by three women; one Tahitian, one Chinese and one French. They were all very nice. It was a very hot day and they stopped when they saw Margaret's umbrella up. We were told later why none of the men gave us a ride. It would have been inappropriate for a man to pick up a lady thumbing. Moreover, none of the women would have stopped for me if I had been bumming a ride alone. So, the only way to hitchhike, is as a couple.

Joe and Kaye drove their dinghy over on Tuesday morning and we motored to Uturoa to re-provision in the Chinese stores and to take in the sights around the old town. We had a wonderful day with Joe and Kaye and decided to leave the next morning for Bora Bora.

"Going to sea has all the advantages of suicide without any of its inconveniences."
— William McFee

CHAPTER EIGHT

BORA BORA

LEAVING THE HOURGLASS

We cast off at 0900 on October 18 and took up a course of 287° T, toward the northern tip of Raiatea at the point of constriction in the hourglass-shaped coral reef that encompasses Raiatea and Tahaa. There is an intersection in front of the airport off Pt. Motutapu where you have the option of turning north to Tahaa or continuing on through Tearearahi Passage between Grand Banc Central to the starboard and a large, unnamed coral formation to port. We came to course 243° T, heading for Rautoanui Pass on the NW end of Raiatea. This passage was well marked and the conditions were optimal for our five mile transit through the lagoon.

Navi-Gator, anchored in Faafau Bay, was ready for us when we arrived at 1000 and weighed anchor as we came within shouting range. Kaye was at the helm as Joe raised the sails and in no time the big ketch overtook us and led us down the NW side of the island towards Rautoanui Pass. We gave a wide berth to Tahunaoe Island, the small wooded motu to starboard. Rautoanui Pass is situated between Tahunaoe Island to the north and the smaller, bare Torea Island to the south of the pass. We came to course 264° T and withdrew from Raiatea's lagoon.

It was a 36 mile passage from the Raiatea Anchorage to the Bora Bora anchorage. After slipping through the pass into the safety of the open ocean, we took up a course of 291° T for the 23 mile stretch to the SW corner of Bora Bora. We motor sailed all day as the wind was very light. It was one of those incredibly beautiful days you see photographed in the travel brochures. The deep blue sea was calm, the sun bright. White puffy tradewind clouds floated above the horizon, accented against the blue sky. We watched the lovely cruise ship *Windsong*, with all her sails rigged, head out of Bora Bora, bound for the Windward islands.

We kept radio contact with *Navi-Gator* during the crossing. They steamed ahead of us and it wasn't long before they were just a dot on the horizon. It was such a clear day we could see them until they got to the leeward side of Bora Bora.

It was very exciting watching Bora Bora grow bigger and bigger as we slowly reeled her in. Another dream was coming true. Eight years earlier I had cut out an aerial photograph of Bora Bora from a chartering brochure and taped it on my computer monitor. That photograph served as my inspiration through many dreadful hours of writing reports. Now we found ourselves only hours away from Bora Bora, described by James Michener as being the world's most beautiful island.

When we reached 16° 33′ S, 151° 49′ 30″ W, our waypoint at the SW end of Bora Bora, we turned north to C-089° M for the 3½ mile run along the western side of the barrier reef. We could clearly see the ocean waves breaking on the reef to starboard. We raised Kaye aboard *Navi-Gator* on our VHF radio. She told us they found *Time-Out* anchored off the SW end of Topua Island in the SW section of Bora Bora's sparkling lagoon. We studied our charts and guides and consulted with Kaye and Joe on the best route to the anchorage and decided to approach along the west coast of Topua.

WINDING OUR WAY INTO PARADISE

Teavanui Pass, "Big Pass" in Tahitian, was fittingly named. Teavanui, the only entrance into Bora Bora's lagoon, is broad, clearly marked and easily navigated. The conditions were perfect for entering the pass. This was the first time we had favorable circumstances for negotiating a coral reef pass. We lined up outside the pass and approached on a course of 112° T with the twin peaks of Mt. Pahia, looking like little devil's horns, directly in front of us. We slid past little Motu Ahuna on the north side of the channel to our port. Margaret took over the helm and I climbed atop the boom at the gooseneck, clutching the chart with my left hand while hanging on to the mast with my right, all the while keeping a sharp eye out for coral heads as we steamed slowly through the watery coral minefields. Visibility down into the azure water was excellent from my perch. After passing Motu Ahuna we turned to starboard and threaded our way past Motu Tapu, through the coral patches off the NW end of Topua Island. We took a very cautious approach to snaking our way through the lagoon. Margaret and I made a good team.

We waived to the people aboard the yacht *Zingara*, anchored all alone off the NW end of Topua. When we were midway down the west side of Topua we saw Joe hightailing it towards us in his little white dinghy. Joe acted as our harbor pilot, leading us the rest of the way to the anchorage. When we reached Pt. Mohio we were grateful to have Joe guiding us as the fringing coral reef extends deceptively far out from the point, nearly to the shallows, affording a very narrow passage to punch through. After rounding Pt. Mohio we could see *Time-Out* and *Navi-Gator* bobbing in an idyllic anchorage off the strait between Topua and Topua-Iti, whose shores were lined with coconut palms bending to the gentle SE Trades. Within a few minutes we were at rest in 35 feet of crystal-clear water watching the Hell Bitch burrow into the white coral sand of Bora's lagoon.

RENDEZVOUSING WITH FRIENDS

It was great to see Rob and Sherry again. They were busy getting *Time-Out* ready for the passage to Christmas Island but we found time to play. There were six boats in the anchorage. Besides *Time-Out, Navi-Gator* and ourselves, there were *Holy Grail, Mika* and *Eliott*.

Holy Grail, a 51 foot custom sloop, was lovingly built over an eight year period by her tenacious owners Howard and Stephanie Conant. *Holy Grail* is unpretentious and ship-shape on deck while below decks she glows in luxurious splendor. We have never been inside a more beautiful, well-equipped cabin. We first saw the boat in Papeete while we were doing the laundry near the De Gaulle monument where *Holy Grail* was tied to the quay.

Mike Salvaneschi bought *Mika*, a sister ship to *Time-Out*, twenty years ago and single-hands the big cutter. He planned to buddy-boat with *Holy Grail* to Suvarov and Samoa. Both *Holy Grail* and *Mika* are from Southern California.

Eliott is a Centurion 36 foot sloop, designed by Henri Wauquiez. Ross and Lorna Thompson purchased the boat in the Caribbean. They found it sunk in 40 feet of water and salvaged it. I inquired as to the meaning of the name *Eliott*, thinking it must have some sentimental significance but was told she had come with the name and they did not want to change it, fearing bad luck. Sinking in 40 feet of water sounds pretty unlucky to me. . . .

For *Eliott* and *Time-Out* to be in the same anchorage was something of a miracle. Ross and Lorna Thompson had dreamed of cruising the world by sailboat after attending a barbecue in South Africa ten years earlier. The barbecue just happened to be at Rob Jordan's mother's house in Durban. After listening to Rob's sea stories, Ross and Lorna decided to go cruising some day. They had left South Africa and sailed to the Caribbean, staying in St. Barts for six years before heading west through the Panama Canal into the Pacific. A few days earlier they had heard Rob talking on the VHF and cut in, asking if he was Rob Jordan from Durban!

TOPUA ISLAND

We had a lot of fun with our merry band of cruising friends anchored off Topua Island in Bora Bora's captivating lagoon. Beachcombing, snorkeling, climbing Hiro's Bell, model sailboat racing and parties on the beach made the days pass quickly.

We were sailing with the *tall dogs*. We were by far the smallest boat we had seen cruising. The other boats had big water tanks, showers, ovens, generators, single side-band and ham radios, radar, hot running water and other creature comforts. We were anchored out in the boondocks, a very wet, hour's dinghy ride to Vaitape Village, Bora Bora's only little town.

A few days after arriving, the yachties organized a bonfire and pot-luck picnic on Topua, just a few hundred yards north of Hiro's Bell. A clearing had been cut back from the beach for a little deserted cottage that sat thirty yards from the lagoon and a dinghy channel had been blasted out of the coral to allow access to the beach from the lagoon. During the afternoon the men mustered on the beach to gather wood for the fire, put up tables and chairs and rig up the large green canvas tarp Joe brought in case of rain. While we were softening up the island for invasion the women prepared their favorite dishes for the feast. For her contribution, Margaret made her fabulous deviled eggs, or as Rob dubbed them, "The Devil's Eggs".

My fondest memory of Bora Bora was this evening on the beach with our cruising friends. The memory of huddling next to the bonfire, of hearing the booming of the waves crashing onto the outer reef, of gazing at the cloud-covered mountain peaks of Otemanu and Pahia, of looking out at the dinghies anchored along the beach with palm fronds waving over them and a magnificent sunset in the background still warms my old heart.

This evening was an emotional one also, because everyone knew the group would break up as soon as the normal SE tradewinds returned. We had been experiencing northerly winds for the last several days which was not suitable for leaving on a long northward leg and we were all a little anxious as the end of October neared and the unfavorable winds persisted. Hurricane season would officially start on November 1. As soon as the normal conditions returned the boats and their crews would strike out towards different headings of the compass. While we would cross wakes with some of our friends eventually, others we would never see again. This is one of the difficult aspects of cruising. *See You in Palmyra*, sung to the tune of *See You in September* became our theme song.

VAITAPE VILLAGE

Topua and Topua Iti are actually the western rim of a volcanic crater. The very deep Pofai Bay, between Topua and Bora Bora, is the center of the collapsed crater. We tied up our dinghy to Vaitape's concrete wharf several times and walked into the village. There is no central "downtown" Vaitape. The village has settled along the lagoon's coastline. The visitor's center, bank, government center, gendarmerie and post office are all close to the wharf.

I was interested in visiting Alain Gerbault's grave. Gerbault was a famous tennis star in France and later a heroic fighter pilot during World War I. He became France's first single-handed sailor to circumnavigate aboard *Firecrest* in the late 1920's. He returned to Polynesia where he lived until World War II when he was captured and executed by the Japanese. We were disappointed to find the Visitor's Center built nearly atop the monument to Gerbault.

We found great ice cream a short walk from the wharf in a little shop just off the road. A second ice cream shop just north of the school also made great malts and shakes.

We had been warned about Bora Bora's high prices and had

stocked up in Papeete. We visited the two Chinese markets in Vaitape and bought some provisions.

One beautiful morning we dinghied into Vaitape with Joe and Kaye McCarthy, rented a little Renault and spent the day exploring the island by car. It takes very little time to get around Bora Bora as there is only one road and it is a very small island. We spent a very enjoyable day stopping along Faanui Bay where the American forces were based during World War II, walking the northern beaches, admiring the motus surrounding the island and stopping for lunch along the southeast corner of the island where the luxury hotels are situated.

BORA BORA YACHT CLUB

The wind finally swung around to the ESE and the boats started to leave the anchorage. *Mika* and *Holy Grail*, both heading to Samoa, were the first boats to leave. A few days later *Time-Out* and *Eliott*, bound for Palmyra, made their way out of the quiet waters of Bora Bora's lagoon. Two days later we waived good-bye to *Zingara*, who had joined the anchorage a day earlier, weighed the *Hell Bitch* and, along with *Navi-Gator*, carefully threaded our way around the south end of Topua Iti and then ran northward up the middle of the deep lagoon between Topua Island and Bora Bora. As *Navi-Gator* steered for Teavanu Pass and Christmas Island, we sailed *Kawabunga* to the Bora Bora Yacht Club and picked up a mooring in front of the club house.

We intended to stay at the club two days but had such a great time we stayed a week. Overall, Bora Bora is not very friendly to yachties but Guy, the owner of the club, provided a congenial haven, furnishing great meals, showers, laundry, a well-stocked lending library and plenty of fresh water only 1¼ miles from Vaitape. The mooring was free if you bought one meal at the club per day. This was a great deal as the meals were delicious and reasonably priced (by Bora Bora standards) and the exotic setting was unsurpassed. Guy's hospitality was exceptional.

We met some wonderful people at the club. We had the pleasure of meeting the Collison family from Newport Beach, California. They were sailing through the leeward islands with their friends aboard *Lady Valerie*, a Beneteau 510, chartered out of the Moorings in Raiatea. They were a delightful family.

Peter La Londe and Mary Miller from New York state were staying in one of the club's lovely over-the-water bungalows. We met them at our favorite ice cream shop on the morning they arrived and struck up a friendship. We joined Peter and Mary for dinner at Bloody Mary's, where we enjoyed an unforgettable evening.

Of course, it is impossible to think of Bora Bora without being swept away by romance. The crew of *Kawabunga* was no exception. On one rainy afternoon we spent several hours in the island's romantic clutches *rebuilding our head*. A more repulsive job I can not imagine, amour or no amour.

Guy gave us a Bora Bora Yacht Club tee shirt and sea shell leis as bon voyage gifts. Guy explained their custom of giving a sea shell lei as a farewell present. This would guarantee that some day we would return to Bora Bora. We hope this is true.

HALLOWEEN GOOD-BYE

At noon on Halloween we slipped the mooring at the Bora Bora Yacht Club, bid farewell to Guy and motored to the Vaitape wharf where we tied up for a last-minute dash into town for goodies. While Margaret walked into the village, I used the convenience of the wharf to break down the dinghy, pack it and to stow away all the loose ends. The cruise ship *Windsong* was anchored in the lagoon and her shore boats provided a constant flow of well-intentioned dreamers who wanted to talk about our voyage. It is amazing how many people dream of sailing away to paradise. I got the impression most of these romantics visualize a much bigger boat — possibly with a cook and a satellite dish.

Margaret returned with ice-cold chocolate malts in hand,

the last ice-cold anything we would enjoy for several months. We were underway by 1400 and within twenty minutes were making our way through the pass out into a calm sea with the sun gleaming overhead.

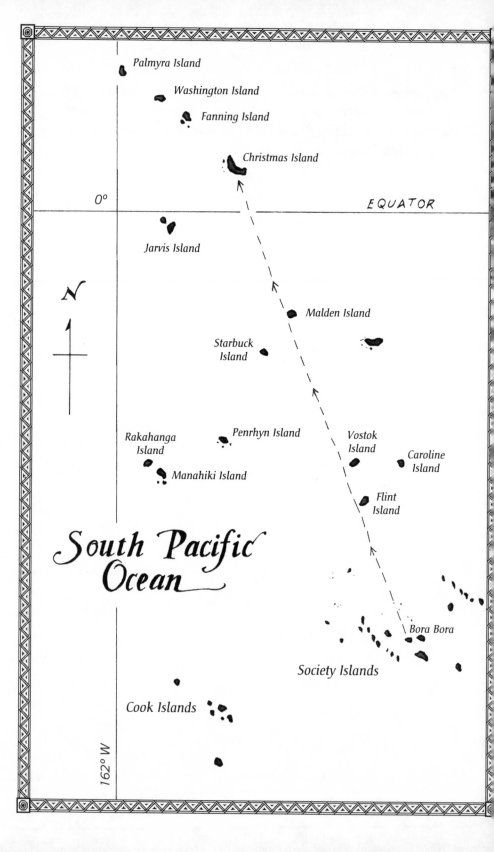

"The only cure for seasickness is to sit on the shady side of an old brick church in the country."

— Old Saying

CHAPTER NINE

LEAVING POLYNESIA

PASSAGE TO CHRISTMAS ISLAND

The first navigational problem confronting us was managing to steer clear of Tupai Island which lies eight miles NNE of Bora Bora. Not only were we able to avoid Tupai, but we were also successful in staying off the reefs of Flint, Vostok, Starbuck, Malden and Jarvis. All of these low islands lie dangerously close to the rhumb line on the way to Christmas Island.

Christmas Island is situated very near the equator at 1° 52′ N, 157° 22′ W. The rhumb line course was 330° magnetic and ran 1,292 nautical miles. We had hoped to make our first landfall at Christmas Island, the Republic of Kiribati, in the Northern Line Group in roughly two weeks. It took three.

THE SMELL OF MUTINY IN THE AIR

We left on one of the most beautiful days I can remember. Unfortunately, there was not a breath of wind. The sky was clear with brilliant sunshine. It was very hot and the ocean was flat-calm. We could see Maupiti off in the distance to the west. Tupai grew larger and larger as we approached while Bora Bora shrank. By 1700 we were safely around Tupai so we shut down the engine and raised our big genoa.

From 1700 on November 1 through the next day the weather was beautiful. We had a 10 knot easterly wind allowing us to charge along under full main and genoa. The moon set at 0230 on the second and the sky was brilliant with stars. I struck the French tri-color and raised Old Glory two-thirds of the way up the topping lift. At noon we changed to the ocean chart of the South Pacific Ocean, Western Part, #4061. Two days later I switched to my old friend, North Pacific Ocean, Southeastern Part, #4051. We scored 88 nautical miles from noon on the first to noon on the second. Our luck was short-lived.

We endured very frustrating conditions for the next four days. We sweltered under the intense heat of the day. What wind we had during the next few days was intermittent, light and variable. We would no sooner get sails hanked on and raised before the wind would die altogether.

The autopilot died after the second day. I took it apart and found it to be very wet inside. I dried it out as best I could, but burial at sea was to be Abe's fate. With so little wind, we ran the engine a great deal early in the passage. Joey the windvane does not steer with the boat under power and no wind, so we were forced to hand-steer for extended periods. This proved to be a great hardship and Margaret was drafted into helmsman service.

We discovered a leak in one of the jerry jugs and the smell of diesel fuel permeated little *Kawabunga*. The boat could not settle into any consistent motion. The heat was unrelenting. These crazy conditions made Margaret green around the gills and her eyes flared with anger towards her beloved ship's captain.

Things came to a head on the evening of November 2. Margaret had endured enough fun. She glared at me and said, "Turn this boat around. Take me back to Bora Bora. I'll take the *Ono Ono* to Papeete and fly home. I'll meet you in Honolulu."

As captain, I had to act quickly and ruthlessly to crush the mutiny. What had Captain Bligh done in this predicament? He had acted too late and spent the next several weeks in an open boat looking for an island to land on that was not crawling with cannibals. The thought of drifting along the South Equatorial Current in a nine foot rubber dinghy, fighting hunger, sunstroke and sharks until washing up on Fiji was not appealing. I had to lay down the law, and fast.

As difficult as it was, I refused to knuckle under to the demands of my crew, my vahine, my soul mate. I had to believe one day Margaret would forgive me for this decision — most likely a month or so after reaching land, after the wild motion aboard *Kawabunga* stopped. I even dared to dream of her thanking me someday. This would likely come after several years of shore-side living.

My verdict was absolute. There would be no turning back. The mutiny was quelled. Margaret resigned herself to my decision, retreating to her bunk to resume her misery. Poor Margaret was seasick throughout the entire three week passage to Christmas Island. But, there was no more talk of mutiny from my beloved first mate. Just in case, I kept all guns, knives and sharp objects under my control.

CHARLIE TAKES A FALL

We clashed with our first major league squall of the passage on November 5 at 2000. I was astonished at the suddenness of the encounter as the conditions had been very fluky over the last several days and we certainly had not even dreamed of scuffling with any squalls. I was caught napping in the cockpit, waiting for the full moon to raise and before I knew what happened, we were hit between the eyes with 40 knot gusts and torrential rain.

We had been tiptoeing along at 3 knots on a starboard tack under main and genoa. I was stretched out on the port cockpit bench enjoying the ride when the assault was launched. *Kawabunga* was immediately overwhelmed, the little sloop lurched to port, nearly rolling me over the cockpit combing into the boiling water that was now only inches from my face. I was almost on top of the jib sheet cleat so it was quick work to release the jib sheet, spilling the wind from the genny. While the genoa tried to flog itself to death I lunged to the main sheet, releasing it, then disengaged the windvane from the tiller and tried to bring some semblance of control to the chaos.

The headsail would be torn to shreds within a few minutes if I did not get it down. It seemed impossible to get the boat turned into the wind so I sheeted the main out as much as possible, set Joey and ran off, charging along at breakneck speed through the night. Before rushing the foredeck, I released the jib halyard at the companionway and, as quickly as I could, made my way up to the foredeck, collecting the jib sheet as I went to assist in yanking down the genny. I wedged myself inside the bow pulpit on my knees and began pulling the headsail down. Unfortunately, as was so often the case during our voyage, the jib halyard got tangled up in its cleat near the companionway and I had to struggle back to the cockpit, untangle the mess, and try to get back to the bow before the halyard got snarled again. After wrestling with the sail for several minutes I was able to get it down on the deck. I laid on top of the sail for a few minutes, struggling to catch my breath before tying the sail securely to the lifelines and climbing back to the cockpit.

We had to run off until 2200 when the wind died enough to come to our proper heading. Heavy rain continued all night. Another trip was made out to the bow to hank on our tiny storm jib. It did not take long to accomplish this task. I turned my attention to putting a double-reef into the main, as I had done countless times. I was standing on the starboard cockpit combing, hugging the boom while gathering up the sail on top of the boom. While I was putting in the last reef knot, the boat suddenly lurched to port, pulling my chest across the cockpit. My feet slipped out from under me and I flipped up in the air, landing on my back, directly on top of the tiller. I was lucky the snap, crackle, pop I heard was our tiller breaking and not my back. We carry a spare tiller for such emergencies, but I was able to mend the old one by lashing nylon line around the base.

By late afternoon the seas had built up and we were involved in some serious rock'n'roll. We were heeled 30° to port, charging along on a starboard tack. At noon on the sixth we we had sailed 45 nautical miles from noon to noon. However, only 17 were miles made good. We were beginning to pay for all those leisurely down-hill days I had enjoyed on the way down to the South Pacific.

THE PRIZED BLUE BUCKET

Margaret had been searching for years for the perfect-sized bucket that would fit into our tiny galley sink. At long last, she found the prized blue bucket at a Chinese store in Raiatea. Margaret was very territorial about the bucket.

As a general rule, Margaret and I find little to argue about. At sea we had one major and recurring disagreement — *water*. I was very judicious with our water supply. Margaret would express it as being stingy. I am happy to report we never came close to running out of water during our voyage.

During the heavy rains of the fifth through the eighth we enjoyed leisurely showers in the cockpit. The weather brightened and we had very little rain the rest of the passage. It was my custom to dampen a wash cloth and wash up each morning. Margaret preferred a complete scrubbing in the cockpit with sea water, followed by a fresh water rinse.

By November 15 Margaret reached her breaking point. She did not like the aroma drifting down into the cabin from the cockpit. She suggested, in no uncertain terms, that I scrub up or ship out. I took the cherished blue bucket and dumped bucket after bucket of sea water over me, scrubbed up and leaned over to scoop up another bucket of water for a rinse. I lost my grip on the handle and the bucket dropped into our wake. I was shocked. Margaret was horrified. She was sure I had intentionally thrown her bucket overboard in retaliation for making me bathe.

We went into a man-overboard drill. Margaret kept her eyes glued to the bucket bobbing in the ocean rollers while I prepared the boat to come about. On my first pass, armed with a boat hook, I came close along the port side, but missed it. I started the engine and began another pass. As we came within twenty yards a funny (peculiar, not ha ha) thing happened. . . . The bucket sank below the surface and vanished.

Prior to this incident I always remembered November 15 as being the opening day of deer season in Michigan. Ever since, I shall remember that day, the day that will live in infamy, as the day I lost the prized blue bucket. It was almost open season on me. All aboard our tiny ship wanted the passage to end soon.

MARGARET BECOMES A SHELLBACK

The weather was excellent during the period of November 8 through 16 and we made incredibly consistent runs of 72, 73, 88, 78, 77, 78, 79, 74 and 76 nautical miles. Although these were not all miles made good, the daily runs were encouraging.

While preparing for our noon plot on November 11, we were startled to look up and see a large container ship close-in, off our starboard bow. The ship's captain altered course to have a look at *Kawabunga*. We were very happy we had a good radar reflector and the ship had a good lookout and radar operator.

Our noon plot on the sixteenth found us 135 miles from Christmas Island and 19 miles from the equator, fighting the west-setting current and, of course, winds directly on our nose. We began watching the GPS computer very closely during the afternoon as we approached the equator.

At exactly 1937 on November 16, 1995, Margaret became a Shellback, crossing the line at 157° 59′ W. We took a photograph of the GPS screen to memorialize the occasion and brewed up some hot chocolate to celebrate. We offered nothing to Poseidon. He already had our bucket. We were now in our home waters of the North Pacific Ocean.

LAND-HO!

As we closed Christmas Island, we fought the Equatorial Current that was setting us west. The currents through the Line Islands are very strong. On Saturday, November 18, we found ourselves ESE of Christmas. We had our heart's set on reaching Christmas Island by sunset. We were used to approaching the high volcanic islands of the Marquesas group and the Societies, but this was our first time approaching a low atoll. At 1530 we had unlimited visibility and were nine miles off Christmas but we could see nothing but the endless blue ocean where the atoll was supposed to be. As we motored directly into the wind and current our boat speed fell to as low as 1.7 knots.

Land-Ho! At 1700 we spotted palm trees. Christmas Island is only twelve feet high. We did not spot land until we were 2¼ miles from the nearest land. . . . Yikes! We could certainly see how easy it would be to crash and burn on the reefs out there. Christmas has a number of wrecks to attest to this. We had 6½ miles to cover in order to reach the open roadstead anchorage off Bridges Point. Now we were in a race to make it to the anchorage before dark.

Sunset overcame us as we approached the island. There were some strong lights on shore so we decided we could cautiously approach in the dark with my eyes glued to the shoreline as Margaret carefully monitored the depth sounder. As soon as we saw five fathoms we released the Hell Bitch and settled into a bumpy anchorage above the outlying coral reef.

IN PRAISE OF MY FIRST MATE

I was concerned as to how Margaret would react to being off-shore for the first time. I must say I was very proud of the way my first mate met the challenge of this significant passage. Please understand, this is not delightful, down-wind sailing. No, not at all. This entailed sailing close to the wind, in strong tradewinds, with the boat heeled 30°, bone in her teeth, (*Kawabunga* not Margaret), bashing into giant seas most of the way. You have to earn these miles and you pay a heavy price. There is no comfort, no fresh food, rationed water and the frayed temper of the captain to deal with on a twenty-four hour basis. Although, I must say in my defense and in the spirit of *gracious living*, I permitted Margaret to have her own bowl and spoon for shipboard meals. Margaret came through this ordeal with flying colors. After such an unpleasant ordeal, many marriages would abruptly cease the very instant the vessel's anchor took hold into the sandy bottom of a calm bay. Ours grew stronger. Quite surprisingly, I had to put down but one *serious* attempt at mutiny, along with a few other minor skirmishes.

Bora Bora Yacht Club

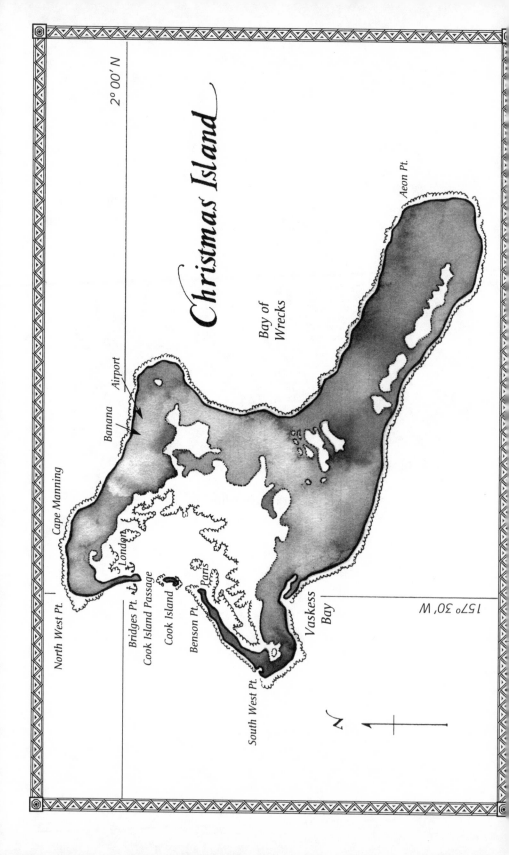

Christmas Island

2° 00' N

Cape Manning

North West Pt.

Banana

Airport

Bay of
Wrecks

Aeon Pt.

Bridges Pt.
Cook Island Passage
Cook Island
Benson Pt.
London
Paris
South West Pt.
Vaskess
Bay

157° 30' W

N

"I know of nothing that will so set a man's blood flowing like a fight with a wind-mad sail."
— Thomas Fleming Day

CHAPTER TEN

CHRISTMAS ISLAND

WORLD'S LARGEST ATOLL

Shortly after anchoring we were both fast asleep. We spent the next day resting up and admiring the beauty of the island from our anchorage. The beach was an idyllic sight, with palm trees towering over a long, white sand beach. The quantity of fish in this area was amazing. There were so many fish in the water they were smashing into *Kawabunga's* hull. Larger fish were herding the smaller fish, putting them into a frenzy for hours.

A welcoming committee of several dolphin swam by early Sunday morning, or what we assumed was Sunday morning, as they made their way up the shore line.

We soon found out that it was actually Monday morning and that we had (presto!) lost a day when we anchored off Christmas Island. Tarawa, the capital of Kiribati, dictates the calendar for Christmas Island. You will note that Tarawa Atoll is located at 1° 25′ N, 173° E, one thousand miles west of Christmas, beyond the international dateline.

As we were napping we would hear boats approaching and would climb out of the cabin to greet the local natives. All of these visitors were fishermen and all had a welcoming smile for us. The majority of these natives are from the Gilbert Group in Micronesia but refer to themselves as I-Kiribati rather than Gilbertese. We asked if we could get into London Harbor. Our guides and the charts indicated we could make it in with our shoal draft. The fishermen told us there was a yacht much bigger than ours in the harbor and we would not have any trouble.

The next morning we studied the charts and used our binoculars to survey the Cook Island Passage. The passage runs between Bridge's Point and Cook Island. As an added bonus challenge, Cochrane Reef lies directly in the middle of this channel. Therefore, it would be sound practice to go to one side or the other of Cochrane Reef on our way into the lagoon.

The thought of staying in this uncomfortable anchorage and of shooting the surf with our dinghy (à là Hawaii Five-O) to get to shore was not an attractive one. We did not savor the thought of leaving *Kawabunga* unattended while we went ashore either, as there was always the chance of the anchor rode parting. Next port — Japan! There would be little chance of anyone seeing such an occurrence as there were no other boats anchored off Bridge's Point. By this time, my confidence in negotiating coral reef passes and coral-speckled lagoons was at it's peak. After all, we had conquered the Societies without suffering a scratch.

In retrospect, it may have been better to take the advice of Earl Hinz when he wrote in his book *Pacific Wanderer*; "Charts and sailing directions say that boats drawing less than 6 feet can find their way into the lagoon via the channels between the village of London and Cook Island, . . . Although it may be possible to snake your way into the lagoon, I would recommend against trying to do so. One steel-hulled yacht had made its way into the lagoon before we had arrived. In stiff trade winds, it's anchor rode parted, allowing it to drift outwards towards the pass where ocean swells picked it up and cast it on the reef. There it still lies."

The smart call would have been to launch the dinghy and motor the 2½ miles into the lagoon to reconnoiter the channel. Without doubt, we would never have attempted to enter the lagoon in *Kawabunga* if we would have followed this level-headed approach.

DAMN THE TORPEDOES, FULL SPEED AHEAD!

We waited for the sun to be high overhead for ideal visibility before we weighed anchor and motored towards Cook Island Passage a few hundred yards distant. After studying the chart we decided to make our way around the south side of Cochrane Reef and to be well east of Cochrane before turning north and snaking through the dangers. We could not depend exclusively on the chart because of the shifting sand and silt. We needn't concern ourselves with red right returning (USA) or red left returning (French Polynesia) as the channel was not marked at all.

My major concern was to successfully negotiate the Cook Island Passage. Our anxiety meters were registering moderate as we said, "Damn the torpedoes, full speed ahead!" We shot through the pass without difficulty and took a prudent route around the east side of Cochrane Reef. As we cautiously headed for the point protecting London Harbor we encountered many dolphin that swam over and played with us. We took this as a good sign. Margaret had her eyes fixed on the depth sounder and called out shallower and shallower soundings. Of course, we expected this, but when the terrain did not come close to matching the chart our anxiety meters shot off the scale. The cartographers were not kidding when they wrote "constantly changing" as concerns the entrance to London Harbor on the chart.

We hailed a couple of young fishermen in a run-about and they pointed the way around the reef extending from the point. We were committed to this course of action so we followed the reef around and snaked through the narrow channel and finally headed for the dilapidated wharf. We could see a 36 foot sport-fisher, a landing craft and the Westsail 32 the islanders had told us about. Now, the depths were alarmingly shallow. The reef off our port side was obvious and menacing. There were numerous coral heads and coral patches to starboard. We felt a jolt, like you feel when you hit a speed bump in a parking lot. Seconds later we struck again. This time, we were hard aground.

HARD AGROUND

Panic set in for a few minutes. Had we come all this way only to lose our boat, our home and everything we own, in a South Seas trap? We were not on the reef — yet. We were aground on coral sand, only a few yards away from reef on both sides of us. To our great relief a local fisherman paddled his pirogue over to us. He rolled out of his narrow canoe into waist-deep water, like John Wayne dismounting his trusty pony, and waded towards us with a broad, reassuring smile.

"Don't worry. Everything is all right. This happens all the time. In an hour you will float off."

The fisherman's reassuring words were just what we needed. Margaret kept the engine running while I went out on the foredeck, released our bower anchor and laid out some rode. I jumped into the water and helped the fisherman carry the Hell Bitch and thirty feet of chain to windward and set it. At least we would not be blown up on the reef when we floated off.

The fisherman came aboard and introduced himself as Luti Vakaliki. The three of us sat in the cockpit drinking fruit juice while waiting for the flood. We certainly ran into the right man on this island. We wanted to express our appreciation for Luti's helping hand so we asked him if we could take him and his wife out to lunch. Luti looked at us as if we had just landed from Mars. There was no bistro in London Village. Instead, Luti invited us to his house for lunch. This was only the beginning of the overwhelming hospitality Luti and his family showered on us during our stay on their island.

Tony Herrick from Durban, South Africa rowed over in his dinghy. Tony, who had sailed through the South Pacific a few years earlier, bought *Shackles,* his Westsail 32 in San Diego and sailed directly to Christmas solo. On his way into the harbor he promptly fetched up on the reef where he lingered for two days. He was pulled off with the help of the local fishermen and their power boats. It was a miracle *Shackles* was saved. He had resigned himself to the fact that he was going to lose his boat and had begun to salvage what he could in order to raise money for his airline ticket home. Tony has been working with the Tourism Board, helping them shoot photographs of the atoll for post cards.

Sure enough, *Kawabunga* floated off within the hour and Luti piloted us into the small anchorage directly in front of the concrete wharf. *Shackles* was the only other yacht at Christmas Island. The anchorage was very rough. Tony told us it had been rough since he arrived several weeks earlier. Thanks to my brilliant decision, we now found ourselves in a rough anchorage with a twenty-five mile fetch and a lee shore. We felt trapped like a rat in the lagoon.

OUR FRIEND LUTI

After we cleared customs we walked over with Luti and Tony to the Ace of Hearts Club for a cold drink and got a taste of Christmas Island's high prices. Luti was anxious for us to see his house so we walked with him through the village to the north end where he had a seaside home.

By this time it was early afternoon and the women were preparing the major meal of the day. Luti's entire extended family made it a point to make us feel at home and welcome. We were invited to sit in their fare, a raised platform with a roof overhead made from palm fronds. Even though it was hot outside, this was a very cool place to sit because we were two feet up off the sand and protected from the sun's rays. We were introduced to Mr. Kamatua Tebaati, Luti's son-in-law and the head of the family. Kamatua, a stevedore, owned the property and structures.

The women grilled the bonefish Luti had just plucked from the lagoon over an open fire in a cooking shed thirty feet from the fare. They had their hands full between cooking and kicking the pigs, chickens, cats and dogs away from the lunch. One big sow received special treatment because she was about to deliver piglets. A few days later she had eight little pink babies.

Luti showed us how to prepare a coconut. With the coconut in one hand and a machete in the other, he chopped away with a few precision strokes to lay open the nut. I expected to see blood gushing over the sand at any time, but Luti had obviously done this before. We drank the coconut juice and ate the coconut meat. We had not eaten any fresh food for three weeks and the thought of fresh fish and fruit made our mouths water. The fish had a lot of bones and we ate with our fingers. Our taste buds exploded in ecstasy.

What an experience. Amorous pigs were running about. Beautiful little girls waved palm fronds around us to keep insects away and to keep us cool. More and more food was served up. We could get used to this.

We were very impressed with Luti's bath tub, which had been fashioned from a segment of an earth mover's rubber tire. It looked like a giant onyx seashell-shaped bath tub.

The next day Luti paddled over to *Kawabunga* with fresh fish for us. He told us his family liked us because we were not shy to eat. . . He said, "Most Europeans are shy to eat. You are not shy to eat." Our friend Luti — the king of understatement!

LONDON, PARIS, BANANA

London Village is actually an old American military base from the 1940's and 1950's. The British were also involved in the 1960's and early 1970's. Atmospheric atom bomb tests were conducted over Christmas Island, making it a creepy place in that respect. We termed the giant flies with red eyes we saw out over the reef as "nuclear flies".

It broke our hearts to see the way the people had to deal with water on Christmas Island. They have very little fresh water and all water has to be boiled. At the time of our visit, it had not rained at Christmas Island for an entire year. They get their water via wells and, even after boiling, it tastes vile. Even though Luti had always boiled his water, he suffered from a worm in his stomach causing him constant, gnawing pain. These people really need a desalinization plant. It is horrible to live without good, fresh water. We bought twelve cans of Diet Sprite for $24 and were happy to pay the price just to have something good to drink.

The government is moving the entire village of Banana (population 666) a mile away from it's present location because of water and sewage problems. We wondered if they would call the new village *The Second Banana*? Paris, located near Benson Point, is at the other end of the island by road, but a short boat ride from London by water across the Cook Island Passage. Oddly enough, there are no bananas in Banana, Paris is deserted and London has no fog.

The people are recruited from overcrowded Tarawa to live on Christmas. Everyone has a job and the people appear happy, untroubled and friendly. Everyone has a smile for you when you walk through the village. The islanders are shy as they do not see very many visitors to their island.

We were told we should lock our boat because there were three known thieves on the island. We did not tell them there were probably three thieves for every block in Santa Monica where we were from.

We had been told we could buy case lots of supplies at Christmas. Once we were settled in, we strolled over to the warehouse to investigate. The warehouse had only two products, apparently staples of the Christmas diet; rice and Foster's Beer. This is no joke. It was a good thing we stocked up at Bora Bora. We bought several pounds of rice at the local store and I made quite a dent in the island's supply of Eskimo Pie ice cream bars while we were there.

Despite the remoteness of Christmas Island and the lack of goods and services, we were miraculously able to buy a brand new VHF radio. Tony Herrick, the only other yachtie on the island, used to own a chandlery in Durban, and had lots of spare equipment on board. He sold us a brand new West Marine VHF radio. Our other ship's radio finally gave up the fight on the way to Christmas. Who would imagine being able to buy radio equipment out in the middle of nowhere? In a situation where he could have charged an exorbitant fee, Tony sold us the radio for the price listed in the West Marine catalog. He was even so kind as to take a personal check for the radio.

THE AIRPORT

While meeting with the Kiribati officials, we saw an unusual sight. The custom's agents were drinking bottled water. We had not found bottled water anywhere. We asked them where they had acquired the thirst-quenching drink. They said they had just been at the airport and got it there. Instantly, visions of a refrigerated display case brimming with bottled water and an airport restaurant where we could stuff ourselves with steak sandwiches leapt into our heads. We also wanted to buy an airline ticket to Honolulu for Margaret for a February departure. We planned to sail back to Christmas from Palmyra so that Margaret could fly rather than sailing the 1,000 miles to Hawaii. Our next question was how to get to the airport.

We were told we could hop on the bus that runs down to the other end of the atoll and get off after the village of Banana, at the road that runs out to the airport. While waiting for the bus, we ran across Father Belmont, the Roman Catholic priest who lives on Christmas. He was riding his bicycle to the wharf where he would board a small boat setting sail for Fanning Island. Father Belmont asked us to say hello to Roger, the caretaker of Palmyra, when we arrived there.

We had been looking forward to meeting John Brydon while at Christmas. Rob Jordan had told us to look John up when we got to Christmas as they had been friends for many years. John came to Christmas Island from Scotland many years ago as a plantation manager and stayed. He had spent a few years on Palmyra also, running a copra plantation. As luck would have it, John had flown to Honolulu to re-stock his store and we missed him.

We boarded a crowded bus in London Village and enjoyed the thirteen mile excursion out past Banana. We were surprised to see Saume Maitonga, a bonefish guide we had met the day before, on the same bus. He was paid quite handsomely to be a bonefish guide. Saume came over and sat with us. He looked troubled when we told him we were going to the airport for lunch. He said, "I will be your guide".

My Los Angeles defense mechanism automatically kicked into gear. I could see that this guy was out to make a quick buck at our expense. "Oh no, we do not need a guide. We're just going to have lunch at the airport and come home. We can't afford a guide."

Saume's response was, "No charge. I will show you the way."

I was offended by Saume's insistence that he accompany us, but resigned myself to the fact we had a guide whether we wanted one or not.

We got off the bus just past Banana. A small, faded, wooden sign pointed us down an unpaved road towards the ocean and the airport. It was just past mid-day and blazing hot. As we approached the airport I began to realize why Saume had insisted on escorting us. The landscape before us looked like a scene straight out of a spaghetti western. The terminal was a small, empty, wooden building. There were no planes, no people, no ticket agents, no refrigerated display cases, and no restaurants in the sky. The place was completely deserted. I expected to see tumble weeds somersaulting past and Clint Eastwood riding up on his cow pony any minute.

The people of Christmas Island are courteous, respectful and polite. Rather than telling us we were too stupid to live, Saume had taken pity on us and insisted on accompanying us to make sure we would be safe and sound.

Margaret reminded me that only mad dogs and Englishmen walked in the noon day sun. Saume took us on a short-cut to Banana where he introduced us to Noere Tonganibeia, the principal of the Roman Catholic school. Father Belmont had founded the school a few years earlier. Noere took us to his home and encouraged us to rest on his porch out of the hot sun while we waited for the bus to take us back to town. We were told the bus would be right along, which to them meant two hours.

Noere was very proud of his school. They had recently built two new, permanent classrooms out of cement blocks. He was quite upset about having to move along with the others in Banana. It will not be quite the hardship on most of the population as their homes are built out of temporary materials. He did not want to leave his new classrooms. A generous benefactor in Canada had given them the money to build and now what would he tell her?

When we got back to London Village we met with Bwebwere Naburennara of the Christmas Travel Agency. Bwebwere explained there was only one flight per week into the Christmas airport. Each flight brings forty fly anglers from Honolulu to fish Christmas lagoon's bountiful stocks of ikari (bonefish). I spoke with a group of anglers who had spent a week fly fishing for bonefish and were preparing to return to their homes in Oregon. They were deliriously happy about the fishing and devastated to have to leave. They return to this distant Pacific atoll every year to fly fish and told me they catch more fish in one morning in Christmas' lagoon flats than they do in an entire week in Florida. In all likelihood, Christmas Island has the best bonefishing in the world.

We told Bwebwere we wanted to sail to Palmyra for two months and return to Christmas Island in February of 1996. It was our intention to have Margaret fly out from Christmas to Honolulu at that time. Margaret could buy a ticket to return to Honolulu on one of those flights. One problem — they did not take the American Express card.

We walked across the street to the little store-front Bank of Kiribati, Ltd. and spoke with the manager, Mr. Marouea Kamraratu. We discussed the best way to get cash from our Bank of America account to Christmas Island so we could pay for an airline ticket. Mr. Kamraratu told us he would take an $800 check from us, send it to the Bank of Hawaii for collection and by the time we returned in February the check would have cleared and he would give us the cash. We wrote Mr. Kamraratu a check for $800 and took a receipt with his stamp and signature affixed to it.

THANKSGIVING FEAST

Luti invited us to a special feast in our honor on their Friday of that week and it just happened to be our Thanksgiving. At 1700 Luti came to pick us up and walked us through London Village on the way to his house. This caused quite a stir with the villagers. Luti wanted everyone to know we were his honored guests. He is a subsistence fisherman and he took the day off from his usual fishing to dive for octopus, dress a chicken and collect special fruits and vegetables for us.

We were seated alone at the place of honor in the comfort of the fare. Set before us was a bountiful platter of food, including calamari, chicken, sweet coconut toddy, tamai (a fruit that looked like a shaving brush), panunes (similar to a yam) and rice. In the center of the platter was the pièce de résistance — canned corned beef.

We were not tutored beforehand in the proper etiquette to employ, but it became apparent we were to eat first, while the rest of the family of about twenty souls watched our every move. While we ate, little girls fanned us with palm fronds. After we finished eating, the platter sat for what seemed an eternity, until Luti and his family were sure we were finished. The men ate after that, followed by the women and then the children.

After everyone had eaten, the women began singing songs. The girls, ranging in age from two to eleven, took turns dancing for us. The family had one grass skirt and each girl took her turn wearing the grass skirt, performing a traditional dance while their grandmother sang in Gilbertese. The dancing entailed graceful, precisely-choreographed, bird-like movements.

We all had a wonderful time. We explained what Thanksgiving meant to us, showed them a postcard picturing our apartment on the beach in Santa Monica and described our way of life in Los Angeles. We had a Polaroid Captiva camera with us for just such an occasion. We took several snapshots of the kids and gave them the photographs. They were honored to share what they had with us and we were overwhelmed by their generosity. As a parting gift, Luti presented Margaret with a large conch shell and several smaller shells. These shells are very expensive in the Society and Line Islands. We gave them a cache of tooth brushes and tooth paste to endure well into the twenty-first century. The children were more grateful for the boxes of Quaker chocolate chip bars. This was truly a Thanksgiving we will never forget.

ESCAPING THE VENUS FLY TRAP

After the difficulty we encountered entering Christmas Island's lagoon, we were very concerned we would meet disaster on the way out. The water is not as clear as in other lagoons due to the free sand in the water caused by the wave action. This makes it particularly difficult to navigate within the lagoon.

I met with Perry Langston at his home on Christmas' lagoon. Perry lives on the site of the old commanding officer's quarters and has lived there continuously since 1982. He previously lived on the island in 1967 while working for the British government. He was the manager of the coconut plantation. Perry had a tide chart for Christmas and we were able to determine the best time for us to cast off. His help was invaluable. Perry made a point of warning me about the violent line squalls on the way to Palmyra.

We arranged with Peter Edwards to have him act as a pilot for us. Peter is the Harbor Master of London Harbor and knows the passage intimately. Luti also insisted on helping us.

We weighed anchor at 0740 on Saturday, November 25. High water would be in one hour so we had an extra cushion should we run into trouble. As we approached the pass between Cochrane Reef and Bridge's Point, Peter told us it was a rarity for yachts to come into the harbor. Just a few years ago they were able to get boats in but the last few years they have lost a great deal of their harbor due to the unrelenting pounding of the surf. The depths have gotten much shallower with all the wave action. One can become trapped inside the lagoon when the wind blows from the south or west. Surfers come to Christmas Island each winter to surf the enormous waves that break over this pass due to the ocean swells striking the outgoing tidal flow from the lagoon. When this occurs, the pass is completely shut down for long periods of time.

By 0805 we were free! We off-loaded Peter and Luti into a launch and set off on a broad reach bound for Palmyra, having cheated death once again.

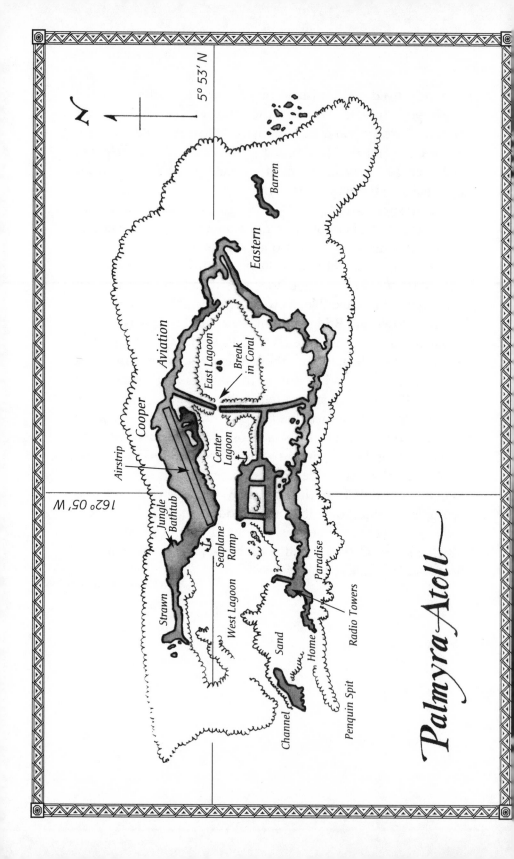

Palmyra Atoll

5° 53' N

162° 05' W

Barren

Eastern

Aviation

Cooper

Airstrip

East Lagoon

Break
in Coral

Center
Lagoon

Jungle
Bathtub

Strawn

Seaplane
Ramp

West Lagoon

Sand

Channel

Home

Penquin Spit

Paradise

Radio Towers

"Danger is where you find it, whether it be the innermost navigable creek that pales to sweet water or the bitter wells of the pounding sea."
— Joe Richards

CHAPTER ELEVEN

PALMYRA

THE ROAD TO PALMYRA

We had a fast downwind leg to Palmyra. It was an uncomfortable ride as *Kawabunga* yawed 35° to starboard and 35° to port, surfing down those big ocean rollers. We were both a little green during this leg, but were encouraged by our daily mileage. This was a short hop of roughly 369 nautical miles on a WNW course.

The first day out we noticed a lift from the current of 1.6 knots. Our Tri Data log showed a speed of 4.2 knots while the computer showed a velocity made good and speed over ground of 5.8 knots. We had to keep close tabs on our position as the current was setting us north as well as west and the Line Islands are on the rhumb line to Palmyra. I jibed away at noon on Sunday, the twenty-sixth as the combination of wind and current was threatening to cast us up on Fanning's SE corner reef. We were relieved when we sighted Fanning Island two hours later.

Our original float plan called for us to visit Fanning for a week to ten days, but we were anxious to meet up with our cruising friends on Palmyra and we were not looking forward to another unruly anchorage, so we bypassed Fanning and steered a course for Palmyra. On Monday, we sighted the palm trees of Washington Island at 0848.

We found ourselves on the flip side of the current problem on Tuesday morning. We were now on top of the ENE-setting Equatorial Counter-Current, struggling with an adverse current of 1.1 knots. At noon on Tuesday our position was 20 miles SE of Palmyra.

Rob had given us detailed instructions for approaching Palmyra while we were in Tahiti. We headed for the rendezvous point to the SW of the atoll, giving Penguin Spit a wide berth. The safe longitude on approach to Palmyra is 162° 08′ West. We were too far east. Most wrecks occur west of the island, beyond the break of the reef. Sailors coming down from Hawaii generally approach from the north and see the reef on the northwest corner and do not realize the reef extends much further to the west. A mile cushion is prudent. Even in deep water, column-like coral heads rise up from the bottom and cause havoc for navigators. We were told not to get caught to the west as the NNW setting current running 1½ knots would sweep us up on the reef. There is a recent and uncharted wreck clearly visible to the west of the channel which should not be confused with the charted wreck which is now overgrown and hard to identify as a wreck. This is an extremely dangerous pass.

Land ho! We sighted palm trees at 1325 on a beautiful, clear day. An hour later a squall hit us 8½ miles from the atoll. Our visibility was reduced to a quarter-mile and Palmyra disappeared. The squall lasted twenty minutes, but the rain continued. Palmyra would appear and disappear in the rain as we approached. Again, we were in a race to make the anchorage before sunset.

We were able to get through to Kaye on *Navi-Gator* on our hand-held VHF. To our surprise, Kaye and Joe had dropped anchor in Palmyra's lagoon only three hours earlier, after enjoying a two week visit on Fanning. Thank God Kaye was on board and monitoring the radio as everyone else was ashore playing. Kaye was able to alert Rob that we were on our approach.

WELCOME TO GILLIGAN'S ISLAND

As we cautiously approached the SE end of the island, we heard Roger Lextrait's voice over the radio. Roger, a Frenchman who lives aboard *Cous Cous* in Palmyra's lagoon, is the resident manager of the island. It was nerve-racking trying to understand Roger's frenzied, fractured-English instructions and steer the boat along the southern reef, looking for the pass in the rain. I was only understanding one of every four words from our sea traffic controller. Do you see a pattern here?

The ruins of the radio towers from World War II days is a distinctive landmark at the south end of the atoll. The remnants of the radio towers are on Paradise Island, 1½ mile ENE of the pass. I told Roger I could see the old radio towers. Roger told me to head straight for the towers.

Rain was coming down in buckets. In retrospect, it is obvious Roger thought we were several miles from the island, on our approach to Palmyra, when we were actually standing just off the reef. We could clearly see a boat bobbing peacefully at anchor in the lagoon and longed to be nestled beside her. This would have been an excellent time to stand off, get an accurate fix on our position, study the chart and proceed cautiously.

We took up a course of 40°, heading for the towers. There was no pass in sight. We could see no break in the reef. We got to within 30 yards of the breaking reef before turning away in time to avert disaster. Rob's voice crackled across our radio. "Where are you?"

"We're trying to find the pass. We're off the reef in front of the old radio towers."

Rob said, "Get away from the reef — you're too far east! You need to come to the southwest end of the island but beware of Penguin Spit. It juts WSW and you have to go out around it and to the southwest side of Sand Island before you'll see the

pass. I'll come out in the dinghy and meet you at the pass."
Margaret and I were greatly relieved. The wind, rain and sea
had taken a toll on our psyches.

We followed Rob's instructions. Roger, Rob and Ross came
out to the pass entrance in *Eliott's* dinghy. Rob brought a hand-
held VHF radio and talked us in. As we carefully maneuvered
around Penguin Spit we spotted the heroic trio being tossed
about in a little dinghy, braving the waves in a cloudburst. If
they had not been there we would not have taken the chance
to go in because the sun was very low, it was raining and
gloomy. With this restricted visibility, we could not make out
the pass or channel at all. We put our complete trust in our
three harbor pilots.

Ross was rarely seen without a fishing pole in his hand. The
fact that the rain was coming down in buckets and the sea was
assaulting his little craft did not dissuade Ross from trolling.
Ross got a strike just as we were about to enter the narrow, fifty
foot wide pass. We were waived off so they could land the fish.
We watched as Ross struggled to reel in a big jack. Just as the
trio was about to land the fish a thieving shark attacked, leaving
Ross with nothing but his pole and a slack line. His jack and,
more importantly, his lure, had vanished in one sudden bite.

Rob and Roger scrambled aboard *Kawabunga* and guided us
into the pass. We gave Rob a big hug and he introduced us to
Roger. Roger's reputation had preceded him, but we still
weren't quite ready for what was standing in our cockpit. His
ensemble consisted of a red weenie bikini, a soiled and torn
oxford long-sleeve shirt, mismatching tennis shoes and feathers
in his hair. A large dive knife was lashed to his right leg. Roger,
thus gloriously adorned and undisputed ruler over his island
kingdom, took a look at *Kawabunga* and exclaimed in his robust
French accent, "Eeez day sailor! Thees eez reedeculous. Ah, you
are crazeee."

In anticipation of our arrival, Margaret put on some
makeup to cover the green from the passage, brushed out her
hair and put on a pretty blue pareu. Roger is not known for his

fondness for American women. He gave Margaret the once over and declared, "You look like you're on your way to the mall." Margaret, defusing the barb, smiled and replied, "I heard there was a party!"

As Rob steered us along the west side of Sand Island and into the West Lagoon, Roger pointed out some of the interesting features of Palmyra. He told us the white splotches in the thick green foliage on Sand Island were the Booby Birds. The island was off-limits as it is preserved as a sanctuary for the birds.

I began to relax as we continued to thread our way into the large West Lagoon. By 1730 we were all squared away, hanging on the hook in fifty-four feet of water along side *Eliott*, out in front of the old seaplane ramp where Roger had his camp. It was a long, hard journey to reach Palmyra and we were looking forward to some serious rest and relaxation. However, the *camp counselors*, who had been there a few weeks and were already tanned and rested, had other ideas.

SUMMER CAMP FOR GROWN-UPS

Palmyra is located at 5° 53′ N, 162° 5′ W, within the inter-tropical convergence zone, roughly half-way between Hawaii and Samoa. It is a horseshoe-shaped atoll with more than fifty islets circling three distinct lagoons. The West Lagoon is connected to the Center Lagoon by a wide, shallow channel running between Cooper Island and an un-named island to the north of Kaula Island. The East Lagoon can be entered by dinghy at high water through a very narrow, shallow pass, broken in the coral causeway running between Aviation Island and Engineer Island. The terrain is very low, the maximum elevation measuring six feet. The islets are overgrown with dense flora, coconut trees and balsa-like trees. The coconut trees grow to ninety feet.

We spent three phenomenal weeks on Palmyra Atoll. Most places do not live up to expectations. Palmyra exceeds its reputation. It is summer camp for grown-ups — unspoiled beauty — wild jungle adventure — incredible white sand beaches — remnants from World War II — underwater paradise — stories of buried treasure — murder and intrigue.

Palmyra was a refueling base for ships and submarines during World War II. A 6,000 foot airstrip was constructed on Cooper Island, a channel was blasted through the coral allowing entrance into the west lagoon and a seaplane landing area was dredged out in the center lagoon. Command posts, a hospital, water collection facilities, roads and mammoth fuel tanks were constructed. The island was able to store an incredible 25 million gallons of fuel. Pill boxes and bunkers were erected along the periphery of the island along with coastal gun emplacements. There were 5,000 U.S. troops stationed on this tiny atoll. At the time of our visit, aside from the channel, the 100,000 gallon fresh water tank and the seaplane ramp, the jungle had reclaimed these projects.

Palmyra is an uninhabited, privately owned island — an unincorporated territory of the United States. The owners live in Hawaii and have contracted with a large real estate developer to manage the property. They have employed Roger Lextrait to be the on-site manager and caretaker of the island to protect the atoll's natural resources and discourage cruisers from over-staying their welcome. The owners have become wary of yachties. In the past, some modern-day Robinson Crusoe-types have fallen out of coconut trees, with less than optimal dismounts. Although Palmyra is a remote atoll, somehow members of the bar were retained and lawsuits filed. I know the lagoon is full of sharks, but this is ridiculous!

The advent of GPS has brought an increase in the number of boats calling on Palmyra each year. Now, an average of 60 boats per year take advantage of Palmyra's secure lagoon for a rest stop either on the way north to the Hawaiian Islands or south to the South Pacific.

PIRATES AND SHIPWRECKS

This idyllic, tropical atoll was not discovered until Captain Edmond Fanning, aboard the American trading ship *Betsey*, stumbled across the island on June 13, 1798. Captain Fanning did not land on the island. Captain Sawle, bound for the Philippines, aboard the American trading ship *Palmyra*, happened across the island on November 6, 1802. Captain Sawle was the first to report the discovery. The crew of the *Palmyra* explored the atoll for a week before naming it after their ship and moving on.

In 1816 the Spanish pirate ship *Esperanza* foundered on Palmyra's reef. The ship was laden with gold and silver looted from Inca temples in Peru. The crew was able to transport the treasure to shore and bury it somewhere on Palmyra before *Esperanza* sank. Tradition has it that the treasure was buried under a banyan tree on Home Island. The buccaneers tired of being stranded on the atoll and built two rafts. The men split up into two groups and sailed away to their fates. Only one raider survived the ordeal but died soon after being rescued by an American whaling ship.

Many ships have met with disaster on Palmyra's treacherous reef. While beachcombing one afternoon we came across the 1993 wreck of a 38 foot Beneteau on the north shore of Cooper Island. The boat had been chewed up and spit out by the unforgiving reef, her bones left to bake on the scorching white sand beach under the tropical sun. Roger told of being startled one evening by a shipwrecked castaway staggering into his camp. Roger had not seen another human being for a while. The yacht could not be saved, but ultimately another boat made a call on Palmyra and gave the man a lift to Honolulu.

In order to get inside the lagoon you have to pass by a Korean longline fishing boat that came to grief across the channel and to the northwest of Sand Island. The passageway into Palmyra is treacherous. Roger told us a high percentage of visiting boats actually strike coral heads or "kiss" the sides of the channel when attempting to enter the pass.

THE PALMYRA CURSE

Before leaving the Bay Club in San Diego, our dockmaster and friend Ann Miller told us, in no uncertain terms, we were not to sail to Palmyra. Since Palmyra was not on our itinerary, complying with Ann's overwrought plea was easy. I had kept a boat at the Bay Club, formerly known as Underwood's Landing, for fourteen years before moving it up to Holiday Harbor in Marina del Rey. We had all heard of the couple who had lived at Underwood's Landing before setting off for Palmyra and never returning. I had watched a television movie of the grisly murders several years earlier, but the only thing I remembered was some crazy hippie cutting down coconut trees with a chain saw. I had not yet read Vincent Bugliosi's extraordinary book, *And The Sea Will Tell.*

In the spring of 1974 Mac and Muff Graham left Underwood's Landing on San Diego's Shelter Island aboard their beautiful 38 foot ketch *Sea Wind,* bound for Palmyra, by way of Hawaii. The Grahams, experienced circumnavigators, were looking for a respite from the pressures and escalating crime of urban civilization.

That same spring Buck Walker and Jennifer Jenkins (a pseudonym) departed Port Allen on Kauai, Hawaii, bound for Palmyra aboard *Iola,* a 30 foot sloop. Buck and Jennifer wanted to escape from life's problems too, but *their* intent was to find a hide-out. Buck was wanted in the state of Hawaii for a drug conviction and feared being sent back to San Quentin on a five-to-life sentence.

The *Iola* arrived in Palmyra on June 27, 1974, followed by the *Sea Wind* five days later. *Sea Wind* departed Palmyra in September of that year with Buck Walker at the helm rather than Mac Graham. Four people had been on the island but only two left alive. The *Iola* was towed out of the lagoon and scuttled. The Grahams disappeared without a trace — until six years later, when Sharon Jordan discovered a human skull while on her morning walk along Strawn Island's south shore. The skull, other skeletal remains and a woman's wrist watch found in and around an aluminum container were the last traces of Muff Graham and spelled the beginning of the end for Buck Walker.

Rob and Sharon Jordan, aboard *Moya*, had been alone on Palmyra for nearly three months before their shocking find. A few weeks earlier, Rob and Sharon had discovered and raised a sunken USAF rescue boat from the bottom of the lagoon and noticed two of the four rectangular storage compartments in the stern of the vessel were missing. One of these containers had been Muff's coffin. Presumably, the second, and still missing, container was Mac's.

DISASTER AT SEA

All news was not good when we arrived on Palmyra. We were slapped in the face with a reality check on the hazards of cruising when Kaye and Joe told us the tragic story of their good friends the Slavins. Joe and Kaye were very close to this family as they buddy-boated with them from Boqueron, Puerto Rico through Trinidad.

Mike and Judy Slavin, from Hermosa Beach, California, were cruising with their two children Ben (age 8) and Annie (age 6) in their forty-seven foot cutter *Melinda Lee*. They had left California, sailed down the Mexican coast and through the Panama Canal to the Caribbean and then back into the Pacific, to Polynesia and then on to New Zealand.

The disaster occurred in November along the New Zealand coast, while we were en route to Palmyra. The weather was bad and they sighted a freighter approaching. They tried to hail someone aboard the freighter with no response. They were run down and sunk within a few minutes. Mike, Judy and Annie were able to get into an inflatable dinghy. Ben was probably killed in the collision. The dinghy kept flipping over and Annie lost her grip and fell away. Mike dove in after her, but both the father and child disappeared. Judy was the only survivor. She washed up on shore in New Zealand and was hospitalized with severe injuries. *Melinda Lee* was fully equipped with electronics and safety paraphernalia and had an experienced and vigilant crew. Joe and Kaye, as you can well imagine, were stunned and grieving.

THE PROFESSOR AND MARY ANN

We had a total of eleven people on the island while we were there. We knew everyone except Roger and the couple aboard *Pilar* prior to our visit. We quickly became friends with Bill and Diane Pool, who built lovely *Pilar* from a bare hull. She is a William Atkins' designed, Ingrid 38 foot cutter. The yachts in Palmyra during our stay were; *Time-Out, Navi-Gator, Cous Cous, Eliott, Pilar* and *Kawabunga*.

Rob was anxious to be our island guide to the mysteries of Palmyra. He is an expert on Palmyra as he has made nine extensive sojourns to the mysterious atoll. He showed us where Sharon found Muff Graham's remains and directed us to secluded anchorages and the best fishing and diving sites.

SNORKELING OVER THE REEF

Our first morning on Palmyra was one of the most beautiful I can remember. Brilliant sunlight made the shallow, coral-riddled water along the shoreline sparkle. We took the dinghy to the seaplane ramp for an orientation meeting with Roger. Roger was relaxing in the shade and comfort of his lovely fare, which provided an awe-inspiring view of the West Lagoon and the southern motus.

We met his two dogs; Tutu and Blackie. The mutts had opposite personalities — Tutu, a friendly pooch — Blackie, a dark, foreboding and dangerous jackal. Blackie, who had been bitten by a shark a few weeks prior to our arrival, was stark raving mad. He bit two people while we were on the atoll. We carried an aluminum fish-basher with us whenever we went ashore. Blackie charged us a couple of times, but he knew I was ready, more than willing and able to brain him with my miniature Louisville Slugger if he got too close.

Roger pointed out the prohibited islands and briefly explained the rules and dangers of the atoll before leading us from his camp down a narrow foot path to the old airstrip. The airstrip was overgrown and covered with millions of sooty terns. The squawking and carrying on by the birds was astounding. We saw the old Lockheed Lodestar airplane that crash landed on the island in 1979. I was able to climb up on it and examine it. Over the years, cruisers have salvaged what was useful for a boat from the aircraft.

We cooled off after our walk with a dip in the swimming hole located just to the north of the end of the runway. This is one of the loveliest places on Palmyra as the coconut trees hang out over the lagoon. While you swim, you can look across the East Lagoon to Sand and Home Islands in the distance. True paradise. Incidentally, this is where Mac and Muff Graham anchored *Sea Wind.*

By 1000 we were back aboard Kawabunga and a snorkeling trip was quickly arranged over the VHF island net. The natives no longer use drums. Joe and Kaye picked us up in their dinghy and we joined two other dinghies filled with island explorers and headed for the pass.

While we drove across the lagoon towards the pass, Ross and Rob, in their respective dinghies, trolled for dinner. As we shadowed the tiny islet on the west side of the pass, Rob had a strike. Sherry steered the boat as Rob expertly reeled in a jack. It wasn't long before Sherry had a strike. Ross and Lorna were playing the same game. We hadn't unpacked our fishing poles so we were reduced to watching the action.

We followed Rob as he led us to a beautiful spot over the reef between the pass and Penguin Spit. Rob took his painter and dove down into the crystal clear water to tie the boat off to a coral head. The other dinghies were tied to Rob and Sherry's little Fatty Knees dinghy.

The snorkeling was magnificent. We marveled at the beauty and life on the reef. The coral formations were spectacular. Multicolored coral fish abounded. It was like swimming in a giant luxury aquarium. I thought the snorkeling on Bora Bora was incredible but it paled in comparison to snorkeling at Palmyra. The reef is as pristine as you will find anywhere on earth.

We snorkeled over the reef at the pass and encountered sea turtles. I fell in love with the Green Sea Turtle and was amazed at how fast they could swim. They would swim to within ten feet and check things out. As long as you kept still they would hang around. If you got too close they would jet away.

We were very impressed with the expert divers we were swimming with. Ross and Lorna were dive instructors in the Caribbean and were very helpful to us. Lorna, who we later dubbed Superwoman, was phenomenal. Not only was she an expert diver, she could sail, navigate, repair any equipment, suffer any hardship and deliver the mail.

Yes, even deliver the mail. Ross and Lorna offered to deliver an important letter and package more than 1,400 miles from Raiatea in the Society Islands to Washington Island in the Line Islands. There is no pass into Washington, so Ross held *Eliott* off the reef at the Ship Lighter's landing site while Lorna swam the correspondence through a narrow gap in the barrier reef, across the lagoon and through the surf to shore. This was an extremely risky and dangerous endeavor and caused quite a stir on the tiny island. The sheepish islanders reported that the addressee had left the island! With that bit of news, Lorna returned to the surf and sharks and began her perilous swim back to *Eliott*.

There were black-tip and gray reef sharks in the water and I was a little hesitant to swim while they were lurking about. They looked huge to me. However, everyone else seemed to pay them little mind and I didn't want to be a big baby, so I jumped in. Rob explained that the sharks are so well fed by the abundance of fish in the area that they do not bother humans. I could understand that intellectually, but it was still hard to accept after having watched *Jaws*. I have also heard sharks are unpredictable, so I always kept track of where the sharks were and never turned my back on them. A few days later we learned the 95 foot commercial fishing boat *South Pacific*, fishing just off the pass, caught a 1,200 pound tiger shark. Yikes!

Spear fishing is a different story. You can not swim in the same area when someone is spear fishing. Spear fishing calls for teamwork — a dinghy driver and a diver. You ring the dinner bell for sharks when you spear a fish, so as soon as a fish is speared the diver swims up and climbs in the dinghy, hauling in the fish before the sharks show up. I would assume that it might be a good idea to be on good terms with your associate prior to setting out on this venture.

We dinghied over to the wreck of the Chinese fishing boat to the west of the channel. This was my first time ever diving on a wreck and it was very exciting. Most of the equipment on the wreck had been salvaged by previous cruisers. Rob found some propane tanks and line. As we made our way about the wreck we were careful not to cut ourselves on steel or coral. Fish swam through cabins and companionways where men once worked and lived.

The tropical sun ravaged my skin and I shuffled about my duties in misery for the next three days. First, I was crimson, then blistery before finally shedding my skin like a snake. I should have taken Margaret's advice and worn my lycra dive suit. But I didn't want to be a big baby. . . .

LOBSTERING BY MOONLIGHT

We took advantage of the low tide brought on by the full moon to execute a lobstering expedition on the barrier reef. We mustered at *Time-Out* at 2130 for a mission briefing before leaving the anchorage in a three dinghy armada, running under the full moon, to the south end of the West Lagoon. We went as far as we could in the dinghies, then anchored and walked in knee-deep water a quarter of a mile to Kaula Island. I was pooped before I even got to the hunting grounds. The full moon illuminated the large Booby Birds and they let out loud squawks when we approached too close for their comfort. We discussed our final tactics on Kaula and then headed out on the barrier reef to the south of Kaula and Paradise Islands on our mission.

Each lobster stalker wore tennis shoes to protect his feet from the sharp coral, leather gloves to protect his hands from the lobster's large spiky carapace and a bag slung over his shoulder in which to stuff the captured crustacean.

The object of this enterprise is to slowly wade through knee-deep water, shining your light into the depths in an effort to identify your quarry. Once identified, you shine the light into the lobster's beady little eyes and while he is stunned you lurch your hand through the water, catching the lobster behind the head and the fight is on. The lobster is not going to go silently into that good night. If you are lucky enough to stuff the lobster into your bag he will calm down. They are expert at escape and evasion and constant vigilance must be maintained to preserve your dinner. We had two hours to hunt before the tide began to rise.

Unfortunately, I can not describe for you the actual first-hand emotion one feels upon capturing a lobster by such means as I proved to be as lousy a lobster hunter as I am a deer hunter — or fisherman for that matter. Fortunately, due to the communal aspects of our troop, the spoils were shared equally among the participants. Joe was able to capture one, Ross and Rob each apprehended three. The next day Kaye prepared a lobster feast aboard *Navi-Gator*.

Kaye, Margaret and I retired early and stumbled back to the dinghies. I would have continued hunting, but someone had to protect the women folk. . . . We each took a dinghy and sprawled out, catching our breath while gazing up at the heavens. The moon was brilliant, illuminating the lagoon, the multitude of stars looked close enough to touch and we all had an overwhelming sense we were sharing a very special moment. It was as though we were transformed into little children and could see God's creation in childlike wonderment. I never want to forget that moment.

BEACHCOMBING AROUND THE EAST LAGOON

On December 5 we moved *Kawabunga* close to shore in a secluded cove in ten feet of water at the southwest corner of the Center Lagoon. *Time-Out* anchored a couple of hundred yards away. We prayed our anchor would hold in the coral sand as the strong NE tradewinds would blow us onto the fringing reef and on shore of the little island if we dragged. We rigged our rain catcher as we were starting to get showers from time to time. This was our favorite anchorage on Palmyra.

One of the benefits of anchoring near *Time-Out* was Sherry's baking. One afternoon I was busy working up on deck. I heard something and looked into the lagoon to see a beautiful brunette mermaid carrying a dish above the water, swimming towards *Kawabunga*. Sherry had baked us some brownies but had no dinghy to bring them to us as Rob had the dinghy out fishing. Sherry can improvise. She put on her mask, snorkel and fins and swam the brownies over. Hot out of the oven — and lagoon!

We were still tired from running up and down the barrier reef in the middle of the night, but when we heard Rob was launching an expedition to the East Lagoon we jumped at the opportunity to join in the fun.

We followed Rob and Sherry closely in our dinghy as we sped across the Center Lagoon for the break in the causeway separating it from the East Lagoon. Once through the narrow passage we turned right and followed the causeway south for several hundred yards until we could snake our way through the coral and into the lagoon.

We motored across the lagoon to Whippoorwill Island on the northeast end of the East Lagoon, pulling the bows of our dinghies across a little shelf of coral and putting anchors out on the beach. This was a beautiful snorkeling and fishing spot. A short walk up the island brought us to a cement, domed-shaped bunker. It looked to me to be a bomb shelter. We walked inside and imagined how it must have been in that structure more than fifty years ago. We spent the day swimming, fishing and exploring.

Margaret and I made several trips back to the East Lagoon to explore. On one occasion we went with Joe and Kaye and Bill and Diane. We motored over to the causeway at the SW corner of the East Lagoon and anchored our dinghies off the jagged shore and waded in. Roger was on his way to go fishing but took the time to give us a tour of the hospital. We waded across more knee deep water, past several little islets to Engineer Island. Single-file, we followed Roger into the jungle. I was looking for a hospital and I certainly did not see one. The building was completely overgrown by green plant life and I would have surely walked by without knowing there was a structure there if Roger had not shown us the entrance. It was creepy inside as there were old hospital beds, pill bottles and other equipment strewn about. Bill commented on how great the condition of the wood was. We used our flashlights to illuminate the hallways and rooms. We were amazed at how camouflaged the hospital was.

Our little troop hiked out of the jungle and waded back to the dinghies. Roger left us to go fishing and we met up with Rob and Sherry and Ross and Lorna and took the dinghies to Papala Island. We decided to take a quick dip to cool off before spending the rest of the day beachcombing. This was one of the most enjoyable days on Palmyra as the weather was absolutely perfect and the scenery was spectacular. As we walked along the beach we could see small white-tipped reef sharks and sea snakes swimming along in the shallow water.

I was fishing one day along the shore and had walked into the shallow water to land a queenie. Just as I was about to land the fish, a black-tip reef shark came in to grab it. We saw each other at the same instant. I don't know who was more surprised — me or the shark. I lost no time wading to shore and fished the rest of the afternoon from the beach.

The entire atoll is a fantasy retreat where you can watch squadrons of manta rays, moray eels, sea turtles and sea snakes swim by. The sea snakes are extremely lethal but so small they would have difficulty biting you. Perhaps they could attack between the fingers or toes. Roger has named a huge moray eel that lives at the seaplane ramp Isabel. Frigate birds robbed from and constantly tormented the other birds on the island. The Booby Birds squawked when you got too close to their nests and their young puff-balls. Huge coconut crabs, with pincers powerful enough to break open coconuts, roamed free and protected. We especially enjoyed the charming fairy terns which hovered overhead, just beyond reach. We usually saw these lovely white creatures whenever we took a walk on Cooper Island.

Rob climbed up palm trees to get us coconuts. I never thought I would tire of coconuts, but by the time we left I had eaten my fill. We found the perfect coconut tree to cut out the heart of palm to make a delicious salad. A tree was recently down and we took turns with our machetes, cutting the heart out of the tree, about twelve inches from where the branches grow out. This was incredibly hard work in the tropical heat. My dull machete was not a big help either.

The only down side to this day was cutting the instep of my right foot on a jagged piece of coral. I was wearing flip flops and should have been wearing tennis shoes or reef runners. We used liberal doses of Hydrogen Peroxide and Neosporen but the wound did not heal until we were nearly to Hawaii.

THE JUNGLE BATHTUB

Our favorite haunt on Palmyra was the jungle bath tub on Cooper Island. An immense bath tub, possibly reclaimed from the hospital, sits in the jungle near the 100,000 gallon water tank, only 50 yards from the north shore and 150 yards from the lagoon. Palmyra is blessed with an abundance of fresh water thanks to the U.S. Navy. You can take a very relaxed bath with a lavish amount of cool, fresh water, shaded by a huge rubber tree and a canopy of ferns and coconut trees and serenaded by the pounding surf on the barrier reef. True paradise, or as Roger would say, "Soopeerb."

The Corps of Engineers recently spent several months on Palmyra removing the old, huge and dangerous fuel tanks. Unfortunately, both the bath tub and water tank were casualties of this operation. What a shame.

I DON'T WANNA LEAVE

While we were on Palmyra, Roger went to Fanning Island soliciting matrimony. It sounded more like he was holding cattle call auditions. He was looking for a mature woman, between sixteen and nineteen, who could bite the head off a live fish, climb a coconut tree and rock the boat. He found Kaybiburi, a lovely nineteen year old within twenty-four hours, and a New Years wedding was arranged with Kaybiburi's family.

After paying for our second week on the atoll, (at $49 per week), we had only $1 aboard the boat. Margaret began searching through her jewelry box and found a gold ring. She asked Roger if he would like the ring to give to "Kabi" for an engagement ring. He was very excited about the idea. Roger said, "I'll give you a week on Palmyra for the ring." Margaret said, "We'll take three".

We had crossed one difficult bridge. We could stay on Palmyra through Christmas and New Years. However, we still had to figure out a way to eat during those three weeks and still have enough food to make it to the Hawaiian Islands. Soon after arriving we had taken out all our stores, reorganized them and packed away enough food for a three week passage to Hawaii. We stowed the Palmyra food, knowing when it was exhausted, we would have to leave. We were running through our Palmyra food at an alarming rate. We had intended on living off the bounty of the lagoon as much as possible, but the fishing went south when we arrived. As soon as we left, the good fishing resumed. Also, we had precious little gasoline to run our dinghy and it was difficult to catch edible fish without trolling. Ciguatera poisoning was a problem with the reef fish, so you trolled for the game fish. Both my father and grandfather were commercial fishermen, but their fishing skills were not passed down to me.

In an effort to minimize fuel consumption, we moved *Kawabunga* to the mooring off Roger's camp for a few days. We could easily row to shore from the mooring. Rob and Roger were generous with their catches and kept us in fish.

We had planned to sail back to Christmas Island, where Margaret would catch a flight to Honolulu. The passage would have been nearly impossible. We would have had to slug it out against both the current and wind the whole way. Margaret decided to sail with me up to Hawaii. We would contact the Bank of Kiribati from Hawaii about getting our $800 back.

On the evening of December 10 we were suddenly blasted with 70 knot winds from the southeast. This came to be known as "The Big Wind Gust of Palmyra '95". We were protected from the worst of the blast as we were tucked behind Cooper Island. Several of the other boats dragged, including Roger, who was out in the middle of the West Lagoon. The next day Roger asked us to give up the mooring because he was moving *Cous Cous* to the mooring. We moved to our original anchorage in front of the camp.

December 17 is the anniversary of our first date and Margaret and I usually do something special to celebrate. Kaye fixed a spectacular brunch aboard *Navi-Gator* for the occasion. Unfortunately, it was also a farewell party as we both had decided to leave Palmyra. Joe and Kaye were sailing to Fanning Island to spend the rest of the hurricane season there before heading back to the Societies and we were heading north for the Hawaiian Islands.

We stuffed ourselves with scrambled eggs, Canadian bacon, hot fruit compote, orange juice and pancakes. This was quite a switch from rice and fish! After brunch Kaye took Margaret into their aft cabin and began filling two large ice bags with canned food. Kaye packed a huge variety of tasty food for our trip to Hawaii. While Kaye was digging out food, Joe was pouring us six gallons of diesel fuel so we would have as much diesel as we could possibly take with us for the passage north.

An hour later, *Navi-Gator* steamed passed us, throwing us a duffel bag of toilet paper they had been stowing for us in their aft cabin. Within minutes they were into the channel and through the pass into the ocean, fighting the current and vicious tradewinds on their way to Fanning. We felt as though we had been socked in the stomach. We did not know when we would see our comrades again. We continued our preparations to leave.

Since we were going to be fighting the NE tradewinds the entire passage to the Hawaiian Islands, I replaced the mainsail we had been using with a narrower cut main. It had been designed as a fully battened main, but I took out the battens before leaving Marina del Rey. The new main worked perfectly for what we wanted. I had a third, somewhat tired, main stowed in the quarter berth.

While we busied ourselves with the million and one things one has to do in preparing for a major passage, Rob busied himself upgrading our computer. He transferred many programs to our little laptop that would come in handy, such as a world tide program, new fonts and games.

We weighed anchor at 1330 on Tuesday December 19, 1995. Rob and Sherry and Ross and Lorna followed us out to the channel in their dinghies and waived good-bye as they fished for yet another Palmyra dinner. I handed down my machete to Ross as we drove by as we would not be needing it anymore. Presumably, Hawaii was civilized. We had chosen a perfect day to leave as the sun was bright and visibility perfect for departing the lagoon. We saw several giant sea turtles as we powered along on a course of 222° M, out the long, narrow channel. The turtles were as big as coffee tables. We continued on until we reached the rendezvous point we had used to approach the atoll before turning directly westward until reaching the longitude of 162° 10′ W.

Palmyra gets into your blood. We would like to return some day. We were sad to be leaving Palmyra and our good friends, but we did not have much time to think about that. In retrospect, we probably should have gone even further west to 162° 13′ W, because as we headed north we went through an hour of being on pins and needles. Coral heads rose up from the ocean depths to within a few feet of the surface. We could actually see coral heads and the depth sounder was going ape as we steamed north. Finally, we found ourselves northeast of Palmyra. Our last radio contact with Palmyra was at 1830 when we said our final good-byes to Rob and Sherry and we continued NE, watching our navigation closely to be sure to stay east of 6° 24′ N, 162° 21′ W in order to clear Kingman Reef.

No wind in the lee of Hawaii

Cruising spinnaker drawing nicely

*"The true peace of God begins at any point
1,000 miles from the nearest land."*
— Joseph Conrad

CHAPTER TWELVE

PASSAGE TO THE
HAWAIIAN ISLANDS

RIDING THE EQUATORIAL COUNTER CURRENT

Our strategy was to steam eastward for three days in order to get as much easting as possible before setting sail northward for the Hawaiian Islands. *Kawabunga's* Yanmar engine burns roughly one gallon of diesel fuel per three hours of operation. We had enough fuel on board to make our easting and motor into an anchorage in Hawaii. If we could find the Equatorial Counter Current, usually encountered just north of Palmyra, we would ride its east-setting current while fighting the contrary wind and waves. We figured three days of bashing into the brutal elements would be about as much as we could take. We were right.

On our first night out we were hammered by tumultuous conditions. We were up all night hand-steering and tending to the boat. Kaye had given Margaret some Stugeron, a Venezuelan drug to prevent seasickness. She was feeling satisfactory on the medication, while I wallowed in the depths of nauseous wretchedness. I found myself hurling for both accuracy and distance as I struggled to steer *Kawabunga*. My broad-brimmed canvas hat shaded my weary eyes from the tropic sun. My eyes were glazed over in a stupor, trying to focus on the compass. Slumped over the tiller, battling mother nature, exhaustion and my queasy stomach, we plodded eastward.

Margaret was pressed into steering duty when fatigue enveloped me. She would steer for an hour at a time while I caught some shut-eye. As morning broke the violent winds diminished, leaving a very sloppy sea.

When Rob learned our autopilot was dead, he insisted we take his back-up autopilot as a Christmas present. We were touched by his generosity. Before leaving Palmyra we stowed the gift away for the trip. We certainly needed it now, so at 0900 I installed the new Abe, rigged it up and crawled into the port cockpit bench for a long winter's nap.

The conditions were just too much for a small autopilot to contend with. After forty-five minutes Abe II coughed, choked and went up in a puff of smoke. That was the short life and times of Abe II.

Our noon observations brought us some much needed good news. Our Tri-Data showed us making 3.7 knots while the computer showed our speed over the ground as 5.1, a lift of 1.4 knots. We were definitely riding the Equatorial Counter Current. Little *Kawabunga* was taking a horrendous beating, so it was nice to know we were getting some easting out of the thrashing.

WILE E. COYOTE — GENIUS

We encountered powerful winds on Wednesday and Thursday, December 20 and 21. At 0200 that Thursday morning I was out on *Kawabunga's* tiny foredeck, struggling to strike our trusty Yankee during particularly nasty weather. Easterly winds hitting 35 knots were ravaging our headsail as we motor-sailed into the terrible seas. The sky was ink black, reflecting the grim mood of *Kawabunga's* captain and crew. I desperately worked to bring the headsail down on the dark and bouncing deck before it was blown out, but the sail was already being viciously torn to bits and parts of the leech snagged on to the headstay and shrouds with a deathgrip, making it impossible to lower the sail. I yanked on the halyard and the jib sheets with every ounce of energy I could muster and after much straining, sweating and swearing I got most of the sail down and secured to the safety netting. The halyard was hung up with the tack stuck 12 feet off the deck, out of reach. Not only was our bread and butter sail blown to smithereens, but I was unable to raise another headsail until I got the remnants of this tangled sail free from our headstay. This was not good at all. I let myself fall into a crumpled heap on the soft cargo bags I had lashed on deck just forward of the cabin, tried to relax and ponder our predicament.

After catching my breath, I decided to go back to the cabin, grab the telescoping boat hook and turn on the spreader lights. It would be good to shed a little light on the subject. It would also be a good idea to let Margaret know there was nothing to worry about. I had been out on the foredeck for a long time and although I am sure she had not heard my indelicate rantings over the howling wind, she certainly would have heard my fancy footwork pounding against the deck directly over her bunk.

From my ditty bag I pulled ten feet of nylon cord. From the quarter berth I pulled the boat hook and from the cabin I pulled myself, after assuring Margaret everything was under control. There was nothing to worry about.

I climbed back to my perch atop the two cargo bags, wiggled into a comfortable position, viewed the chaos of Dacron flailing above me and set about lashing my rigging knife to the end of the boat hook. Suddenly, I had the feeling I had slipped through a storm portal into Toon Town and found myself on the set of a Road Runner cartoon. The Pacific Ocean was the setting rather than the American Southwest. The part of the Roadrunner was being played by the storm. Yours truly was playing the part of Wile E. Coyote. The "genius" had just received the latest weapon from ACME — a rigging knife, line and boat hook. We all know who ended up crumpled at the bottom of a canyon or smashed into a non-existent tunnel or pulverized by a falling boulder. I did not like the casting.

After rigging the knife, I began, with limited success, cutting away the sail from the standing rigging with my boat hook spear. With the wind howling through the rigging and the seas pounding little *Kawabunga*, I stood on my tip-toes on the teak bow platform, hanging on to the forestay for dear life with my left hand while slashing away at the jib with the jury-rigged harpoon in my free hand. This gymnastic fiasco was challenging, frustrating and hazardous. After flailing away at the perversely tangled sail like a teenage girl at a rock concert for what seemed to be an hour, I had an overwhelming premonition the knife was going to break free. In my mind's eye I saw the knife falling in slow-motion; tumbling down, until it executed a half-gainer into my chest. Degree of difficulty; 3.2. Enough. This could wait for morning. I decided to make a tactical retreat in order to live to fight another day. . . .

The next morning the conditions had improved and I was able to cut the sail away from the headstay, raise the little storm jib and run the jib sheets through the deck blocks back to the cockpit. I had not taken the double-reef out of the main from the previous day's gale. We would have to make our way one thousand miles into hearty NE trade- winds without our perfect-sized head sail for these conditions. There were still pieces of the sail clinging to the port upper shroud when we arrived in Hawaii — our souvenir of the affair.

LUCKLESS LATITUDE

There were very few entries into *Kawabunga's* log for the first three days out of Palmyra due to the brutal motion of the boat. The challenge of hand-steering during this time, twenty-four hours per day, was nearly unbearable. Margaret would spell me for an hour when I simply could not go on. It seemed as soon as I closed my eyes the hour was over and I was at the helm again. Again and again while steering I would close my eyes and put my head down on the tiller for an instant only to find us 30 degrees off course. I can not remember anything in my life being harder than continuing the struggle. I felt like a boxer on the ropes, trying to cover up against the onslaught of jabs and upper cuts, hoping I could make it through the round so I could regroup and refresh in my corner.

We continued motor-sailing ENE until Saturday morning December 23 at 0900 when the engine croaked. The filter was clogged and we were out of spares. This tragedy occurred at 9° 10′ N, 159° 4′ W, within two degrees latitude of my previous engine failure. The last engine-failure position was 6° 52′ N, 129° 11′ W. Not my favorite latitude.

We had run north of the Equatorial Counter Current the day before, so motor-sailing at this point was not effective anyway. We would have to fight for every minute east we could gain on our way north.

A CHRISTMAS STORY

Our physical and mental conditions were at an all time low as we fought our way north. My little cockpit bunk was constantly wet and I suffered from saltwater boils on my bum. An air vent cap on one of the diesel cans lashed to the side deck had worked itself loose and leaked fuel down the deck, so the smell of diesel fuel permeated our tiny environment, igniting more mal de mer. A major piece of equipment was failing daily under the horrendous stress. It was difficult to read and nearly impossible to write anything under the conditions Margaret termed, "The Twenty-Four Hour Earthquake". We were wet, weary and waiting for the next bomb to detonate.

My idea of Christmas Eve is walking through the snow to a midnight service at a little church surrounded by family. Christmas morning means eating my sister's cookies while watching the excitement in the eyes of my two nieces as they opened a mountain of presents piled around the Christmas tree.

I was feeling overwhelmed with guilt for putting Margaret through such hardship and taking her away from her family at this time of year.

On Christmas Eve we sat together on the starboard settee in *Kawabunga's* tiny cabin and celebrated Holy Communion. We had packed away grape juice and saltine crackers for this occasion. Later that evening we were able to listen to Dr. Vernon McGee, broadcast on AM radio out of Honolulu. His familiar southern drawl was a great comfort.

We had been feeling a bit sorry for ourselves out on that lonely ocean, without friends and family and worrying about whether we would be able to make Hawaii. "Jehovah-Jireh" (God provides) was brought to mind. He had certainly provided for our needs. We had plenty of food, were in good health and had a seaworthy vessel. Margaret reminded me of all the canned food drives we had participated in over the years. We used to think that *canned food* was not a very appetizing gift. We discovered when you're hungry, canned food is a welcome gift. Hooray for canned goods. We never thought we would be so grateful for something as simple as canned yams, chicken and beans. It was delicious.

We shifted from a state of depression to feeling overwhelmed with gratitude. We realized we had been concentrating on ourselves and had lost our perspective. What began as our worst Christmas was transformed into the best Christmas of our lives. Even though we were physically uncomfortable, spiritually we were soaring. We never felt closer to God than on that Christmas Eve in 1995.

The minor trials we were experiencing were trivial compared to the horrible ordeal my sister Bonnie was enduring at the time. We did not know until we reached Hawaii that Bonnie had very nearly died on Christmas Eve. She had been rushed to the hospital for emergency surgery to save her life.

We could not wait for Christmas morning to open our presents. We pulled out all the packages from our hanging locker and began tearing open the presents wrapped in old newspaper, charts and plastic bags. Of course, we already knew what Joe and Kaye and Rob had given us. Ross and Lorna hosted a delectable Christmas dinner before leaving Palmyra. Sherry had packed away a pair of earrings for Margaret and had written us a lovely poem that brought tears to our eyes.

Bill and Diane's package had piqued our interest. We were like two little kids who had found presents hidden away in a closet. We had come close to succumbing to our curiosity many times. Finally, the time had come, and we opened the package and started removing presents. First to be extracted were two old *People* magazines. We read them cover to cover many times over the next few days — even the advertisements. A map of Hawaii with Bill and Diane's personal notes on things to do and places to go provided many hours of entertainment as we hashed over where we would go when we reached Hawaii. Next were several individual baggies full of goodies; cocoa, Hershey's kisses, butterscotch and peppermint candies, prunes and wheat berries. We tried to ration these treasures over the next several days, but they disappeared all too soon. Also included was a crisp twenty dollar bill so we would have some cash on hand when we made landfall. They knew we were broke and would need to somehow get to an ATM machine before we could get anything to eat.

Christmas morning broke clear and beautiful. We tuned in Christmas music on the radio and we both celebrated with a bath. I still could have used some of Bonnie's cookies!

CHANGES IN LATITUDES

We were able to get AM radio stations in Hawaii and heard the north shore of Oahu was bracing for twenty foot waves. The midwest was in for "The Blizzard of 1995 - 1996". We were in our own battle with the elements. As we slugged our way north, I found out the true meaning of living the life of a sea dog. I lived on the port cockpit bench in my foul weather gear. The bibs were holding up fine but the jacket was parting around the shoulders. Since I was taking water into the bench every couple of minutes I resorted to wrapping myself in a blue plastic tarp in an effort to stay dry. The boat and crew were taking a tremendous pounding.

At 0300 on December 26 I was awakened by what sounded like a gun shot fired a foot away from my right ear. *Kawabunga* was close-hauled, charging through the night, when the port jib sheet fair-lead block blasted off its track atop the cap rail. I replaced the block and reduced sail. The crazy wind and rain continued throughout the night.

During the last week of December we began suffering disturbing losses in our easting war. We were feeling the full affects of the North Equatorial Current, setting us west at an alarming rate. Our noon position on December 29 was 15° 18′ N, 160° 34′ W. We were in a very poor position and began to seriously question our ability to make Kona, Hawaii. We prayed in earnest for fair winds.

Our prayers were answered later that day. The sky cleared and the winds blew from the east at 15 knots. *Kawabunga* was able to make between 4 and 5 knots on a course of 045° M. I rigged up the kevlar 120% headsail and pushed *Kawabunga* for every extra ¼ knot. Thanks to SE and then S winds, we made a giant leap northeast on the 29th, with smaller steps northeast on the 30th, 31st and 1st. If this wind held we would be in Kona during the first week of the new year.

NEW YEAR — NEW DIET IN THE LEE OF HAWAII

On New Year's Eve we were only 190 miles from Kona. We were enjoying a fine broad reach with southerly 10 knot winds and it looked like we were within striking distance of our target.

What happened next was foreboding indeed. We were able to tune in the Rose Bowl game from Pasadena and learned that Southern California was playing Northwestern. Not Michigan. Not Ohio State. *Northwestern.* Surely, this was a sign of the End Times!

As the game concluded, the sky darkened, the wind rose and the rain began. By 1800 we were hunkered down, preparing for a long, soggy night.

Thanks to Joe and Kaye we enjoyed an ambrosial New Year's Day dinner of turkey, yams and cranberry sauce. This was the last of our tasty food.

Our food stores lacked variety and imagination. We were down to cans of tuna and fruit cocktail. I had exhausted my tolerance for fruit cocktail on the way to Nuku Hiva. The mere smell of it made me gag. So, my options were further reduced. The next eighteen meals consisted of tuna and fruit cocktail. We had no condiments and no vegetables. There was no way we were going to starve as we had more than enough cans, but the menu was monotonous. Food fantasies ranged from prime rib to custard pie. We even thought about opening up a bakery when we returned from cruising. How does Kawabunga Cookie Company sound? We were stark raving mad.

For the next nine days we were becalmed in the lee of Hawaii and the prevailing NE tradewinds. We covered only 172 miles made good from the first through the ninth, an average of 19 miles per day. I have never seen the ocean so azure blue or so flat calm. It was also extremely hot. This was absolutely perfect motoring weather. . . .

We welcomed the calm weather for the first day as we were able to rest up and make some repairs on the boat. Nevertheless, the novelty of drifting along, sometimes actually losing miles, soon waned.

During this time we acquired a pet Dolphin fish, or Mahi Mahi as they are known in the islands. This fish swam up to *Kawabunga* late each afternoon and looked up to see what we were doing out there. We named her Flopsy because her dorsal fins were so big they looked like rabbit ears. We had the meat hook rigged up but we were never going fast enough to catch anything. She would have been an easy target with our spear gun, but even though we were hungry for a change of diet, we would not have harmed our pal Flopsy.

We were lucky to be within reach of Hawaii's AM radio and passed the time listening to Dr. Laura Schlessinger, Dr. Vernon McGee, Michael Reagan, Rush Limbaugh and Ken Hamblin. They entertained and informed us and made the time go faster. Dr. Laura's psychological help was particularly valuable. On the down side, have you ever noticed how many food commercial spots there are on the radio? Listening to a grocery store's pitch for fresh vegetables or a fast-food restaurant describing its juicy hamburgers was torture.

On Sunday morning January 7, we were off the southwestern tip of the Big Island of Hawaii, sixty-six miles from Kona, fighting the strong winds and currents that whip along the southern edge of Hawaii. Near the cape, the onshore current sets against the wind, causing disturbed waters. At 0800 we could see the sun coming up behind Mauna Loa, the 13,680 foot volcano. We could not see land, but could tell the sun was rising over a mountain. Since Hawaii has mountains exceeding 13,000 feet, we thought we would be able to see the island from about sixty miles out. We did not take into consideration the volcanic activity from Kilauea causing a haze or vog as it is known. This vog greatly restricts visibility and makes the island appear to be just another cloud on the horizon.

While we were tacking our way northward, towards what Earl Hinz describes as Polynesia USA, the East was expecting the snow storm of the century. A little cool weather sounded just fine to us.

KONA STORM

The next morning we began receiving Kona Storm warnings over the VHF and AM radios. We were forty-two miles from Kona, on the leeward side of Hawaii. I pulled out my *Charlie's Charts for the Hawaiian Islands* and studied our options. We had intended on anchoring in Kailua Bay, where the Ironman Triathalon is staged. Unfortunately, Kailua Bay is an open roadstead anchorage with a coral and rock bottom, exposed to swell. It would be particularly unsuitable during a Kona storm.

There are only two sheltered harbors on the west coast of Hawaii. Kawaihae Harbor is only five miles from Upolu Point, the northern-most tip of the Big Island and twenty-nine miles north of Kailua. Honokohau Harbor, just two miles north of Kailua, appeared to be our best bet. It was close by and had a shipyard.

We struggled through calms interspersed with very light and variable winds until Tuesday January 9 at 1330 when the Kona storm hit. We were fourteen miles off Honokohau Harbor when we were struck with 35 knot winds from the south. Finally, we were up and running and making up for lost time. According to the computer we were rapidly closing the Kona coast, but we did not sight land until we were seven miles off and on our final approach to Honokohau Harbor. When we were five miles off we raised Ken Denton, the Harbormaster for Honokohau and Kailua Bay, on the VHF radio. Ken told us he would have customs and agriculture agents meet us at the fuel dock.

As we approached the coast we could see several sportfishing boats heading for the harbor. As we closed further we could see Keahuolu and Kaiwi Points, giant lava formations jutting out into the sea, separating Kailua Bay from Honokohau Bay. The entrance to Honokohau Harbor is only about 175 feet across. Once through, we would have to make a 90° turn and tack about 400 feet through a crowded harbor to the fuel dock on the southeast corner of the entrance. Damn the torpedoes — full speed ahead.

People were lined up along the south side of the harbor entrance watching the crazy Californians racing the Kona storm. My favorite khaki hat flew off into our boiling wake at 1600 as we surfed through the entrance. No time for sentiment. How much fun did you want to have? I put the helm hard over, hardened up the main, trimmed the jib and tacked into the anchorage, all the while averting a PT-109 landing. Dozens of tourists and fishermen were at the docks watching the sportfishing boats exhibiting their catches and they applauded as we approached the fuel dock. We must have been a sight. Two local men came forward to catch our bow and stern lines and *Kawabunga* was quickly settled into an American port once again. We had won the race. The harbor was closed the next morning as twenty foot waves were breaking over the navigational lights high atop the lava at the harbor entrance.

Honkohau Harbor entrance, Kona Coast, Hawaii — calm conditions

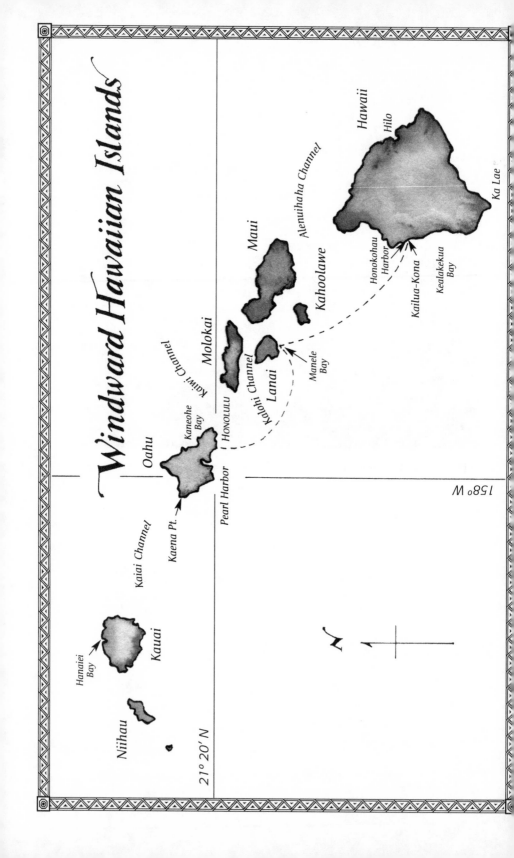

"The loveliest fleet of islands that lies anchored in any ocean."
— Mark Twain

CHAPTER THIRTEEN

THE SANDWICH ISLANDS

ALOHA POLYNESIA USA

The crowd parted, allowing two gigantic, uniformed and armed customs agents to greet us. I handed over our ship's papers to one of the agents while the other helped me climb off *Kawabunga*. My knees were wobbly, I was eager to assault the deli and I was not looking forward to the long, drawn-out bureaucratic dawdle we had come to expect from foreign customs officials. To my utter astonishment we were quickly and efficiently cleared into the USA. It was wonderful to be on US soil again. One of the agents handed our ship's papers to me and said "Welcome home". Although we still had 3,000 miles to sail to get to California, they made us feel like we were home. These agents exemplified the aloha spirit.

While I was with the customs agents Margaret met with the agricultural agent. With a twinkle in her eye, she asked Margaret if we had any livestock, fruits or vegetables on board. Margaret explained we had eaten nothing but canned tuna for the last six days. If we would have had a heifer, bananas or green beans aboard, they would have been slaughtered, peeled or sautéed long ago.

While I got *Kawabunga* settled in at dockside, Margaret took the twenty dollars Bill and Diane Pool had given us and headed for the deli. The deli was closed, but the woman locking up took pity on Margaret and made her a roast beef sandwich. It was delicious.

When the customs agents shoved off we were greeted by two guardian angels. Tom and Arlene Riley from Redding, California were enjoying their yearly Kona vacation and had driven down to the harbor to watch the sportfishing boats come in with their catches. They had crossed their fingers and watched as we sailed into the harbor and up to the fuel dock. They knew it would be a long walk into the little town of Kailua-Kona and also knew we could use a good meal, so they offered to drive us into town. Within thirty minutes of landing we were seated at the Kona Inn, marveling at the view and giddy on a fresh salad, prime rib and custard pie.

Over the next week we struck up a wonderful friendship. They entertained us at the Kona Reef, their seaside condo, and introduced us to the lovely town of Kailua. We felt lost when we hugged good-bye at Keahole Airport a week later.

ROAD TRIP

We rented a red Mustang convertible from Avis and hightailed it for the south end of the island. This was an impromptu departure and we left with little more than our shorts, shirts and sandals.

We stopped at Kealakekua Bay where Captain James Cook was dispatched from this world in 1779 by the locals; the tragic consequence of poor judgment, deadly confusion and terrible timing. There is a monument to the great mariner on the far side of the bay.

As we drove down the west coast of Hawaii we decided to continue on to Volcanoes National Park. There are two active volcanoes within the park; the smaller, more recently active Kilauea, and Mauna Loa which towers 13,679 feet. Mauna Kea (13,796 feet) is north, in Mauna Kea State Park. The Kilauea Caldera continues to spew out sulfur and steam along the inside of the crater and lava continues to flow from Kilauea into the sea. Apparently, Pele, the Hawaiian goddess of fire, continues to harbor hard feelings about something or other.

We were very excited to stay at the Volcano House, where Mark Twain had stayed in 1866 when writing for the Sacramento Union. The Volcano House, at an elevation of 4,000 feet, was built on the rim of the Kilauea crater in 1846. The fire in their fireplace has not gone out in 121 years, a good thing since the temperature was very cool and we brought only light clothing. It was wonderful to smell the scent of pine trees and warm ourselves before the giant fireplace. We savored a wonderful dinner and breakfast at the Ka Ohelo dining room. We stayed in the Ohia Wing, which has a handsome anteroom with a library, a huge stone fireplace and lovely rare koa wood furniture. We had a queen size bed in our room, arrayed with Hawaiian quilts. But the pièce de résistance was the shower with unlimited hot water.

After a superb stay at the historic hotel, we drove around Crater Rim Drive, seeing Halema'uma'u Crater, (the legendary home of Pele), the Thurston Lava Tube and Kilauea Iki Crater. The terrain where the lava flowed and cooled is astounding. It looks as though you could be walking on the surface of the moon. We drove from moonscape to rain forest and then to beaches and the blue Pacific, all within a few minutes. The contrasts were staggering.

We left the park and headed for Hilo where we found out that they weren't kidding when they told us the windward side of the island is wet. Very wet. But the moisture makes the lush rain forest possible. We drove through sugar cane fields to Akaka Falls State Park which is a rain forest gulch filled with tropical plants. We walked in a pouring rain, through bamboo groves, ferns, orchids and bougainvillea to Kahana Falls where we saw a rainbow. After hiking up to Akaka Falls, where the water cascades down 400 feet, we had endured enough rain.

We continued up the northeast coast of Hawaii past one lush gulch after another. We passed Laupahoehoe Point, where Captain Mitchell and fourteen men from the ill-fated clipper ship *Hornet* landed on Hawaii after escaping their burning ship and sailed in an open boat for forty-three days. Mark Twain interviewed the survivors and reported the news to the world. We continued to circumnavigate the Big Island, passing Parker Ranch, Waimea and the Kohala Coast, finally arriving back at the Kona coast in the late afternoon.

HONOKOHAU HARBOR

Ken Denton is the Harbormaster for Honokohau Harbor. Moorings are scarce in this harbor and we were very grateful to Ken for digging one up for us. He made our stay at Honokohau a very pleasant one.

Our Tahiti-style mooring at Honokohau Harbor took some getting used to. We had to constantly adjust the aft mooring lines, letting them out with the high tides and taking them in with the low tides. The harbor is exposed to a great deal of surge during Kona storms. Soon after we arrived, our beautifully varnished bowsprit was damaged during the night when *Kawabunga* was slammed into the lava wall. Honokohau is a completely man-made harbor, blasted out of solid lava and there's not a lot of give to those lava walls.

We constantly risked life and limb while attempting the transition from boat to sea wall or visa versa. Fortunately, we managed to suffer no serious injuries. That is, if you don't count wounds to our pride as a serious injury. It's a good thing no one was video taping these desperate leaps, vaults and hops, as it would have made excellent footage for *America's Funniest Videos*.

There are no shower facilities for the boaters at Honokohau. The harbor caters to its 115 sportfishing charter boats based there. I rigged a make-shift shower by attaching our hose to the lava wall 7 feet above the sidewalk atop the sea wall. We donned our swim suits and took turns soaping up under it, enduring a heart-stopping, mind-petrifying, flesh and bone-freezing shower. After a few weeks of Polar Bear showers, our friend Rick Ebenezer took pity on us and offered us access to the shower in the shipyard. Rick even gave us our own key. A private shower with hot water. What opulence, splendor and lavishness.

Rick owned Honokohau Marine Maintenance and he, along with Dan and Craig from Honokohau Diesel Services, tinkered with our diesel engine, getting it up and running again. It has run perfectly ever since. Their assistance was required as my usual regimen of swearing, pleading and threatening had proven ineffective.

NORTH KONA COAST

We fell in love with the little town of Kailua-Kona and spent as much time as we could enjoying the small town charm of this historic village. The 8,271 foot Mount Hualalai towers skyward, acting as a snow-capped backdrop to tropical paradise, Kailua-Kona. The locals term the contrast "fire and ice".

We attended the Mokuaikaua Church, the first Christian church in the Hawaiian Islands. Missionaries arrived in the brig *Thaddeus* and founded Mokuaikaua Church in April of 1820. The church is built of coral and stone. Across the street from the church stands the Hulihee Palace, built on the beach in 1823 from the same materials as the church. This was a summer home for King Kalakaua and remained a royal vacation retreat until 1916. We spent several Sunday afternoons on the grounds of the palace enjoying concerts under the towering palm trees. From the royal grounds you could see the palm trees hanging out over the ocean to the south. To the north is the pier of Kailua-Kona where the Ironman Triathalon is staged each October. The pier begins at the base of the King Kamehameha Hotel where the great king had built his heiau of Hale O Lono.

Some of the best swordfish, sailfish and marlin fishing in the world is only minutes away in the deep waters just off the Kona coast. Warm, dry weather makes Kailua-Kona an ideal spot for snorkeling, surfing and swimming. Until just a few years ago Kailua had only one traffic light. The town has grown by leaps and bounds, now even offering a Wal-Mart and Price Club.

When I was in Nuku Hiva I missed the voyaging canoes by one month. Several Oceana island nations sent representatives in voyaging canoes to the Marquesas, Societies and Cooks. While in Kailua, Rick introduced me to Nate Hendricks, a native Hawaiian who sailed on the Polynesian Voyaging Canoe *Makalii* from Tahiti back to Hawaii last year. We had lunch on the beach and swapped sea stories. He knew the captain from the Cook Island canoe we had met in Tahiti. Nate is a member of the Polynesian Voyaging Society and his local group is called Na Kalai Waa, meaning "canoe builders". He is part of the crew of the *Makalii*, named after a great Hawaiian navigator. Makalii is also part of the constellation Pleiades. Nate teaches "way-finding" or navigation by way of currents, winds and celestial. We were honored to welcome Nate aboard *Kawabunga* later in our stay.

HAPUNA BEACH

Margaret and I met Sef and Kay Godinez one afternoon while picnicking at the Honokohau Harbor entrance. We were marveling at the waves kicked up by the most recent Kona winds and started talking to this affable pair. Sef and Kay live in Southern California, but spend several weeks each year in Kona. Sef retired from the Los Angeles Fire Department as a Captain. They told us about their favorite beach on Hawaii and before long we were sitting in the back of their Jeep Wrangler, heading north up highway 19 towards Hapuna Beach State Park. They were right. Hapuna's wide, white sand beach was the most beautiful we had seen on Hawaii.

Sef and Kay took us under their wing, sharing their favorite places on Hawaii with us and entertaining us at their condo. We had a great time with them bombing around in their Jeep Wrangler. I have had a burning desire to get a Wrangler ever since.

THE CROW'S NEST

Early one Sunday morning while hitchhiking into Kailua we had the good fortune of being picked up by Jim Crow. Jim and his wife Madge are blue water sailors who have cruised through the South Pacific, down to Australia and back, on a 34′ sailboat and plan on setting out again on *Pacific Pearl*, their 41′ Morgan Out-Island ketch. They had us up to their house for dinner and a few weeks later, when Jim and Madge flew to California on business, we house-sat for them at "The Crow's Nest", their home nestled in the middle of a coffee bean plantation in the mountains overlooking the entire Kona coast. They let us use their car, their guest bedroom, their washer and dryer. . . luxury for a week! We were exposed to cable TV for the first time in a very long while. Again, I was in sleep deprivation as channel surfing has its own appeal. It was pure delight to watch Gilligan's Island at 0200. Our only duties were to look after Cazamero, the world's friendliest feline, and not burn down the joint.

Jim and Madge interviewed us aboard *Kawabunga* for *Sail Hawaii,* their video cruising guide of the Hawaiian Islands, released by Aikane Video Productions. We hope they sell a million copies.

ALENUIHAHA CHANNEL

Our schedule called for us to leave the Big Island by the end of February, but, as the month drew to a close, the weather turned ugly, putting our sailing plans in limbo. Severe weather programming was in effect as a cold front was passing through the islands causing strong north winds and rain. Our target date of Tuesday the twenty-seventh had to be postponed and our crossing plans went into a holding pattern as we vigilantly followed the weather reports. On Wednesday night the forecast for Thursday was northeast winds at 20 knots with 8 foot seas. The front was breaking up and moving southeast. We would have a weather window for 24 hours.

Charlie's Charts of the Hawaiian Islands, by Charles E. Wood, has this to say about the channels between the Hawaiian Islands. "Though strong and gusty trades and the mature waves of an open ocean passage can be both exhilarating and tolerable downwind, they are far less desirable when they must be handled in restricted waters and with the need to make a specific heading." It had this advice for crossing the Alenuihaha Channel. "It is best to work one's way up the west side of the Big Island to Upolu before heading across the Alenuihaha Channel to Maui."

I had read about how treacherous this channel could be and had talked with a lot of local sailors in order to get a feel for what lay ahead. After assessing the data, I decided to take a direct route across the Alenuihaha Channel between Hawaii and Maui. In order to minimize the slot-effect as much as possible I would steer a course for the southwest end of Kahoolawe Island, a crossing of 56 nautical miles before skirting Kahoolawe and heading across Kealaikahiki Channel to Lanai, another 25 miles down track. I should have taken Charlie Wood's advice. If I would have, I could have sailed on a broad reach and could have run off with the wind and current. So much for Monday morning quarterbacking.

We left the dock Thursday, Leap Day, February 29, 1996 at 1410. We timed our departure so we would be in the center of the channel during the middle of the night, when the conditions are relatively calm. The storm had left some lumpy seas, but nothing to worry about. When we cleared Keahole Point the winds dramatically picked up and by 1630 we had reefed down the main and were motor sailing into increasingly wicked weather. I struck the mainsail at 1700 and secured the boat the best I could. By this time the waves were building larger and larger and they were breaking, so I placed the drop boards in the companionway and secured the sliding hatch, leaving Margaret to fend for herself in the cement mixer below.

I must admit we were concerned (read that *frightened*) because we were not expecting the channel to be so violent. It was unnerving to have the wind build and build and build. Each time we felt we had reached a plateau it seemed the wind was ratcheted up another notch! The deafening sound of the wind roaring through the rigging and of the horrendous breaking seas approaching was terrifying. This was ten and a half hours of mortal combat.

Fortunately, visibility was good as we had nearly a full moon and a clear night. Through my salt-caked glasses I could see the intimidating waves barreling down on us. I steered the boat 45° into the breaking waves and about fifty percent of the time the breaker would engulf little *Kawabunga,* filling her cockpit, producing an instant Jacuzzi. How long can you tread water in the cockpit? It sounded as though we were crashing into a brick wall. The wave would roar on by like a run-away freight train careening down the tracks. Fortunately, the cockpit would drain quickly, sometimes leaving interesting flotsam. After one such assault I found I was sharing the starboard bench with a squid, so I quickly flipped him back into the sea. He was one lucky calamari.

At 0300 the conditions began to moderate and I began to appreciate the beauty of the evening. We skirted around Kahoolawe and headed towards Manele Bay on Lanai, arriving off the 110 foot high Puupehe Rock at 0930 Friday. This seemed a good time to start adding up the damage. Our wind vane gears were tweaked, my favorite coil of rope was lost overboard and the radar reflector was blown right off the mast. We had been in a brawl with the Alenuihaha Channel. It would be wild exaggeration to say we had won. The Alenuihaha Channel allowed us to pass — only after we were sufficiently humbled. Now I grasp the "ha ha" in Alenuihaha!

THE PINEAPPLE ISLE

I had been ridden hard and put away wet. Every muscle, every joint, every fat cell, shrieked in pain. It reminded me of yesteryear, of my glorious Saginaw Arthur Hill High School football days when I was routinely thrashed every autumn Friday evening. Our miserable record as seniors was 1-7-1. At least on Lanai, while deliberating my "to give up the ghost or cling to life" verdict, I was wearing a swim suit, shaded by swaying palms and cooled by tradewinds rather than dressed in my smart blue blazer with gray slacks, crawling along Atwood Stadium's parking lot on my hands and knees.

When we were motoring slowly through the little harbor we were surprised to hear, "Over here, Charlie". We looked at each other. Who knew us here? We spotted a couple waiving to us from an open dock so we headed in. As we approached I recognized Mike and Gisela Curray whom I had last seen in Nuku Hiva. Margaret had never met them, but had talked with them over the telephone. After meeting them en route to Nuku Hiva, they had called Margaret when they arrived to tell her I was all right.

Sherry Menze is the Harbormaster of the Manele Bay Small Boat Harbor, a charming, crescent-shaped port, with room for twenty-four boats. Sherry's husband owns a sportfishing boat and takes hotel guests on daily fishing trips. They are a very friendly, helpful couple.

A short walk brings you to Hulopoe Bay and one of the most beautiful beaches we have ever seen. The snorkeling there is magnificent. Humpback whales can be seen from the beach, playing in the bay only a few hundred yards off the white sand beach. Children play in the tide pools. Margaret and I took several hikes up to the cliffs between the two bays, enjoying the majestic views of Kahoolawe and Maui.

After a few days of R&R from the Alenuihaha, we were ready to explore the interior of Lanai. Mike and Gisela had access to a Jeep Scrambler, a perfect vehicle to explore the back trails of Lanai. We all piled into the Jeep and headed up to Lanai

City, seven miles from Manele Bay. Lanai City is located on the high plateau of the island and is ten to fifteen degrees cooler than the beach. It is an old plantation town with a lovely park filled with Cook and Norfolk Island pine trees. Mike and Gisela showed us around town and drove us up the Munro Trail, an eight mile trail that winds up to Lanaihale, the highest point on Lanai (3,370 feet). We stopped at Hookio Gulch and tried to imagine what it was like over two hundred years ago when an invading Hawaiian Islander force massacred the Lanai defenders. We continued on to Lookout Point where we were knocked out by the panoramic view of Maui, Molokai and Kahoolawe. The color of the water was breathtaking.

We frittered away many afternoons nestled in the shaded comfort of *Kawabunga's* little cockpit, sipping a cool drink, watching the sun sink into the Pacific and counting the deer grazing along the side of the hill. Not a bad way to end a hard day at the beach.

Axis deer outnumber the 2,700 residents of Lanai. One morning several deer trotted right through the harbor picnic area. There is no bag limit and Mike's hunting expertise keeps *Albatros* stocked with venison. *Albatros* is the only boat I know with deer antlers mounted on the bulkhead!

The Aloha spirit is definitely alive and well on Lanai. We have been told that Lanai is "Old Hawaii." We were adopted by Sequndo Asuncion, better known as Pops, or CQ, a cook for Trilogy, the charter company that runs catamarans over from Lahaina, Maui every day. Pops invited us to a barbecue and camp fire on our very first night on Lanai. He made it a practice to bring us barbecued chicken, home-made cinnamon rolls, chocolate-chip cookies and steak stir fry. He even brought us ice for our ice box.

While out snorkeling, we met Robert Jaramillo and Grechen Mills, a delightful couple from Santa Cruz. They entertained us at their camp site and introduced us to fellow campers Patricia and Dale Hursh from Boulder, Colorado. Robert regaled us with stories of his perilous hike through

South America. The last Saturday night on Lanai we all got dressed up and walked up to the Manele Bay Hotel for drinks, hors d'oeuvres and dancing — playing the role of "tall dogs". The hotel is one of two luxury resorts with world class golf courses recently built on the island. Lanai is transforming itself from a pineapple plantation to a high-end tourist destination. Patricia and Dale attest to Lanai's romantic island setting as "Hawaiian made" Keenan Sullivan Hursh was born nine months later.

SAILING UNDER THE LAST QUARTER MOON

Our eighty-one mile crossing of the Kaiwi Channel between Molokai and Oahu was a dreamy, overnight sail. We shoved off at noon on March 13, sailing along the lovely south coast of Lanai, clearing Palaoa Point before setting course directly for the Ala Wai. Joey was on the injured reserve list so I had to steer all night. That was the only drawback on an otherwise perfect passage.

We were treated to a romantic, South Seas sunset while we dined on delicious barbecued chicken, a farewell gift from Pops. We cuddled in the cockpit, savoring the sights, sounds, smells and motion of the vast Pacific. We knew this would be our last night at sea together on the cruise we had dreamed of, sacrificed and planned for so many years.

During the early part of the evening we were protected from the strong northeast tradewinds by Molokai and were lulled by the gentle winds carrying us along at 5 knots. As we approached Laau Point on Molokai we were jolted back to reality by 25 to 30 knots of wind howling through the Kaiwi Channel. I struggled to reduce sail, finally settling on a double reefed main and no jib. *Kawabunga* bolted off on a broad reach, in a hurry to get to Honolulu.

Listening to talk radio helped me stay awake through the wee hours. The big story on Art Bell's show was a Denver Nuggets' basketball player who refused to stand for the national anthem. The host was outraged. The callers were outraged. I was outraged. How quickly we can jump back into the concerns of shore-side life. The Makapuu Point light, combined with the adrenaline generated by the radio discussion, kept me awake all night.

As morning broke, we could make out Koko Head at the southeast end of Oahu. As we closed Oahu, Diamond Head came into view. What a thrill to see Diamond Head from the sea. By 0900 we were rounding Diamond Head and gliding along Waikiki Beach. Margaret could barely contain her excitement as we sailed along the famous beach with its luxury hotels crowded together in the lee of Diamond Head.

SOUTH PACIFIC GURU

As we steamed through the reef into the Ala Wai Yacht Basin at 1000 we kept a sharp eye out for surfers riding the waves just off the channel. We made our way down the fairway, passing the transient and fuel docks, looking for the Harbormaster's office. As we passed the Hawaii Yacht Club to starboard, we noticed a tall, distinguished gentleman motioning us in from the Aloha dock. I turned the boat around and brought Kawabunga alongside the club's guest dock. Margaret tossed our bow line to the gentleman as I stepped off the boat and secured the stern line. I recognized him as Earl Hinz, the prolific writer and guru of South Pacific cruising.

I stuttered and stammered but was finally able to tell him I had read all of his books and actually had three of them aboard as reference material and had used them extensively during our cruise. My brother John and I had attended one of his cruising seminars in Long Beach several years earlier. It was a big thrill to talk with Earl and his wife Betty, who have cruised the Pacific and written extensively about their experiences. They had sold Horizon and lived aboard Kumulani, a 36 foot Monk Trawler. Their book, Sail Before Sunset, was an inspiration for us to go cruising when we did, instead of waiting for a bigger boat, more equipment, a bigger cruising fund, retirement pensions and all the rest.

HAWAII YACHT CLUB

We had a marvelous stay at the Hawaii Yacht Club. Generally, a cruising boat can stay three days at the club. We were allowed to stay out on the Aloha dock for two months, enjoying their unending hospitality. The members treated us like royalty and *Kawabunga* was soon becoming the club mascot. Richard Ali, the dockmaster, Arlene Schade in the office, and Patty Deacon the club's Hospitality Chairperson, simply could not do enough for us. Several members offered us rides into town, directions to tourist attractions and advice on where to have work done on the boat. Most of the members have made significant offshore passages and know the value of a kind word, good food and creature comforts.

Steve Jackson has been a member of the club since he was a young man. Steve, a professional seaman working for Matson Lines, sailed his sloop from California to Oahu one year before our arrival and is preparing it for a South Pacific cruise. Steve was very helpful to us, always making sure we had a ride into town and alerting us to special bargains of interest to cruisers.

A few days after arriving in Honolulu we met Ted Trimmer. He pulled up to the Aloha dock in *Lea*, Flicka hull number 415, built in 1992. Ted is a commercial pilot for Hawaiian Airlines. He has sailed *Lea* out to Midway Atoll and back. Ted was kind enough to come back a few days later and drive us to West Marine where we picked up a back-up hand-held GPS computer. Ted docks his Flicka at Ke'ehi Lagoon.

The Hawaii Yacht Club is very active in cruising, racing and fishing tournaments. There is always something going on there. We had to move to the Ala Wai on two occasions; once when they had a fishing tournament and once when they had their Mardi Gras party. Patty called the Ala Wai Harbormaster and cleared the way for us to get a temporary slip for a few days.

When we walked into the Harbormaster's office and introduced ourselves, Robert Rutherford's face lit up in instant recognition and he said, "Oh, you're the little boat that's come such a long, long way."

We will never forget the warmth we felt as guests of the Hawaii Yacht Club. The delicious food, especially the Wednesday night two-for-one prime rib dinners, lovely facilities and generous hospitality were unparalleled. They epitomize the aloha spirit.

FOXY TOO

Ron DuBois helps to coordinate the Pacific Maritime Mobile Net for licensed Ham operators every evening at 1730 Honolulu time on 14.313. He provides an invaluable service to all the yachties in the Pacific by being on board *Foxy Too* every night after work. He also runs his own net (Ron's Net) on 12.353 for those not Ham certified. Boats with medical emergencies or other difficulties are invited to come up on the air first. Ron is the yachtie's lifeline to emergency medical care, ordering repair parts for yachts in transit, relaying messages to worried family members and keeping track of boats making passages all over the Pacific. This is an enormous responsibility and commitment of time that Ron takes on for absolutely no remuneration. His dedication to duty is laudable.

After we settled into the club we struck out to find Ron and Janice DuBois. We wanted to meet him and tell him how much we, and all the other yachties, appreciated his efforts. *Kawabunga* doesn't even have a Ham or SSB radio, but Ron found ways to help us by relaying messages to our family.

Earl Hinz directed us to *Foxy Too*, the immaculately maintained Westsail 42′ that serves as home for Ron, his wife Janice and their two poodles; Maile and Summer. Ron invited us to come aboard and use their radio any afternoon to talk with our friends aboard *Time-Out* and *Navi-Gator*.

Ron stays in shape physically and financially by selling yachts, maintaining and managing yachts, arranging boat deliveries, flying as a corporate pilot for Molokai Ranch and Bank of Hawaii and hauling new-friend yachties around Honolulu in his pickup truck. Janice does topnotch custom canvas creations. She loves to run on the beach and paddle her kayak off Waikiki. Pacific Yacht Care is the name of their company.

THE ZINGARA RESCUE

While aboard *Foxy Too* one afternoon we listened to a drama unfold as Ron coordinated medical doctors in Honolulu with U.S. Navy SEALS that had parachuted into Fanning Island's lagoon to save Dave Baker aboard the ketch *Zingara*. Many articles have been written about this heroic operation. Dave suffered a puncture wound to the instep of his foot while landing a tuna. One day later, Dave's foot was infected and he was burning up with fever. His temperature was 104°. The antibiotics aboard *Zingara* and those available on Fanning were useless. Luckily, Dave had a radio and contacted Ron, who coordinated the rescue involving the U.S. Navy, Army and Coast Guard. There was a significant logistics problem as Fanning Island is 1,050 miles south of Oahu, had no landing strip and was five days away by USCG cutter. The commandos parachuted out of a C-130 Hercules into Fanning's lagoon, boarded *Zingara*, stabilized Dave, sailed Dave's boat three days into stiff tradewinds and currents to Christmas Island, where another C-130 transport plane flew Dave to Honolulu where he was hospitalized at Tripler Medical Center for several weeks.

Can you imagine what the natives were thinking when they looked up and saw commandos jumping out of an airplane into their lagoon? Aside from one tractor, there are no vehicles on Fanning Atoll, no roads and very few people. This was probably the most excitement to hit that island since World War II.

We first encountered *Zingara* in October when we were anchored near them off Tapua Island in Bora Bora's lagoon. Dave was very embarrassed that he had caused such a fuss because he is a self-sufficient cruiser, but he was very grateful to

Ron and the SEALS for risking their lives to save him. In the very least Dave would have lost his leg. He could have lost his life. Rob pointed out that Dave was lucky he was an American, because there is no other country that would go to such lengths for one of its citizens. How true.

OAHU BY BUS, CAR AND FLIP FLOP

We spent two months on Waikiki Beach, one of the most beautiful, exciting and expensive places in the world. Since we sailed to Oahu, we paid United Airlines zero, zilch — absolutely nothing. Ditto for the Ilikai or the Hilton Hawaiian Village as we brought along our own beach-side bungalow. Our only expenses were food and club slip fees, which were considerably cheaper than staying in the luxury hotels just a stone's throw away.

The bus system on Oahu is first rate and absurdly economical. For a dollar you can ride the bus around the entire island. A monthly bus pass sets you back twenty-four dollars, roughly the cost of a taxi from the airport to Waikiki. You rarely have to wait long for a bus, the drivers are helpful and friendly, and the riders, for the most part, are normal people. I say normal, because I am comparing the Oahu ridership with those in Los Angeles.

A few years ago, in the bad old days, I found myself in the position of riding the bus from my apartment in Manhattan Beach to my mid-Wilshire office and back each day. For over a year I spent between three to four hours each day rubbing elbows (and worse) with the most demented, deranged and dangerous creatures the City of Angels ever dredged up. And those were the drivers!

We used the bus for multiple visits to Pearl Harbor, the Honolulu Zoo, the Aloha Tower, Ala Moana Shopping Center and historic downtown Honolulu. We took the bus across the Pali to Kailua Bay, Waimanalo Beach, Sea Life Park, Hanauma Bay and Diamond Head. On one of our excursions into Waikiki

Beach we shopped at the International Marketplace. A guy approached me while I was walking through the open booths and offered to sell me marijuana — apparently his idea of authentic Hawaiian crafts. At that time and place I became conscious of the fact that I no longer appeared to the outside world as *Charlie Dewell, Insurance Man*, but something different — I know not what. . . .

RENDEZVOUS WITH FRIENDS AND FAMILY

After spending five months in Palmyra's lagoon, *Time-Out* set sail from Palmyra. Ron gave us updates on their progress and we counted the days until our old playmates would arrive. Eight days after shoving off, and during particularly strong tradewinds, *Time-Out* tied up right in front of us at the Hawaii Yacht Club at 0330. We had a cold beer waiting for Rob and an ice cold Coke for Sherry and hugs all around.

Rob has left a slew of friends in his wake from his world cruising. Honolulu was no exception. As soon as Rob and Sherry arrived at the club, Don Ross and Autumn Whitehurst, who are club members and live aboard their Mariner 30 *Aegir* at the Ala Wai, came by and offered Rob the use of one of their vehicles for the duration of their stay. Rob and Don met in Pago Pago in 1981. Getting around Honolulu was much easier now, as Rob would drive us where we needed to go.

A few weeks after *Time-Out* arrived we finally got to meet John Brydon. John is another old friend of Rob's from Christmas Island. We missed John when we sailed to Christmas as he was in Honolulu on a buying trip for his store at that time. John is a very important man in the Line Islands so I took the opportunity to petition his help in recovering our $800 from the Bank of Kiribati.

I told John we had faxed the bank manager twice with no response. We had made several telephone calls and two visits to the Kiribati Consulate in Honolulu in an effort to personally meet with the Kiribati Counsel General. We had hand-delivered letters to the Kiribati Consulate asking for their help. We were stiff-armed and stonewalled at every turn. This was a prolonged, frustrating and expensive venture.

John Brydon is a man of few words. He means what he says and says what he means. John told us he would look into it when he returned home. A week later, Ron DuBois drove up with an envelope from John. In it was a check from John's personal account for $800! Ron knew we would have trouble cashing the check so he drove us down to his bank and cashed the check for us against his own account. There really are noble human beings in this old world. You just have to go cruising to find them.

We were thrilled when my niece Becky Gowan flew out from Minnesota for a few days. When I think of my two nieces Beth and Becky, I think of little girls with long blonde hair and pink bikinis, romping with Woof, their tan collie and building sand castles on the beach in front of my sister's cottage on Manistique Lake. Now, their romping is in the courtroom or the boardroom as they are both hard-charging professionals.

Becky was a big hit with all the yachties at the club. Ron and Janice graciously invited Becky to stay aboard *Sequoia,* a Westsail 32', so that she would have her privacy. She used our dinghy to shuttle between the club and *Sequoia.* In between middle-of-the-night business conference calls, we circumnavigated Oahu by rental car, beachcombed along Waikiki Beach and enjoyed a day snorkeling at beautiful Hanauma Bay. We took the dinghy out the to the harbor entrance to watch the surfers riding the waves into Waikiki Beach and to watch the outrigger canoe races with Diamond Head as a backdrop. Late one afternoon we hopped into the dinghy and ran up the Ala Wai Canal, past the University of Hawaii and watched the canoe racers train. It was hard to keep up with Becky as her half-speed is our full throttle. After a whirlwind four days, Rob drove us to the airport where Becky boarded a plane back to Lake Minnetonka, her Wellcraft Scarab and her broad-shouldered, charming and devoted husband Brian.

The day Becky flew home, Dave Baker was discharged from Tripler Medical Center and moved aboard *Sequoia*. We kept Dave stocked with ice from the yacht club via *Thumper* until we left Honolulu.

PREPARING FOR THE LONG JOURNEY HOME

When early May arrived, we started preparing *Kawabunga* for her return passage to California. This was not something I was looking forward to and the work was like pulling teeth.

I shudder at the thought of going up the mast — even *Kawabunga's* relatively short mast. I am downright cowardly when it comes to heights and view with horror the notion of working for hours at a time in a boson's chair. Rob spent three days running me up and down the mast. By the third day he no longer had to use the whip. I am trainable.

I replaced the bulb in the tricolor light at the top of the mast, removed the halyard-snatching spare block, reattached our radar reflector to the upper port shroud and wrapped rigging tape on anything that could tear sail cloth. During my inspection of the rigging, I noticed that the starboard rear lower shroud was beginning to fray. The forestay and backstay were in good shape and the two uppers appeared fine also. Rob and I took the four lower shrouds down and Rob drove me to Art Nelson's loft where we met with the rigging manager, Larry Stenek. We picked up the new shrouds the next morning and installed them that afternoon.

I had been fretting over how to repair the wind vane. Our Monitor Windvane manual was stored in my leather legal bag which had been soaked in the Alenuihaha debacle. I wish I could blame someone else for this snafu. For some reason I had not encased the manual in plastic like my other equipment manuals. I will not even get into why I had a leather briefcase aboard a cruising boat. . . .

I tried to separate the pages and dry out the manual but essential passages were indecipherable. I thought I might have to resort to turning the problem over to a welding shop. I telephoned Gordon C. Nash at Scanmar Marine Products in Sausalito where I purchased the vane. He immediately faxed me the few pages we needed. The diagram made little sense to me. In my case, there is a deficit of basic intellect associated with anything remotely mechanical. My studying an engineering diagram is like a golden retriever sitting in front of a television set critiquing the evening news. No comprende.

Rob did not bother with the blueprint, the soggy manual or my appraisal of the enigma. Wasting little time, he took a quick glance at the vane, sorted through our spare parts kit and repaired the thingamabob before I could re-pack the spare gear.

WAIKIKI NUPTIALS

The morning of Tuesday May 7 found the ship's company of *Kawabunga* in a downcast and somber spirit. Margaret's bags were packed and her flight was scheduled to leave early that afternoon. After breakfast Sherry stopped by and pitched us the following proposition: Would Margaret stay another week if she and Rob got married that Friday?

We were looking for any excuse to remain together a while longer, but wasn't this a bit extreme? Suddenly, we were caught up in a wonderful, whirlwind of wedding preparations. The next four days were a flurry of planning and excitement that climaxed Friday at sunset on Waikiki Beach. The wedding ceremony was officiated by our good friend Steve Jackson from the Hawaii Yacht Club. Steve's faithful flock can generally be found communing with God in the bar at the club. Rob and Sherry hosted a lovely party at The Tahitian Lanai which had a lush, tropical setting. We had dinner in a thatched hut along with fellow cruisers and friends from *Bananas*, *Foxy Too* and *Aegir*. We could think of no finer end to our stay in the Sandwich Islands. By some miracle, I kept expecting Joe and Kaye from *Navi-Gator* to walk into the thatched hut in the middle of the party and for Joe to say, "It's always somethin'."

The next day we accompanied Rob and Sherry on *part* of their honeymoon. We drove into the mountains behind Honolulu and found a creek winding through the forest where we stretched out along the trail and enjoyed a picnic lunch. There was a small waterfall that created a shady little pool for swimming. We were very honored to be a part of their celebration. Within a few days we would part wakes again, *Kawabunga* bound for Los Angeles and *Time-Out* bound for Victoria, British Columbia.

"It is commonplace that we cannot answer for ourselves until we have been tried. But it is not so common a reflection, and surely more consoling, that we usually find ourselves a great deal braver and better than we thought. I believe this is everyone's experience... I wish sincerely, for it would have saved me much trouble, had there been someone to put me in good heart about life when I was younger; to tell me how dangers are most portentous on a distant sight, and how the good in a man's spirit will not suffer itself to be overlaid and rarely or never deserts him in the hour of need."
— Robert Louis Stevenson

CHAPTER FOURTEEN

HOMEWARD BOUND

ALOHA ALII, KAHUNAS AND HAOLES

On Monday, May 13, 1996, Rob drove us to the Honolulu airport where Margaret and I kissed good-bye once again. We were no longer rookies and had put thousands of miles under *Kawabunga's* keel. We knew the return passage would be a challenging one and did not take the risk lightly. Moreover, we did not savor the thought of being apart for another long passage.

Interestingly enough, I was a bit more apprehensive about this passage than I had been for the others. I remembered my old skiing days and knew it was always the last run at the end of the day that can be your Waterloo. That's when you're tired and you can slip up and get injured.

We had done all we could to prepare the boat. We had off-loaded several boxes of equipment and clothes that would not be needed on the return voyage and shipped them home. Margaret also took as much excess as she could on the plane with her. The boat was laden with stores, spare parts, extra sails, charts, guides, safety equipment and plenty of books. The boat was ship-shape. As my hero Cap'n Ron would say, " Best thing to do is get her out on the ocean. If anything's gonna happen, it's gonna happen out there."

Although *Kawabunga* was chafing at her dock lines to move into the vast tracks of the open ocean, I was not. I was struck down with a migraine headache for two days, simply unable to function at all. It's always tough when people know you're getting ready to go and asking when you're shoving off with comments like, "I thought you were leaving yesterday".

I researched the passage home prior to leaving Honolulu. The prescribed route for the month of May would take me directly north from Oahu, turning northeast at about 30° N. The course would then curve gradually NE, aiming for 38° N, 150° W. I should be able to sail east with the westerlies of the higher latitudes. The position of the North Pacific High would influence the whole problem. Rob suggested that whenever I hit any NE winds I should immediately head north and sail until I hit the westerlies. I did not want to get sucked into the North Pacific High, sometimes known as the Pacific parking lot.

I was given a rousing send-off at the Hawaii Yacht Club at noon on May 16th, one year and two days after shoving off from San Diego. It was a magnificent day; bright, sunny and warm. Just before hugging Rob and Sherry for the last time and stepping aboard *Kawabunga,* I telephoned Margaret in Los Angeles and said good-bye. Sherry handed me a stack of *Readers*

Digest magazines. What a treasure. Many new friends wished me a safe passage, including Patty and Arlene from the club, Buzz Taylor aboard *Ishi* from San Francisco and Peter the South African and his girl friend. Patty bid me a safe passage by placing two fern leaves on my stern pulpit, a traditional Hawaiian good luck promise. I was able to keep these in place nearly the entire passage.

As *Kawabunga* steamed up the Ala Wai channel and through the fringing coral reef into Mamala Bay, I thought of the warm people we encountered, the beautiful sights we would never forget and the good times we shared in the extraordinary Hawaiian Islands.

I set to work getting used to life at sea again. Trimming sails, preparing meals and navigating, all while reading a good novel, takes some practice. Fortunately, it did not take long to slip into my seaborne routine.

By 1530 I was directly abeam of Barber's Point on the southwest end of Oahu. At 1545 I was hailed on the VHF radio by Rob and Sherry who had taken their hand-held radio with them to Barber's Point to pick up their newly galvanized anchors. They walked out on the beach and saw *Kawabunga*, just a little white speck, in the distance. We had a nice farewell conversation, the last contact with friends for five and a half weeks.

The Waianae mountain range was a breathtaking sight from the sea. I savored these serene panoramas along the Waianae Coast during the late afternoon and early evening. As night fell, the wind picked up and *Kawabunga* scooted along at 4.3 knots under a single-reefed main and working jib. The last navigational hazard was rocky Kaena Point, which juts out into the Pacific, the western-most point on Oahu.

As usual, seasickness had its hold over me for the first three days out. I came to accept the malaise and nauseous sensations, knowing they would eventually recede. I made great mileage during this period though, averaging 90 miles per day. It was very hot during the early stages of the passage.

One of my favorite times aboard *Kawabunga* during our cruise was in the evening with a bright moon glimmering on the waves as we charged along through the night. It brought me back to the times as a child when I would watch the *Victory At Sea* films about World War II in the Pacific. Those films always closed with a shot of the ocean as seen from the deck of a war ship with the moonlight shining on the sea. An ominous feeling enveloped me when we were 200 miles north of Oahu on May 19. This was the same patch of ocean where the Japanese Imperial Navy launched their attack on Pearl Harbor fifty-five years earlier.

On May 21 at 1220 I came close to running into a pod of seven False Killer whales that were basking in the sun on top of a very calm, glassy sea. We were steaming at 5 knots and I spotted them only 40 yards off the port bow. I spooked them and they gradually came to life and swam away. Off in the distance I spotted several more swimming atop the calm sea.

Our Autohelm Tri-Data gave me trouble off and on during the passage back from Honolulu. I hired a diver to clean the bottom two days before shoving off, but I should have gone down to double check to make sure the little paddle was totally free from growth. From time to time the instrument would read a lot like my grade point average the term I pledged my fraternity at Ferris State — 0.0.

Margaret and I had provisioned as well as we could. We did a good job of not only stocking plenty of tasty food, but a nice variety also. Unfortunately, I just get sick of eating all together while at sea. I force myself to eat during these long, lonely passages, eating only to survive, taking little of my customary glee in meal time. Two things I never tired of were tapioca pudding and Dinty Moore Beef Stew.

A CHANGE IN WEATHER

God threw the weather switch on May 24. We went from warm, bright sunshine with consistent, strong winds to cold and damp, with fluky winds and a dark, threatening sky — all within a few hours. It remained that way, getting colder by the day, until two days before my arrival in Los Angeles. Our noon position on May 24 was 30° 28′ N, 153° 01′ W. The water temperature was 65°, 5 degrees cooler than the day before. We were surrounded by dark, menacing clouds. We were not in the tropics anymore. I moved down into the cabin, started wearing my Patagonia woollies and broke out the hot chocolate.

On Memorial Day I scored my best noon-to-noon mileage to that point, making 92 miles. We were on the same latitude as Avalon on Catalina Island and ran into our first fog of the passage. I thought the June gloom looked familiar.

The cold weather had to have something to do with the Memorial Day weekend. As a kid growing up on Lake Huron, we made it a rule that we had to go swimming over the Memorial Day weekend — no matter how cold the water was. I swear there was ice floating around the lake on some of those polar bear dips.

My food fantasies returned during this period. The thought of prime rib, custard pie and ice cream danced in my head. Other subtle and not so subtle delusions came over me. I began reading Judy Carter's book, *Stand-Up Comedy*, contemplating my next career as a stand-up comic. Some of you may remember my aspiration of becoming a cookie baker during the Palmyra to Hawaii passage. . . . What I really wanted to do was play baseball for the Detroit Tigers.

CLOSE ENCOUNTERS

One thing I would do differently the next time around is to have radar aboard. It would be much more reassuring to be able to take a cat nap while the radar is operating with a guard zone up. I will describe some of my ship sightings during the passage from Oahu to Marina del Rey.

On June 2, I saw four ships within three hours! Our noon position was 37° 16′ N, 148° 09′ W. We were 1,500 miles from home in the shipping lanes between Japan and the Panama Canal. I felt like a paranoid terrier on the west-bound lane of the Santa Monica freeway on a get-away Friday afternoon.

At 1604 I spotted the first ship, a super tanker, off my port beam on a SE course. A second super tanker was sighted off my starboard quarter at 1808. At 1920 I spotted two ships at the same time. The first ship was a cargo freighter sailing from Japan to Panama and then New Orleans. The second was a Greek freighter loaded with coal from New Orleans on its way to Japan.

I had a nice talk with the skipper of the cargo freighter. They had been tracking me on radar and told me of a storm they had just passed through. We wished each other a safe passage. After I signed off I heard them talking to a third ship in the area, one that I never saw at all.

My favorite radio communication with a ship's captain came on the early evening of June 12. At 1936 I spotted the bulk carrier *Beaumare 2*, three miles off my port quarter. I enjoyed a long conversation with Captain Sekou, the ship's master. Captain Sekou was a very kind man, interested in our cruise, what I did for a living and my safety. He was surprised I was sailing solo and was amazed that I was aboard a twenty foot boat in the middle of the Pacific. He had the habit of responding on the radio, "Well understood". Captain Sekou wished much happiness to Margaret and me. By 2010 *Beaumare 2* melted into the horizon off my starboard beam, leaving me feeling a bit lonely.

On June 17 I sighted two ships within two and a half hours. *Winter Spring*, bound for Los Angeles, was sighted directly astern at 1800. She was coming right at me. I hailed the ship on the VHF. The sea was wild at the time causing sea clutter and they did not have me on radar. They were able to locate me visually after I gave them my position. I changed course to give her plenty of room and the ship passed me to starboard. Let the big dog eat!

My nerves were jumbled at the thought of *Kawabunga* being invisible on *Winter Spring's* radar screen. The conditions were deteriorating fast. At 2030, while in the middle of reefing down again, I sighted the second ship of the evening off our starboard quarter. I dropped the jib and a melee ensued in which the jib halyard wrapped around the topping lift and I was unable to untangle the mess. I decided to wait until morning to attack the problem. During the skirmish with the halyard I lost sight of the ship's lights and never found them again.

During this passage I observed eighteen ships at sea. I was able to raise most of them on the VHF radio. All but one told me they had me on their radar screens, a tribute to our Mobar radar reflector.

DISCOVERING THE WESTERLIES

The westerlies were officially declared at noon on May 31. Trekkies would say we were at warp speed. Kevin Costner would say we were carrying the mail. I say we were forging ahead with reckless abandon. *Kawabunga* was zooming along at a steady 5½ knots and we posted 101 miles noon to noon. The wind was howling out of the west, the sky was completely overcast and the waves were serious, mature ocean rollers. The sea temperature had dropped to 59°.

Our position was 35° 22′ N, 149° 55′ W. I updated our routing information on the GPS computer and found our great circle course to Marina del Rey was 1,508 miles distant on a course of 72° M. I did not head on a direct course for home yet, preferring to continue NNE.

I dropped the jib, put a reef in the main, rigged a preventer on the boom and began running before the westerlies. Kawabunga dude!

STORM AT SEA

The seas continued to build once we hit the westerlies. We had a particularly rough afternoon on June 3 and I was looking forward to the wind tailing off after sunset, the usual phenomenon. I needed sleep as I had very little rest the night before. By 1800 we were in a full gale running 5½ knots under a double-reefed mainsail alone. I prayed for no more unscheduled ship visits. I dropped all canvas at 2330, lashed everything down tight, and ran under a bare pole. We were still making 2 knots running before the gale-force winds and mountainous, breaking seas without a stitch of sail up. The only canvas we had up was the dodger. The chain teeth for the windvane line had trouble staying in the tiller. It acted like a horse spitting out its bit. I spent a terrible night below with the sliding hatch locked in place, hoping against hope the conditions would moderate. Waves would strike *Kawabunga* from abeam making the entire ship shutter. In short order the little ship would press on, staggering through the heaving ocean. Without the mainsail up we were yawing savagely, making for a most uncomfortable motion. There was no fun in Mudville!

The conditions were the worst I had experienced. I would estimate a 9.5 on the Beaufort Wind Scale, between a strong gale and a very strong gale. We had high waves, foam blown in dense streaks with overhanging crests and the wind was screaming consistently in the fifties with stronger gusts. The sound of the wind howling through the rigging was unnerving. It was not yet time to panic but the thought of breaking out the marine grade Depends crossed my mind.

In the early morning hours of June 4, I seriously considered deploying my parachute sea anchor. The thought of climbing out on deck and crawling to the bow to deploy the brute in these atrocious conditions made me cringe, but I was fearful of lying ahull in the breaking seas. A 360° roll would ruin my whole day. We were taking some vicious shots and water was shooting through both large portholes onto my bunk and stove.

The scene reminded me of the old World War II submarine movies where a depth charge would explode just outside the boat, causing leaks to erupt and the crew would go to work with wrenches to repair the damage. Then they would sweat it out, knowing the destroyer would return for another attack.

I set about dragging the bag with the sea anchor out of the quarter berth. What a job. Next, I crawled to the very forepeak and pulled out a canvas bag containing 300´ of nylon line and 25´ of chain out and into the cabin. I found a large block in my rigging bag and was all set to deploy the monster. Now, the problem was that I had made myself seasick by all the weird activity below. I really needed to sprawl out on my bunk, keep down lunch, and marshal some backbone before literally "braving the storm". My best judgment at the time, for the conditions I faced, was to not over-react and to just stay put, to see if the weather would improve. I was in a win/win situation. Odds were that I would survive this deadly peril. If I were killed, I would surely feel better than I did at the time. In my misery I thought of my friend Doug Giese and thought that he would probably love this situation. He and I used to go storm sailing off Point Loma in San Diego. What a madman. . . .

After resting for a couple of hours the conditions slowly began to moderate. The gale gradually blew itself out and by noon we had bright sunshine and winds of 25 to 30 knots. There was still a big sea running and we still had 1,240 nautical miles to sail, but we had cleared a major hurdle with no damage other than some deep psychological scars.

During that awful night I prayed ceaselessly for my sister Bonnie who was going in for surgery the next morning, and I must admit, I slipped in a few prayers for *Kawabunga* and me too! He must have heard me over the shrieking wind because we all kept body and soul together.

A LULL IN THE ACTION

I scored good noon-to-noon runs on the two days following the storm but by June 7, the party was over. My mileage was insanely disappointing for the next week, averaging a measly 51. These were tough, hard-fought miles. I was up and down constantly changing sails, trimming the sails and the vane.

I ran the little diesel engine quite a bit during this period. I was very grateful that the engine ran flawlessly during this entire passage. Abe III, the new Autohelm autopilot we bought at West Marine in Honolulu also performed admirably.

After three weeks at sea, frustration set in. I was losing my patience with the weather, the food and the ship's library. I had stocked the library with a glut of lawyer-books and now was stuck with courtroom dramas ad nauseam. Little things got on my nerves; a squeak in the hanging locker, another ugly meal, halyards constantly getting wrapped around the mast fitting, my saltwater-soaked bunk. I had endured enough fun and adventure, learned enough about patience and preparation and challenged myself enough against the perilous, deep blue sea. It was time to wind up the adventure and get home to pine trees and fireplaces. Who do I see about resigning?

Sometimes it was so calm I would swear you could see the curvature of the earth. This made filling the ship's tanks with diesel fuel from the jerry jugs on deck an easier job than in some anchorages we had been in. Other times I was battling squalls. The squalls in this region are not as violent as those in the South Pacific, but they pack a wallop and demand a lot of work from an increasingly lazy crew. I was afraid to admit out loud that I was bored to tears, for fear that I would immediately find myself fighting another North Pacific gale. I kept my thoughts to myself and this period was marked by fluky winds, rain and cold. I was appalled at the cursing and swearing I heard coming from above and below deck during this time.

One of the highlights of my day was picking out a big, fat orange to savor after lunch. I had foolishly rationed them out, allowing myself only one per day. By the third week, many of them had spoiled and I had to go through them and toss two bad oranges for every good one. I did not bother with rationing them after that, enjoying them until they ran out. I also had to throw out several dozen eggs. I had been turning them every few days, but it was starting to smell like a barn down below. Something was rotten and it wasn't in Denmark. I'm sure I was smelling a little ripe at the time too, but no one complained.

KAWABUNGA SMELLS THE BARN

On June 10 I calculated a course for my approach into Marina del Rey. My original course had me going between Pt. Conception and the Channel Islands. I did not want to do that so I designed a new course giving Pt. Arguello and Pt. Conception a wide berth and approaching Marina del Rey from the west, taking San Nicholas and Santa Barbara Islands to starboard and Santa Cruz and Anacapa to port. We had 870 nautical miles to sail on a course of 83° M and then a final 106 miles on a course of 55° M.

We had very strong westerly winds for the last ten days of the voyage. *Kawabunga* smelled the barn and skedaddled for home during those boisterous conditions, crossing time zones and lifting my spirits. I was airborne quite often and my back was giving me some trouble, but the mileage was heartening. Madness prevailed whenever I would attempt cooking. A pot of hot water and pasta was dumped on the ice box and onto the cabin sole but I escaped any scalding episodes. I fell into the habit of hesitating before putting in another reef as I wanted to get as much speed as we could without losing our rig. Dreaming of home, I drove *Kawabunga* hard, pushing her to the edge of the envelope.

We were confronted with another gale on the evening of June 17 and all day June 18. The storm-tossed sea was wild and we enjoyed more nautical hijinks. "How much fun did you want to have?" We took some tremendous shots during that time and my bunk was completely soaked with sea water. The comfort level had bottomed out at this point. More fear, loneliness, exhaustion and frustration. But, I had no one to blame but myself. I had chosen to be there, to be tested and forged into a true blue water sailor.

As we approached the continental shelf, the conditions not only remained very rough, but actually got more perilous as we ran before a westerly wind under a double-reefed main. During this time, the Coast Guard came on the air announcing there were two fishing boats sending out EPIRB alerts at the same time! The spray was so bad it was as though it was raining. I hated even going from the relative comfort of the cabin into the chaos of the cockpit. I rigged the trim adjustment on Joey the windvane so I could adjust it from the cabin. Why didn't I do that a year earlier?

I was grateful for satellite navigation. Without it, I would have been running under dead reckoning for the last ten days until within 120 miles from the coast. There had been no way to shoot any celestial body during that time. We were completely socked in. One sign we were getting close to home came on June 20 when the water changed from a deep blue to a green-gray color.

On June 21, the first day of summer and Margaret's favorite day of the year, I sustained three injuries. Perhaps I was careless, being on the doorstep of home, or maybe I was just exhausted, getting only one hour sleep the previous night, but I had been very careful during the entire voyage and now the wheels were coming off. Early that morning I twisted my right knee changing head sails. About 0900, while running down wind, we jibed. The main sheet ran across my face ripping off my glasses and hat. My hat was thrown into *Kawabunga's* wake but my glasses were attached to my neck and saved. I felt as though Rosie O'Donnell had slapped me up. In the early afternoon we jibed again, causing the boom to fly across from starboard to port. I took a George Foreman-like whack upside my head and went down like a sack of potatoes. I was dazzled and stayed curled up on the port cockpit bench for several minutes, making sure I still had all my faculties. As Curly of the Three Stooges would say, "Not in the head. You know I'm not normal".

While still 90 miles out I was able to raise the San Pedro Marine Operator and contact Margaret. I had been weary and depressed up until that time and talking with Margaret made my spirits soar. Shortly after making radio contact the wind speed accelerated and we had one last gale to contend with off Pt. Conception. So, for six hours on my last night out, we fought our final battle. By 0200 the storm was over and the night sky was radiant in starlight. I was chilled to the bone after the gale. I took off my foul weather gear, put on clean, dry clothes and put on my second set of foul weather gear. I was ready for civilization. By 0700 there was not a breath of wind and I steamed the last eleven hours to the Marina del Rey breakwater.

A DREAM FULFILLED

When I sighted Pt. Dume with the familiar Santa Monica Mountains in the background at 1440 it struck me that the cruise I had dreamed about for so many years was ending.

I was returning a changed man. I had learned the value of time. Life was in session while we were away and we returned to many of our friends who were facing death, disease, divorce or bankruptcy. During the short period we were away living out our dream, two of my good friends, both forty-one years old, passed away; came to a full stop; died.

When my time comes, I will not look back on this cruise with regret. I can not imagine looking up from my death bed and saying, "Gee, I sure wish I would have worked in insurance during those two years in the 1990's instead of going on that darn cruise." How absurd that sounds to me.

As *Kawabunga* steamed into Santa Monica Bay, I reflected back on the many incredible places we had visited and people we had met on our cruise. I recalled the sadness and anticipation I felt while waving good-bye to Margaret in the rain at the tip of Shelter Island; the excitement of encountering two sailboats at sea, the delight of navigating by the Southern Cross as the cruising spinnaker drew me to the heart of the South Pacific; the thrill of sighting Ua Huka after forty-two days at sea and the awe-inspiring beauty of the Marquesas Islands; the rush from being surrounded by hundreds of whales for seven hours on the Fourth of July; the pure joy of swimming in Margaret's fantasy waterfall pool in Tahiti; the satisfaction of anchoring *Kawabunga* in Cook's Bay, Moorea; the delicious dinners at the Bora Bora Yacht Club; the overwhelming generosity of our friend Luti and his family on Christmas Island; the fun we had lobstering by moonlight on the reef at Palmyra Atoll; the gratification of sitting down for dinner at the Kona Inn on our first night on the Big Island of Hawaii; the night of terror in the Alenuihaha Channel; the hospitality of the Hawaii Yacht Club; Friday night fireworks on Waikiki Beach and the fight of my life with a North Pacific storm. These adventures would have remained only dreams, had I commuted into the insurance district during that time.

I also looked back to the magical, fateful night in 1992 when *my* dream became *our* dream. Margaret and I were sailing *Kawabunga* from Avalon to San Diego. In the middle of the night, under a full moon, we were visited by several spinner dolphin that entertained us for fifteen minutes. We stood out on the bowsprit, hanging over the pulpit, watching the show. The little creatures darted through the ocean, leaving a sparkling, phosphorescent, corkscrew trail. They jumped in choreographed perfection in the light of the moonbeams. Their splashes and *Kawabunga's* frothing wake made the sea glitter. It was a captivating, momentous encounter. Margaret signed on for the cruise that instant.

Margaret had arranged a slip for *Kawabunga* on the same dock where we had lived at Holiday Harbor in Marina del Rey. It was wonderful to sail into this familiar harbor on a busy Saturday afternoon after being absent for two years. I stepped onto the dock at 1815 on June 22, after thirty-seven solitary days at sea.

We are extremely pleased with "the little blue boat", *Kawabunga*. She did everything asked of her, carrying us safely to the South Pacific and back, without ever a worry and without ever missing a beat. She is quite a little ship. After 10,000 blue water miles under her keel, *Kawabunga* has returned home.

The author inspecting the rigging before leaving Honolulu

APPENDIX

SHIPS ENCOUNTERED HONOLULU TO LA

1	Monday	5/20/96	5*	1240 Got on VHF — bound for Philippines. Stb. beam.
2	Wednesday	5/29/96	14	1100 Yang Ming Line container ship. Crossed close to stern, less than 2 miles.
3	Sunday	6/2/96	18	1604 Port beam — tanker 5–7 miles SE course Super Tanker
4	Sunday	6/2/96	18	1808 Freighter off stb quarter. Super tanker. We are 1500 miles from home!
5	Sunday	6/2/96	18	1920 two ships @ once!! #1 Cargo freighter Japan to Panama to New Orleans. Had nice VHF conversation. Had me on radar. Wished each other safe passage.
6	Sunday	6/2/96	18	#2 Greek Coal from New Orleans to Japan. They talked of a storm. Then, they had a conversation with a third ship!
7	Tuesday	6/11/96	27	0230 Ship to port— several miles off.
8	Wednesday	6/12/96	28	1936 Freighter off stern. VHF Capt. Sekou 2.9 miles off. *Beaumare 2*, a bulk carrier. Japan to Panama — long talk about our cruise. Interested in what I did for a living, Margaret. Wished much happiness to Margaret & me. He had a habit of saying; "well understood". By 2010 ship melting into the horizon off stb beam.
9	Monday	6/17/96	33	1800 Ship directly astern 8 miles off. VHF 1820 did not have me on radar due to sea clutter — found us visually after I gave him our position. Sounded like a nice guy. Exchanged pleasantries. *Winter Spring* bound for LA. 1900 passed. Took photographs. Sea is wild. Changed course to give him room. "Let the big dog eat!"
10	Monday	6/17/96	33	2030 Another ship! Stb quarter. Gale force winds. Lost ship's lights in melee of halyard & toping lift. Single-reefed main.
11	Wednesday	6/19/96	35	2310 Ship's lights to the north.
12	Thursday	6/20/96	36	2135 Ship to port. Passed to stern by 2145. (Tonight will cross two main ship traffic lanes).
13	Friday	6/21/96	37	1440 VHF Capt. said 7 miles off. Horrible conditions.
14	Friday	6/21/96	37	1825 Ship going north.
15	Friday	6/21/96	37	2000 2 ships seen during gale.
16	Friday	6/21/96	37	2000 (see above)
17	Saturday	6/22/96	38	1130 *Evergreen* — a container ship. I steaming.
18	Saturday	6/22/96	38	1330 N-bound ship going 30 kts.

*Number of days at sea

SAIL PLAN

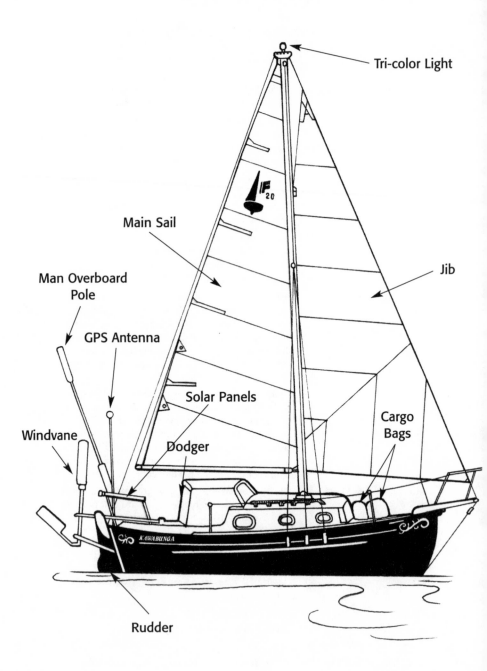

Tri-color Light

Main Sail

Man Overboard
Pole

GPS Antenna

Jib

Windvane

Solar Panels

Dodger

Cargo
Bags

KAWABUNGA

Rudder

CABIN LAYOUT

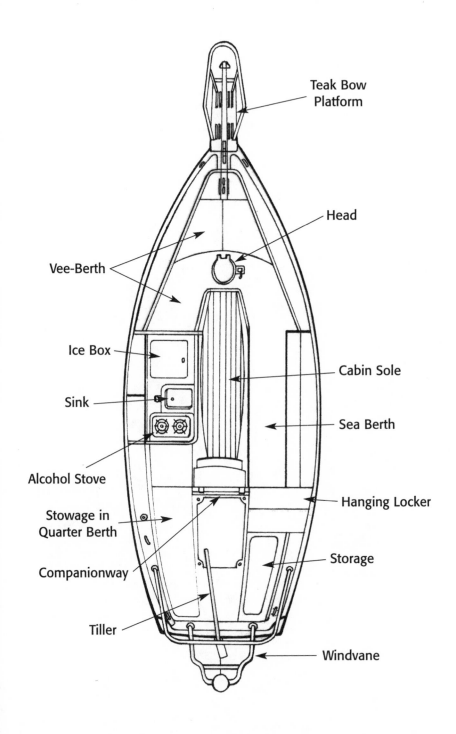

Teak Bow Platform

Head

Vee-Berth

Ice Box

Cabin Sole

Sink

Sea Berth

Alcohol Stove

Hanging Locker

Stowage in
Quarter Berth

Storage

Companionway

Tiller

Windvane

KAWABUNGA!
EQUIPMENT LIST

Navigation:
OmniBook 425 laptop computer & Citizen Notebook
    Printer II with
Pelican Box
Magellan 5000 GPS Receiver
Garmin GPS 38 Personal Navigator (Back Up)
Plath Classic Sextant
Davis Plastic Sextant
Astro Celestial Program
Autohelm TriData
Autohelm Auto pilot
Monitor Wind vane
Gemini Compass
Airguide Compass for in cabin with levogage
West Marine Orion VHF Radio
Grundig Yachtboy Shortwave Radio with Pelican Box
Chart Kit Weems & Plath Chronometer Weems
    & Plath Barometer
Fujinon Polaris binoculars with compass & light
    Handbearing compass
Electronic handbearing compass
Handheld anonometer Spotlight Loran HandHeld
Flash Lights Air Horns (compressed)
Blow air horns (2) Brass

Abandon Ship Bag (Floating)
Avon four man offshore double bottom life raft
Litton 406 EPIRB
Speargun
Flares
    Nine (9) Orion 12 gauge red aerial flares & pistol
    Seven (7) USCG/SOLAS Red Parachute Rocket
        launched (PainsWessex)
    Three (3) Orion HandHeld Orange Smoke Signals
    Three (3) Orion 12 gauge practice flares
Signaling Mirror

Emergency Fishing Tackle
ICOM VIV Radio with Pelican Box (DC, AC & alkaline)
Survivor 06 manual water maker
Emergency Blanket
Two (2) personal strobe lights
First Aid Kit & Marine Medical First Aid Kit
Seasick pills
Small pair Mirador 8 x 21 Binoculars for abandon ship bag
Emergency rations

Tools
Tool Box
Rigger's Bag #1 (Electrical)
Rigger's Bag #2 (Misc.)
Socket Set

Ground Tackle
25 lb. CQR Anchor: 60 ft. 5/16" chain. 300 ft. line
16 lb. Bruce Anchor: 25 ft. chain. 200 ft. line
11 lb. Dansforth Anchor: 15 ft. chain. 200 ft. line
Simpson-Lawrence Manual Anchor Windlass with winch
Parachute anchor 9 foot diameter
Drogue
Small mushroom dinghy anchor with chain & nylon rode

Photography
35 mm Minolta with lenses
35 mm SLR with lenses
VCR video camera
Captiva instant camera
Minolta underwater camera
2 Pelican Boxes

Fixtures
Hurricane Oil Lamp
Weems & Plath Oil Lamp
Anchor Oil Lamp
3 dome lights
2 adjustable chart lights

Cooking Equipment
Two burner alcohol stove
Pressure Cooker, pots, pans, utensils, plates
Propane Bar-B-Q grill with custom cover & propane bags

Sails
Three (3) main sails
Yankee
120% genoa
130% genoa
120% Kevlar genoa
Cruising Spinnaker
Storm Jib
Storm Trysail
Sail cover for main and jib bag @ bow
Forespar telescoping whisker pole
Four bronze winches (with covers) with all lines leading
    to cockpit

Misc.
Hammock (large)
Hammock (chair)
Bronze Opening Port Holes (four 5″ x 8″ and two 8″ x 13″
Custom mosquito netting for cockpit
Prescription dive masks, flippers & snorkels
Two sets lycra dive suits
Cockpit cushions & cockpit pillows
Two West Marine Cargo Bags for storage on the foredeck

Electricity
Two (2) six volt deep cycle batteries (Bank #1)
One (1) 12 volt deep cycle battery (Bank #2)
Two (2) solar panels Battery Charger

Sun
Custom tropic awning with side panels
Spare canvas awning
Kite Shade/rain catcher
Dodger with covers Two (2) triangle canvass shades

Flag Kit
  Dress Up Flag strings
  Signal Flags
  Courtesy Flags

Rope Bag
  Bosun's Chair
  6 to 1 gantline
  Various lengths & diameter rope

Safety
  Two (2) fire extinguishers
  Two safety lines, gates & jib netting
  Screens for ports
  Two Jack Lines
  Two harnesses
  One (1) Sospenders inflatable harness
  Two (2) Tethers
  Underwater Epoxy (2)
  Many AA batteries.
  Man Overboard Pole with cover.
  Foul weather gear (two suits of gear with boots)
  Henry Lloyd Bags (4)
  Two sets of Frogwear (sun repellent clothes)

First Aid Kit / Dental Kit

Fishing Gear
  Meat hook, Gaff, Fish Basher bat, Lures & case

Dinghy
  Avon Redcrest Inflatable (AVB66704KO9 1) with canvas cover
  Suzuki 2 hp outboard & tiller extension with canvas cover

Water Jerry Jugs
  Five 6 gallon jerry jugs
  Four 3 gallon Jerry jugs

CHART INVENTORY FOR KAWABUNGA!

Tube A — French Polynesia

83021   Iles De La Societe
Manuae to Tahiti
French — Scale 1:592,000

83383   Moorea — Northwest Coast of Tahiti
Iles De La Societe
USA — Scale 1:50,000

83382   French Polynesia
Iles De La Societe
Approaches to Tahiti & Morea including Maiao
& Tetiaroa
French — Scale 1:173,000 @ Lat 17° 30′

83392   South Pacific Ocean — French Polynesia
Iles Sous Le Vent
Leeward Islands including Huahine, Raiatea, Tahaa, Bora
Bora, Tupai, Maupiti, Manuae, Maupihaa, Moto One
USA — Scale 1:174,383 @ Latitude 16° 35′

998   Archipel des Tuamotu
Overall Tuamotos — Including Tahiti
Ile Makemo to Lle Tahiti
French — Scale 1:750,000 @ Latitude 16°

83020   Iles Marquises
Marquesas — Overall chart
USA — Scale 1:962,050 @ Latutude 9°

Tube B — Hawaii & Marquesas

19340   Hawaii to Oahu
        USA — Scale 1:250,000

19380   Oahu to Niihau
        USA — Scale 1:247,482

19320   Hawaii
        USA — Scale 1:250,000 @ Latitude 20° 30´

3931   Archipel Des
        Ile Nuku-Hiva
        French — Scale 1:69,800

3997   Iles Marquises
        Iles Hiva-Oa, Ta Huata et Motane
        French

Tube C — Ocean Charts

5245   Great Circle Sailing Chart for Panama to Japan
        USA

4051   North Pacific Ocean — Southeastern Part
        USA — Scale 1:10,000,000 @ equator

4061   South Pacific Ocean — Western Part
        USA — Scale 1:10,000,000 @ equator

81   Pt. Vicente to Dana Point & Pt. Vicente
        USA

18740   San Diego to Santa Rosa Island
        USA — Scale 1:234,270

5160   Pacific Yacht Races
        San Pedro to Honolulu including Acapulco & Mazatlan
        USA — Scale 1:4,790,000

Tube D — Samoa — Tonga — New Zealand

83567   Tonga Islands
Nuku' Alofa & Approaches

76040   New Zealand
North Island — North Coast
Cape Maria Van Diemen to Tutukaka Harbor
USA — Scale 1:300,000 @ Latitude 34° 50′

76050   New Zealand — North Island — East & West Coasts
Manukau Harbor to Maunganui Bluff & Tutakaka
Harbor to Mayor Island
USA — Scale 1:293,940 @ Latitude 36° 27′

605   New Zealand to Fiji and Samoa Islands
USA — Scale 1:3,500,000 @ Latitude 22° 30′

83560   Tonga — Tonga Islands
USA — Scale 1:400,000 @ Latitude 20° 25′

83555   Tonga Islands
Va Va'u Group
USA — Scale 1:74,460 @ Latitude 18° 50′

83425   Islands & Anchorages in Cook Islands
USA

83026   Samoa Islands
USA — Scale 1:1,000,000 @ Latitude 13° 22′

83473   Samoa Islands — Western Samoa
Savai'I & Upolu
USA — Scale 1:200,000

5122   New Zealand — North Island East Coast
        Bay of Islands
        New Zealand — Scale 1:50,000

Charts for the Line Islands, including Christmas Atoll, Fanning Atoll, Washington Island, Palmyra Atoll and Kingman Reef were acquired while in Tahiti.

Chart Books and Atlases taken included:

Cruising Guide to Tahiti and the French Society Islands by Marcia Davock, edited by Julius M. Wilensky.

Charlie's Charts of Polynesia (The South Pacific, east of 165° W. Longitude) by Charles E. Wood.

Charlie's Charts of the Hawaiian Islands by Charles E. Wood.

Marine Atlas of the Hawaiian Islands (Complete charts for mariners cruising the waters in and around Kaua'i, Ni'ihau, O'ahu, Moloka'i, Maui, Kaho'olawe, and Hawai'i) by A.P. Balder.

Mariner's Atlas of Southern California, Complete NOAA charts from Monterey Bay to Cabo Punta Banda, Baja California, Including all bays, inlets, channels, passages, approaches and harbors of Southern California, the Channel Islands, & Santa Catalina Island by A.P. Balder.

GLOSSARY

abandon ship bag: Bag kept at the ready to be transported to the liferaft in case of a catastrophic event such as sinking. The bag would include safety gear such as an EPIRB, hand-held VHF radio, portable watermaker, food, medical kit, flares, etc.

aft: Towards the stern or back of a boat.

anchor rode: The chain and / or line attached to the anchor.

anchorage: An area appropriate for anchoring.

archipelago: A large group or chain of islands.

atoll: A ring-shaped coral reef or series of closely spaced small coral islands surrounding a lagoon.

Autohelm Tri-Data: On *Kawabunga*, this instrument's transponder is in the hull at the bow and transmits data to the screen located in the cockpit. Reports speed, depth, water temperature and is a trip odometer. Can be set with a depth alarm.

autopilot: Known as "Abe" aboard *Kawabunga*. An electronic steering system which runs on batteries. Can be set to maintain a magnetic course.

bare poles: Having no sails up, usually due to storm conditions.

bearing: The direction of an object — described as either a true bearing on a chart or as a bearing relative to the heading of a ship.

bilge: Interior of the hull, below the floor boards.

bollard: Post set into a wharf or in the ground to which a ship's mooring can be tied.

boom: Spar extending from a sailboat's mast, used to extend the foot of a sail.

bosun's chair: Short board or canvas chair attached to a bridle and a block and tackle. A sailor can go aloft to do work on the mast by sitting in the chair while a crew member hauls on a halyard.

bow: The forward area of a boat.

bow pulpit: Safety rail generally made of stainless steel located at the bow of the boat to which the lifelines are attached.

bowline: A knot tied to form a temporary loop in the end of a line. It has many uses at sea.

bowsprit: A spar extending forward from the bow of a sailboat.

celestial navigation: A method of determining your position at sea using sun, stars and moon, a sextant, a Nautical Almanac and a chronometer and an assumed position.

chart: A mariner's map of an area of the sea, showing any coastline, harbors, anchorages, lighthouses, navigational information, latitude and longitude, depths of the sea, dangers.

cleat: A fitting to which lines are made fast.

cockpit: An opening in the deck of a sailboat where the boat is steered and affords access to the cabin.

companionway: Ladder/stairway leading from the cockpit to the cabin.

companionway drop boards: Aboard *Kawabunga*, the three boards which slide together to form a door separating the cabin from the cockpit.

cruising spinnaker: A three cornered sail of light cloth used in downwind conditions without the need of a spinnaker pole.

dinghy: A small boat used as a yacht tender.

dismasted: A sailboat is dismasted when her mast falls down, usually due to storm damage or a catastrophic event like pitchpoling or a severe broach.

dodger: A structure, usually built of canvas with stainless steel frames, over the companionway to protect from spray, rain and sun.

doldrums: The belt of calm and frustrating winds north of the equator between the north and south tradewinds in the Pacific and Atlantic oceans.

draft: The vertical distance from the waterline to the lowest point of the keel. Therefore, the minimum depth of water in which a boat will float.

drogue: A hallow cone, usually constructed of canvas or plastic, used to slow down a boat in following seas to prevent her from being pooped by waves coming up from astern.

electronic navigation: The use of GPS, SatNav, Loran, radio direction finders, radar, and computerized charting devices for navigation. Usually refers to GPS.

EPIRB: Stands for Emergency Position Indicating Radio Beacon. It is a small, battery operated emergency radio which can be activated to declare a vessel in distress at sea. A mariner's "911". The position is pinpointed allowing search and rescue to locate the vessel.

foredeck: The forward part of the deck of a boat.

gale: Winds ranging from 34 to 47 knots.

galley: The boat's kitchen.

gendarmes: French police officer.

genoa: An overlapping jib.

GPS: Global Positioning System — electronic system which uses satellites to fix a vessel's position (latitude and longitude).

great circle route: A circle of which a segment represents the shortest distance between two points on the surface of the earth.

halyard: A line used to hoist a sail aloft.

hank: A small snap hook that secures the jib luff to the headstay.

Haole: Hawaiian for Caucasian or Mainlander.

hatch: An opening in a deck providing access below. Usually, a hatch cover (either sliding or hinged) is fitted.

hawsepipe: Pipe in the bow of a vessel through which the anchor rode passes.

head sail: Any sail in the fore triangle — any sail forward of the mast.

heaving to: Setting the sails so a boat makes little headway, usually in a waiting or storm condition. Helm lashed downwind, storm jib sheeted to windward and a storm trysail sheeted to leeward.

Hinano: A brand of Tahitian beer.

jackline (jackstay): Nylon covered wire running fore and aft on both starboard and port sides.

jib: A triangular sail, set on the headstay.

jibe: To change tacks by heading off until the sails swing across the boat.

keel: The deep appendage or fin under the hull whose lateral area counteracts leeway forces and whose weight counteracts heeling forces.

knot: One nautical mile per hour. A nautical mile is 6,076.12 feet.

leech: After edge of a mainsail or jib (both edges of a spinnaker)

life raft: Inflatable boat (stored in a valise below decks or canister on deck) for use in emergencies.

lifelines: Lines, usually wire rope covered in plastic, running along the side decks to keep crew members from going overboard.

M (magnetic) course: Ship's heading based on the magnetic compass.

mainsail: A sail hoisted on the after side of the mainmast.

mast: Vertical spar and the main support of the sailing rig.

masthead tricolor light: Light at the top of the mast showing green, red and white.

mooring: Permanent ground tackle.

painter: A towline or bow line on a dinghy.

parachute sea anchor: On *Kawabunga* we had a 9′ parachute rigged as a sea anchor with 300' of nylon line running off the bow to be used in storm conditions.

passage: One leg of a voyage.

pitch pole: To somersault.

pollywog: Someone who has yet to cross the equator.

port: The left side of the boat looking towards the bow from the cockpit.

Q-Flag: Yellow quarantine flag. Flown when entering a foreign port. It is lowered after satisfying customs and immigration.

quay: Concrete structure at the water's edge where boats tie up.

reef: (1) To reduce sail by tying in reef points. (2) A shoal made of coral or rock.

rhumb line: A straight line laying out a course on a Mercator chart. (A great circle is actually a shorter distance.)

safety harness: Harness worn like a vest and attached to a jackline (running along the deck) by a tether.

sheet: A line used to control a sail's lateral movement. (jib sheet/main sheet)

shellback: A person who has crossed the equator aboard a boat.

solar panel: A bank of solar cells providing electrical energy to the ship's batteries.

Southern Cross: A constellation in the southern hemisphere near Centaurus, forming the shape of a cross.

squall: A sudden, violent windstorm, usually accompanied by rain.

starboard: The right side of the boat looking towards the bow from the cockpit.

stern: The after portion of the hull.

storm jib: A strong, small, triangular headsail used in strong winds or storm conditions.

storm trysail: A triangular sail having it's luff bent to a mast. Used to heave to in storm conditions.

tiller: A wooden lever fitted to the rudder, providing steering control for the vessel.

transom: The stern cross-section of a vessel.

trim: To set sail or adjust the sails via sheets and rigging lines.

T (true) course: A course steered by a ship's compass which has been corrected for variation and deviation.

VHF radio: Very high frequency marine radio using line-of-sight, with a normal range of up to 25 miles.

wahine: Hawaiian for woman.

weigh anchor: To raise anchor or depart.

winch: A geared drum, mounted on deck or on a spar, turned by a handle used to haul halyards and sheets or other lines under strain.

windlass: A special type of winch used for raising the anchor rode.

windvane: A mechanical self-steering gear. Uses no electricity but rather is wind sensitive and is set for a desired point of sail.

INDEX

South Seas Publishing Company

14025 Panay Way

Marina del Rey, CA 90292 U.S.A.

(310) 305-4123

Fax: (310) 305-3757   e-mail: cdewell722@aol.com